Fiction and the Camera Eye

*Visual Consciousness in Film
and the Modern Novel*

Fiction and the Camera Eye
*Visual Consciousness in Film
and the Modern Novel*

Alan Spiegel

University Press of Virginia
Charlottesville

THE UNIVERSITY PRESS OF VIRGINIA
Copyright © 1976 by the Rector and Visitors
of the University of Virginia

First published 1976

Library of Congress Cataloging in Publication Data

Spiegel, Alan
   Fiction and the Camera Eye

   Includes index.
   1. Fiction—History and criticism.   2. Moving-pictures and literature.
Title.   PN3491.S65   809.3'3   75-22353   ISBN 0-8139-0598-2

Printed in the United States of America

For

my mother and father

Anita and Albert Spiegel

Contents

Preface ix

Part One: The Origins of Cinematographic Form

I. Concretized Form 3
    The Legacy of Flaubert 5
    Cervantes and Narrative Form 8
    Flaubert and Concretized Form 16
II. The Oval of Vision 28
    Flaubert and the Camera Eye 28
    The Development of Interior Form 39
      Zola, Lawrence, Woolf
    The Development of Cinematographic Form 53
      James, Conrad, Joyce

Part Two: Film and the Modern Novel

III. Joyce and Company 71
    Joyce and the Cinema 71
    The Ontology of the Camera 82
IV. The Adventitious Detail 90
V. The Anatomy of Motion 109
VI. Depthlessness 131
    Animation and Dehumanization 136
    Black Graphics 150
VII. Montage 162
Epilogue: *Comment C'est* 185
Index 201

Preface

THIS BOOK EXAMINES the nature, origin, and development of a particular form of the modern novel from its first systematic crystallization around the middle of the nineteenth century (in the work of Flaubert and others) through its refinements, intensifications, and modulations in the twentieth century (in the work of Joyce and others) and on to the present day. The spectrum of analysis and illustration covers over one hundred years of prose fiction and draws upon a wide range of international novelists—including Zola, James, Conrad, Faulkner, Nabokov, Robbe-Grillet, and many others—whose work, by virtue of this form, may be said to constitute a continuing tradition. I take this tradition to be central to the history of modern fiction.

Many of the novels that embody this form, those of Zola and Conrad, for instance, have also been described in literary histories as *realistic* or *naturalistic* or as examples of *psychological realism*. In a sense, I do not suppose that there is anything very wrong with these terms since most people seem to recognize the kind of novel you are talking about whenever you use one of them. The problem arises when you try to examine the categories themselves to determine whether any kind of novel could legitimately fulfill them. Most critics nowadays are willing to admit that the term *realism*, or any of its near relations, represents a presumptuous, ambiguous, and philosophically loaded designation.

Because I do not mean to carry any excess metaphysical baggage, I have attempted to describe *all* of the novels in this tradition not according to their different modes of expression—which in certain instances may seem to be "realistic," in others "romantic" or "grotesque" or whatever—but according to the form they share; according, that is, to those elements of style, texture, technique, and structure through which their authors have *concretized* human experience. I have thus described these novels as examples of *concretized form*. I do not insist on this name, but I do think that this form needs a name and one that does descriptive justice to it.[1]

I began this study because I wanted to find out the answers to a couple of questions. One of them was, Why is there so much to look at, so much purely visual information, in the nineteenth-century novel—particularly in the latter half of the period—and so much less to look at in earlier novels? It was the visual richness of the concretized novel which first caught my eye (literally, seriously) and which now more than ever continues to impress me as one of the defining and most striking qualities of this form. One can *see* the figures of Nana and Emma Bovary, as well as all the actions they engage in, but not those of Pamela or Emma Woodhouse. I wanted to know how to account for this.

The second question was related to the first, but at the time I was not yet fully aware of it. In what way could one legitimately account for the original visualizations in the work of James Joyce in terms of the photographic arts? Critics had often discussed Joyce's work in conjunction with film, but I could never tell from what they said whether Joyce was actually influenced by film or

---

[1]Only after Adam had named all the animals in the Garden could he take his first Edenic nap. To give a thing its proper name is, in part, a way of creating it all over again, and until he picks the right name, a fussy creator might well have cause for a period of sheet-rumpling insomnia. Before naming this literary form, I considered three roughly synonymous adjectives—"reified," "concretized," and "materialized"—and originally chose *reified* in deference to its freshness, brevity, and smoothness of vowel. I even went ahead and published an article using this term in connection with this form ("Flaubert to Joyce: Evolution of a Cinematographic Form," *Novel,* 6 (Spring 1973), 229-43). I was immediately taken short, however, when friends, colleagues, and some readers, too, informed me that this term "belonged" to the Marxist philosophers (Lukács, Marcuse, and others) and that unless I was using it "their" way, I had better not use it at all. I obviously was not using it their way, though I had long been aware of their way and, given my preference for this term, was naive enough to believe that a university audience would recognize (and welcome) this little word when used in another way; that is, a way that could be found, not in *One-Dimensional Man,* but in any standard dictionary. Unfortunately, the political takeover of *reified* seems to be a fait accompli. So be it: in order to avoid further confusion, I have discarded the term and replaced it with the sharper, tougher, but less melliflous *concretized* (though in itself still more mouthable and less tainted than its faintly satanic alternative *materialized*).

Preface

whether the alliance was simply (or not so simply) metaphorical.[2] At any rate, on what grounds could Joyce and the film be related?

Later I came to realize that while Joyce's visualizations were "cinematic," they were also not without their literary precedents and anticipations; that they were in fact the point of culmination, as well as transition, for a whole tradition of visualization in literature that first appeared in the formal procedures of the nineteenth-century novel; that many of the cinematic effects to be found in Joyce's work were also to be found in Flaubert's, though Flaubert was not, of course, influenced by the cinema. Later I also came to feel that Joyce, too, was not specifically influenced by the cinema. Did one really need film, then, to account for the technique of Joyce or, for that matter, of any novelist?

In spite of logic, in spite of history, it was hard to shake my original intuition: here was the cinema and here was a certain kind of novel and here were the two of them, still looking—to my mind at least—remarkably alike. Maybe my intuition had been based on little more than whimsy and cheap sentiment. Maybe I had gone to too many movies and could not get them out of my mind whenever I read a book. Still, here was a precinematic Joseph Conrad in 1897 telling us that when he wrote his books, the task he was trying to achieve was to make us "see," and here sixteen years later was an ex-poet and playwright, D. W. Griffith, telling us the same thing in virtually the same words ("The task I'm trying to achieve is above all to make you see")—except that now Griffith was trying to make movies.[3] Griffith wanted to make us "see" in and through and finally *past* those truncated surfaces on the screen—those voiceless, disembodied heads and

---

[2]Levin, Kenner, Kain, Tindall, and Magalaner, to name only some of the more widely known Joyce critics, have all remarked upon the cinematic character of Joyce's art (especially *Ulysses*), yet none of these critics seems to imply the specific or conscious influence of film. Robert S. Ryf, however, does imply such influence in *A New Approach to Joyce* (Berkeley and Los Angeles, 1962), pp. 171-91, and so too, following Ryf, does Edward Murray in *The Cinematic Imagination: Writers and Motion Pictures* (New York, 1972), pp. 124-26. My own view of the problem appears in chapter 3.

[3]Quoted by Lewis Jacobs in *The Rise of the American Film: A Critical History* (New York, 1939), p. 119; Conrad's famous remark is from the Preface to *The Nigger of the "Narcissus,"* in *A Conrad Argosy* (New York, 1942), p. 83.

floating torsos—so that we could finally "see" how they added up as part of a conceptual design, a continuing and cohesive narrative action. He wanted us to look at those images and "see" them as indicators of the story he was trying to tell. Conrad wanted to make us "see" in and through and finally *past* his language and his narrative concept to the hard, clear bedrock of images that he hoped in themselves would be impervious to anything he could say about them. I think he wanted his images to have the visual immediacy of unmediated objects that would, as it were, tell the story for him. Conrad wanted us to understand his story as something to be seen, while Griffith wanted us to see his images as something to be understood. Generally speaking, I would say that Griffith's aim was the more novelistic, Conrad's the more cinematographic. Both Griffith and Conrad, however, were starting from opposite ends of the same line and moving toward the same point in the middle: a union of image and concept, of visual fact and value. At the time he made his remark Conrad had probably not seen a movie; yet he and Griffith shared a common aesthetic.

I did not think there was any cause for whimsy or sentimentality in this. One began to understand where film and certain kinds of novels came together as soon as one began to understand the film as something more than the sum of its mechanical devices. One really learns about film technique when one realizes that film technique as such embodies values and attitudes which are vital *outside* of film; that film technique as such relates to a way of thinking and feeling—about time, space, being, and relation—relates, in short, to a body of ideas about the world that has become part of the mental life of an entire epoch in our culture. This body of ideas not only exists outside of film, as well as in it, but in fact precedes the invention of the motion picture camera and in part determines the shape and texture of novels by pre-cinematic artists like Conrad, Zola, and Flaubert. These ideas also explain why there is so much to look at in the work of these novelists; and how later Joyce, Hemingway, and Faulkner could draw upon these novelists for their own visualizations; and how finally the advent of the cinema itself could come to seem but the final fruition of intellectual tendencies developing in the culture for over half a century.

By the time Joyce was writing *Ulysses*, a novelist need never

Preface

have gone to a movie to know what was meant by one. The film "idea" had become so much a part of a general cultural style that one could catch the tone and rhythm of what Arnold Hauser called "the Film Age" in the ordinary events of one's daily life.[4] One could learn all about camera angles from the ads on billboards and in magazines; or all about dolly shots and tracking from the window of a moving car; or all about montage by simply trying to keep up with what was happening all around one during a rush hour in any major international city. Any artist could be influenced by film and know all about it simply by being alive and visually alert in the modern world.

This book, then, while substantially not an "influence study," will try to explore the common body of thought and feeling that unites film form with the form of the modern novel; it will try to describe the shape of the consciousness that in part determines the shape of these forms and is in part embodied by them; and it will try to present a series of terms (such as *adventitious detail, anatomization*)—a grammar, if you will—through which this consciousness and these forms may be approached with facility and precision. (I need hardly add that this grammar exists to help the reader—and the author—take hold of the subject, but the reader should understand that it is the subject, not the grammar, which is the end and purpose of the book. The reader is free to disregard the grammar if he wishes to take hold of the subject in another way: but if nothing else, this book will try to show him that there is a subject to be taken.)

Throughout the discussion I place most emphasis on the work of two men, Flaubert and Joyce (and particularly on the latter as a transitional figure between the centuries). I see both of these novelists as pivotal and prototypical figures, indeed, as the foremost exponents of the concretized form and manner. I take Flaubert as its central practitioner in the nineteenth century and Joyce as a comparable figure for the modernists, the post-Flaubertians. I do not think, however, that Flaubert "invented" this form any more than I think that Joyce "invented" the interior monologue. Flaubert drew together the dramatizing and visualizing tendencies of his immediate predecessors (Balzac, Dickens, Gogol, Hawthorne) and presented them in a definitive form.

[4]Hauser, *The Social History of Art*, IV (New York, 1958), 226-59.

Before Flaubert, there were certain random and unrelated writers writing in a certain way; after Flaubert, there was a literary movement.

Chapter 1 serves essentially as an introduction to the central argument. It discusses the necessity for a visualized narrative in the art of Joyce and his literary predecessors, describes the nature and origins of such a narrative in the work of Flaubert, and contrasts this narrative with the prototypical literary form of the pre-Flaubertians. Chapter 2 examines the evolution of Flaubert's narrative form as it branches off into two related but essentially different directions: first into its important but noncinematographic antitype, interior form; and then into its modern counterpart and subtype cinematographic form, the appropriate designation, I think, for the concretized narrative in the twentieth century. Chapters 3 through 7 form the center of my argument; they explore the various components of cinematographic form in the fiction of Joyce and numerous other twentieth-century novelists. Some of these components are adventitiousness, anatomization, depthlessness, and montage. The Epilogue attempts to determine the fate of the novel in relation to the present cultural situation.

In the recent past there have been critical studies that bring together novels and films on the basis of a common body of narrative technique.[5] Some of these books have been quite use-

---

[5] These books include George Bluestone's *Novels into Film* (Berkeley and Los Angeles, 1961), Robert Richardson's *Literature and Film* (Bloomington, Ind., 1969), William Jinks's *The Celluloid Literature: Films in the Humanities* (Beverly Hills, Calif., 1971), and Edward Murray's *The Cinematic Imagination*. None of these studies attempts to establish a common metaphysics between the film and the novel, but certainly the most intellectually ambitious is Richardson's, a rather brief but panoptic survey of literary and cinematic analogies from the Bible to Wallace Stevens. Richardson finds examples of the cinematic imagination in a variety of literary forms throughout history but places special emphasis on drama and poetry. Considering the enormous scope of the project, Richardson's treatment of the modern novel is predictably thin (ten pages). His greatest weakness, however, is a failure to distinguish finally between visual description in general (practically a constant in the literature of almost any era) and visual description of a specifically cinematic nature (a special condition of the modern literary situation).

One work that does indeed establish the necessary philosophical relationship between novel and film is Claude-Edmonde Magny's brilliant 1948 study *The Age of the American Novel: The Film Aesthetic of Fiction between the Two Wars* (New York,

ful, but I am inclined to think that the trouble with many of them has been that they have told us *only* about technique and therefore not enough about it, and have ended by reducing technique to trickery and effect. It was Lionel Abel who once said that formalists "are too interested in form itself to really understand it."[6] In this book I hope to come a little closer to a proper understanding of two modern art forms.

One final note on method: all talk about "common aesthetics," "general cultural styles," and "Film Ages" will mean less than nothing and will probably be worse than nothing if such talk is not sanctioned and validated by specific examples of an artist's work. If the grand and sweeping correspondences between two art forms cannot illuminate something about specific works of art in either one or the other, why bother to make these correspondences at all? Since my primary interest here is in the novel, I

1972). This book has recently been translated from the French and was brought to my attention after my own study had been completed. Though the late Mme. Magny examines only four modern American novelists—Dos Passos, Hemingway, Steinbeck, and Faulkner—she manages to set up an excellent theoretical and historical framework for any discussion of film and the post-Flaubertian novel. Since she approaches her subject in a manner similar to my own and comes to some similar conclusions, I will note her remarks wherever we seem to agree—or violently disagree.

Two notable studies have each discussed in a single chapter the cinematic influence on all modern cultural styles, but particularly on painting: Arnold Hauser's "The Film Age," in *The Social History of Art,* and Wylie Sypher's "The New World of Relationships: Camera and Cinema," in *Rococo to Cubism in Art and Literature* (New York, 1963), pp. 257-94. Both studies provide an excellent intellectual framework that relates ideas in modern philosophy to the ideas behind the camera, cubist painting, and the modern novel. Unfortunately, neither Sypher nor Hauser has time to illustrate sufficiently his general principles. Sypher finds the "widest application" of the "montage principle" in *Ulysses* but quotes from the novel only once. Hauser does not quote from it at all.

Beyond these, there is notably Marshall McLuhan's study of the interdependent and hybrid nature of all the modern arts in "Hybrid Energy: Les Liaisons Dangereuses," *Understanding Media: The Extensions of Man* (New York, 1965), pp. 48-55, and László Moholy-Nagy's similar study in *Vision in Motion* (Chicago, 1965).

The only full-length treatments of the impact of cinematic form on a specific novelist appear to be Roger Shattuck's excellent *Proust's Binoculars: A Study of Memory, Time, and Recognition in* A la Recherche du Temps Perdu (New York, 1967), and Alfred Appel's hectic catalog of Nabokov's borrowings and conversions from popular culture, *Nabokov's Dark Cinema* (New York, 1974), published after the completion of this study.

[6]*Metatheatre: A New View of Dramatic Form* (New York, 1963), p. viii.

have tried to work as closely as possible with specific and representative visualizations from the work of various authors and have tried to determine before anything else what the words in each visualization ask us to see and how they ask us to see it—that is to say, how the space is visualized in each literary object we are considering. I have tried to make most of the general remarks (about film and the novel) either merge with, or directly follow from—but never supersede—these specific analyses. Thus, if you do not find the meaning of the generalization confirmed by the art of the visualization, you probably will not find it confirmed by anything else—nor, I think, should you.

More people have helped me in the making of this book than I probably have the space to record or the capacity to remember. But here are the names of some friends, colleagues, and generous counselors that I don't want to forget: Professor Robert Langbaum of the University of Virginia, who read various drafts of this work, offered much encouragement and a myriad of valuable suggestions; Professor Robert Kellogg, also of the University of Virginia, who provided insight and support throughout the early phases of the project; Professors Charles Bernheimer, Stefan Fleischer, Martin L. Pops, and Howard Wolf of the State University of New York at Buffalo, who read the manuscript in its final stages and inspired many useful emendations of fact, style, and organization. Further aid and advice were offered by, and taken from, Malcolm L. Call, Ernest Callenbach, Dr. Anthony Foti, George Kaplan, Hugh Kenner, Peter Lushing, James Raimes, Margaret Rundell, and Judith Sawyer. I also want to thank Professor A. Walton Litz of Princeton University for his kindness and support, and special thanks to Dwight Macdonald for the keenness of his mind and the pleasure of his witty company during a time when it was needed most.

Parts of chapter 2, "The Oval of Vision," originally appeared in a somewhat different form in *Novel: A Forum on Fiction*. My thanks to the editors for permission to reprint this material.

Part One

The Origins of

Cinematographic Form

Chapter I
Concretized Form

In *Ulysses*, Stephen Dedalus talks to himself as he wanders along Sandymount strand: "Ineluctable modality of the visible: at least that if no more, thought through my eyes."[1] The first phrase—with its Latinate diction and florid march of resonating consonants—is one of the richest and most haunting expressions in a book that lacks little in the way of the rich and the haunting. The phrase also helps us to understand Stephen as a young man who needs to *see*, as one of the great spectator-heroes of modern fiction. We do not often find a literary character of equal gifts who wishes to confront so much of life yet who remains so much the nonparticipant—sitting in rooms, standing before windows, walking through streets, watching, waiting, yet refusing to engage in any part of the living spectacle that passes before his eyes. By the end of *A Portrait of the Artist as a Young Man*, the visual modality has become for Stephen unavoidable and inevitable, that form of reality without which one cannot do or know or be. And what has become true for Stephen is true as well for James Joyce. In this respect at least, if not in all others, the artist and his creative offspring are one.

Italo Svevo once described Joyce as "a being who moves in order to see," and Joyce once described himself as "Ireland's eye."[2] He named his daughter Lucia after the patron saint of eyesight, and in Trieste wore a little metal ring on his finger to ward off blindness.[3] In the end the ring proved to be not without its charms, for Joyce never went blind. Still, his amulet could have served him better than it did, for in his later years frequent

---

[1] James Joyce, *Ulysses* (New York: Random House, 1961), p. 48. Subsequent reference to this edition will appear in text.
[2] Svevo, quoted by Richard Ellmann in *James Joyce* (New York, 1965), p. 281; Joyce quoted on p. 585.
[3] Ibid., pp. 272, 352.

attacks of glaucoma reduced his sight to minimal vision.[4] An imperiled eye can charge the act of vision with special urgencies, and Joyce worried over the condition of his eyes throughout his life. Perhaps this partly explains how one of his students at the Berlitz school in Trieste could watch Joyce analyze a lamp for a full half hour and describe the performance as nothing less than a display of "descriptive lust."[5]

But such a lust did not make Joyce unique in his time; rather, it made him a typical member of the literary movement in which he worked. What was ineluctable for Stephen and for Joyce was ineluctable also for Joyce's literary contemporaries and immediate predecessors. Joyce grew up and, as it were, came of age during that period of literary history in which Joseph Conrad announced his credo for visualization in the Preface to *The Nigger of the "Narcissus"* (1897): "My task which I am trying to achieve is, by the power of the written word to make you hear, to make you feel—it is before all to make you *see*. That and no more and it is everything."[6] It was also in this period that Henry James wrote of Guy de Maupassant (1888): "His eye *selects* unerringly, unscrupulously, almost impudently—catches the particular thing in which the character of the object or the scene resides, and, by expressing it with the artful brevity of a master, leaves a convincing, original picture."[7] It was James, too, who much later (1914) concluded his own preliminary sketch for *The Sense of the Past* with the famous words "Above all I see—."[8] And all of these instances had been prefigured—and in certain ways, actually fostered—by the example of Gustave Flaubert, who announced his credo for visualization in 1852: "*The less you feel a thing the fitter you are to express it as it is.* ... But you must have the capacity to *make yourself feel it*. This capacity is what we call genius: the ability

---

[4] From 1917 to the end of his life Joyce experienced very brief periods of "half-blindness," usually immediately before, during, and after one of his eye operations. But as Professor Ellmann states, "Joyce could see; to be for a period half-blind is not at all the same thing as to be permanently blind" (ibid., p. 729).

[5] Ibid., p. 353.

[6] *A Conrad Argosy*, p. 83.

[7] "Guy de Maupassant," in *Major Writers of America*, ed. Perry Miller (New York, 1962), II, 242.

[8] *The Notebooks of Henry James*, ed. F. O. Matthiessen and Kenneth B. Murdock (New York, 1947), p. 369.

to *see*, to have your model constantly posing in front of you."[9] It should come as no surprise to us, then, that Joyce's "descriptive lust" finds its exact and intriguing adumbration in Flaubert's remark "I derive almost voluptuous sensations from the mere act of seeing."[10]

The Legacy of Flaubert

Who can say when a literary movement begins? Who can say when it ends? It is, of course, as difficult to pinpoint the precise origins of any literary trend as it is to pinpoint the moment when day becomes night. The clock tells us when it is noon or midnight, but the clock does not tell us when it is evening or dawn. Knowing this, one can still observe that something remarkable was beginning to happen to literary procedure and form before the middle of the nineteenth century. In 1840, for instance, Balzac writes, "I don't believe it is possible to depict modern society by the methods of seventeenth-century and eighteenth-century literature. I think pictures, images, descriptions, the use of dramatic elements of dialogue are indispensable to the modern writers."[11] He calls the old method a "literature of ideas"—or what nowadays we might want to call a literature of authorial commentary. Balzac calls the new method a "literature of images," but significantly describes his own method as a combination of the "new" and the "old." And one can see the effects of the new method, as well as many remnants of the old, in the "pictures," "images," and "descriptions" of certain early nineteenth-century novelists—in the landscapes of Scott and Cooper, in the caricatures of Dickens and Gogol, in the emblematic tableaux of Hawthorne, and, of course, in the urban decor of Balzac himself.

By the time we encounter Flaubert, however, all of the old

[9]Flaubert to Louise Colet (1852), *The Selected Letters of Gustave Flaubert*, ed. Francis Steegmuller (New York, 1957), p. 136, Flaubert's italics.
[10]Flaubert to Alfred Le Poitteven (1845), ibid., p. 35.
[11]Honoré de Balzac, in a review of Stendhal's *The Charterhouse of Parma*, quoted by Georg Lukács in "Balzac and Stendhal," *Studies in European Realism* (New York, 1964), p. 67. Balzac's distinction has been most famously updated (and somewhat transmuted) in our own time by Wayne C. Booth in his examination of novelists who "tell" and novelists who "show" (*The Rhetoric of Fiction* [Chicago, 1965]).

influences have been refined away and all the new descriptive tendencies have been consolidated, have become part of a definite and permanent form. In 1857 Flaubert published *Madame Bovary*, and the influence of this book upon the literary generation of Joyce's youth and, in fact, upon practically all subsequent literary generations—including the present one—cannot be overestimated. I do not think it is too much to say that after the appearance of *Madame Bovary* one either tried to write a book that was like it or one tried to write a book that was not like it; in any instance, if one wished to take the novel form seriously, one did not try to write without bearing it in mind. Much of what we mean today by "the conventional modern novel" is actually our way of referring to the standardization—indeed, the formularization—of what Flaubert first did in 1857.

What he had done amounted to no less than a presentation of the narrative as a totally concretized form. By this I mean precisely what Ezra Pound meant when he described Flaubert's efforts as "an attempt to set down things as they are, to find the word that corresponds to the thing, the statement that portrays, and presents, instead of making a comment, however brilliant, or an epigram."[12] Concretized form, then, is a way of transcribing the narrative, not as a story that is told, but as an action that is portrayed and presented, that seems to reveal itself to the reader apart from the overt mediations of the author.

The effects of this form can be found in the novels and stories of the great literary practitioners (those novelists quite uselessly called "realists") who followed Flaubert and who, consciously or unconsciously, in one way or another, assimilated his general approach to the problems of fiction: Tolstoy, Turgenev, Chekhov, de Maupassant, Mérimée, Conrad, Ford, Hardy, Howells, James, Crane—and, of course, Joyce himself (it is well known that Joyce considered Flaubert one of the few masters of the novel and that he committed whole pages of Flaubert's work to memory).[13] The effects of what Flaubert had done can also be found most strikingly in the formal assumptions of the group of

[12]*ABC of Reading* (New York, 1960), p. 74.
[13]Frank Budgen, *James Joyce and the Making of Ulysses* (Bloomington, Ind., 1964), pp. 176-80. Many critics have written about the relationship between these two writers, but none at greater length than Richard Cross, *Flaubert and Joyce: The Rite of Fiction* (Princeton, 1971).

novelists known as the naturalists, particularly Zola and those men working in the tradition of Zola: Bennett in England; Moore in Ireland; and Norris, London, and Dreiser in America. (The influence is obvious even though Flaubert officially dissociated himself from naturalism—that is, the specific literary program of the naturalists.)[14]

Some of these names represent superior achievement. Some of the others, however, do not mean much to us nowadays. Certainly we do not like to think of de Maupassant, Norris, and Howells as the primary determinants of our literary situation. And I suppose there is a good deal that is just in this attitude: we are probably right to reject the pseudoscience of a Zola, the genteelisms of a Howells, the slick sensuality of a de Maupassant, the brutalized heroics of a London, and even the sentimentalities of such a master as Turgenev. But these personal attitudes and qualities of temperament represent only half of the picture: the half that is embodied by all the dead issues and exhausted emotions of a literary era that, in this respect, could not seem farther away from us. We tend to ignore the other half of the picture: the half that shows us a large group of novelists of greatly varying gifts who either attempted or achieved remarkable, and remarkably permanent, transformations of novelistic procedure and form.

It is the formal tradition of the Flaubertian novel that, despite outmoded moral and social passions, determines the textural and structural foundations of the modern novel. *The Sound and the Fury, In Our Time, Mrs. Dalloway,* and *Ulysses* all find their formal roots in *Germinal, Fathers and Sons, The Bostonians,* and *Dubliners* in much the same way that the cubist achievement of Picasso and Braque finds its roots in the impressionist experiments of Monet and Degas; and the serial structures of Berg and Schoenberg find theirs in the late romanticism of Wagner and Mahler.

We like to think of *Ulysses* and *The Sound and the Fury* as specimens of a literary revolution, but we would probably do better to think of them as specimens of the final stages in a literary evolution. And in order to appreciate this evolution, I think that

---

[14]"Speaking of my friends [the naturalists], you call them my 'school.' But I am wrecking my health trying not to have a school" (Flaubert to George Sand [1857], *Letters*, pp. 247-48).

we must understand the nature and the implications of concretized form—the highly sensuous and visualized narrative that was the legacy of Flaubert; a legacy, we must realize, which did not merely offer a gratuitous assemblage of stylistic tricks but rather a decisive and fully achieved narrative form—which is to say, a mode of apprehending the world, a way of seeing one's experience as determined by one's idea of experience. We must understand the way in which novelists like Joyce, Hemingway, and Faulkner developed and refined this legacy. But unless we appreciate the formal vision of the past, we will never fully understand how the modernists made it part of the formal vision of the future.

Cervantes and Narrative Form

Every time he read *Don Quixote* Flaubert felt like breaking his pen: "What dwarfs all [other books] are beside it! How small one feels, oh Lord, how small one feels!" He loved this book not only for its comic realism but even more for its poetic qualities. Cervantes appealed to the romantic in Flaubert and set him dreaming: "Whenever I read *Don Quixote* I long to ride my horse down a white and dusty road and to eat olives and raw onions in the shadow of a rock."[15]

In 1914 Ortega y Gasset described Emma Bovary as a "Don Quixote in skirts" (a remark that has since become a critical commonplace). But Ortega added that Emma, unlike the Don, had a "minimum of tragedy in her soul" and went on to reproach Flaubert and his contemporaries for lack of the very qualities that Flaubert himself admired in Cervantes: "poetic sensibility" and "poetic dynamism." And Ortega concludes his brilliant *Meditations on Quixote* with a lament for the dead: "One night Bouvard and Pécuchet buried poetry in the Cemetery Père Lachaise—in honor of verisimilitude and determinism."[16]

I think that there is more poetry in *Madame Bovary* than Ortega would probably allow, but he is perfectly just when he contrasts

---

[15]Flaubert to Louise Colet (1852), ibid., p. 142; Flaubert to Ivan Turgenev (1863), ibid., p. 205.
[16]Jośe Ortega y Gasset, *Meditations on Quixote* (New York, 1961), pp. 161, 165.

Concretized Form

Cervantes with Flaubert as novelistic antipodes. In their formal qualities, at least, no two authors could tell us more about where the novel has been and where it has gone. Here is an example of the narrative mode that would ultimately be replaced by Flaubert's generation:

> In a village of La Mancha the name of which I have no desire to recall, there lived not so long ago one of those gentlemen who always have a lance in the rack, an ancient buckler, a skinny nag, and a greyhound for the chase. A stew with more beef than mutton in it, chopped meat for his evening meal, scraps for a Saturday, lentils on Friday, and a young pigeon as a special delicacy for Sunday, went to account for three-quarters of his income. The rest of it he laid out on a broadcloth greatcoat and velvet stockings for feast days, with slippers to match, while the other days of the week he cut a figure in a suit of the finest homespun. Living with him were a housekeeper in her forties, a niece who was not yet twenty, and a lad of the field and market place who saddled his horse for him and wielded the pruning knife.
>
> This gentleman of ours was close on to fifty, of a robust constitution but with little flesh on his bones and a face that was lean and gaunt. He was noted for his early rising, being very fond of the hunt. They will try to tell you that his surname was Quijada or Quesada—there is some difference of opinion among those who have written on the subject—but according to the most likely conjectures we are to understand that it was really Quejana. But all this means very little so far as our story is concerned, providing that in the telling of it we do not depart one iota from the truth.
>
> You may know, then, that the aforesaid gentleman, on those occasions when he was at leisure, which was most of the year round, was in the habit of reading books of chivalry with such pleasure and devotion as to lead him almost wholly to forget the life of a hunter and even the administration of his estate. So great was his curiosity and infatuation in this regard that he even sold many acres of tillable land in order to be able to buy and read the books that he loved, and he would carry home with him as many of them as he could obtain.[17]

This, of course, is the well-known opening of *Don Quixote* (1605), and Cervantes's method of depiction can easily serve as the model for novelistic exposition in a pre-Flaubertian era (that is, for the seventeenth and eighteenth centuries, and even for many

---

[17]Miguel de Cervantes Saavedra, *The Ingenious Gentleman, Don Quixote de la Mancha,* trans. Samuel Putnam (New York, 1949), pp. 25-26. Subsequent references will appear in text.

novelists of the early nineteenth century). Allowing for the very obvious differences in style, subject, and individual temperament, you will probably not find very different expositional strategies in *Tom Jones, Emma, The Red and the Black,* and *Eugene Onegin*. (Even Gogol and Balzac do not introduce characters in a radically different manner.)

Perhaps what is most immediately striking about the passage is the simple fact that it is indeed a real exposition. The story has begun, yet it has not begun: before the action can proceed, the character must be exposed in toto. Don Quixote is removed from his spatial context, extricated from the temporal flux, and examined by the author as an autonomous, self-contained whole. The entire sequence of action that follows this examination and continues almost for the duration of the novel can be deduced from the information about Don Quixote directly stated or suggested in these first three paragraphs. (He neglects his estate because he loves to read books of chivalry; because he loves to read books of chivalry, he spends all his time reading them; because he spends all his time reading them, he goes "completely out of his mind" [p. 27]; because he goes out of his mind, he decides to become a knight-errant.) Each time a major character enters the story, the action itself stops. Time and space, as it were, cease to exist as the character is plucked from the realm of experience and held in the timeless suspension of exposition. When the character returns, the action begins again: but now it is shaped and modulated by the pressures of the characteristics revealed in the exposition. In the pre-Flaubertian novel, the action is always a function of the character, and it is in terms of character that the action is always explained.

Another striking quality of the passage is the tone of voice that seems to permeate it: relaxed, genial, modest—yet wonderfully confident too; it seems to flow all around its subject like a warm current of affectionate curiosity. It is a remarkably human voice, and in its accents we detect the shape of an individualized personality with a temperament ("the name of which I have no desire to recall") and conviction ("But all this means very little so far as our story is concerned, providing that in the telling of it we do not depart one iota from the truth") and a sense of humor ("on those occasions when he was at leisure, which was most of the year round"). Cervantes is so assured of, and at ease with, his subject that he can afford to tell us what he does *not* know about Don Quixote's history: "They will try to tell you that his surname was Quijada or Quesada—there is some difference of opinion among those who have written on the subject." Cervantes knows that these admissions will not shake the reader's confidence in him as a narrator but, on the contrary, will insure the reader's belief in him as an honest historian, one who refuses to fake points of information about which he is uncertain. He also knows that these admissions will increase the illusion of verisimilitude that he is trying to create for Quixote. The lives of real persons do contain areas of ambiguity; it is only characters in fiction who are entirely transparent to the author who invented them.

Cervantes is superbly confident, then, both about what he knows and what he does not know. He is not only certain of the story he is telling but also to whom he is telling it: he knows his audience, trusts it, and relies upon it in a number of significant ways. First of all, he knows that he really has got an audience to speak to, a body of listeners who presumably want to hear his story and for whose benefit he, in turn, wants to tell it. The rapport between author and audience is at times so keenly felt that it seems in these moments as if the reader were actually drawn into the process of creation and were telling the story *with* Cervantes ("this gentleman of *ours*," "*our* story," "they will try to tell *you*," emphasis added). The sound of a personalized voice directly in touch with its audience and using the audience in various ways to shape the story are characteristics not only of Cervantes's fiction but also of Fielding's, Sterne's, and Smollett's; as well as Austen's and Stendhal's, which speak, however, in less personal tones. (And in spite of their departures from this model, Gogol, Balzac, and Dickens often employ a voice that is almost as familiar with its audience as is the voice of Cervantes.)

Moreover, Cervantes and his audience share certain assumptions about the world in which they live, assumptions about the structure of society and the various categories of experience, that enable the author to take certain matters for granted in the telling of his story. For instance, Cervantes can rely on this audience to identify the type of nobleman he is describing in the first paragraph without naming him. In the key phrase "one of those gentlemen," which governs all the concrete details in the first paragraph, Cervantes reminds his audience of its familiarity with the particular social category to which Don Quixote belongs; that is, a social category which at one time "not so long ago" could easily be identified by the "lance in the rack," "an ancient buckler," "a skinny nag" and the like. All the details of Quixote's economy, costume, and domestic staff are pressed into service to solidify this general social classification. By the end of this first paragraph the reader knows that Don Quixote is indeed "one of those gentlemen" called a hidalgo, an impoverished member of the landed gentry. The description itself is purely illustrative: a sequence of precise signs that designate for the reader a particular social typology. Cervantes can assume that all the members of his audience will recognize this typology, for both author and reader live in a stable and hierarchic society that operates according to fixed laws, reasoned precepts, and a clearly defined and orderly system of values. And these laws, precepts, and values are true not only for Cervantes himself but—because they are objective and unified—are true for all his readers, for all the members of this stable seventeenth-century Spanish society.[18]

The stable society that permits Cervantes to rely on his audience's recognition of Quixote's social category also permits Cervantes to ignore the accidental and transitory elements in Quixote's character. Reality for this stable society does not reside in the fortuitous. The traits enumerated in the first paragraph are not only typical, they are also habitual and recurrent. Cervantes is not interested in those odd moments in the life of his hero when—for one reason or another, or for no reason at all—he might presumably vary his diet, or change his attire, or simply reverse custom by wearing homespun on feast days and broadcloth during the week. The author is not interested in those exceptions to the general law of Quixote's social conduct: the hero is one of those gentlemen who "always" has a lance in the rack, a stew with more beef than mutton, and lentils on Friday and pigeon on Sunday. His pattern of behavior—at least at the outset of the story—has, like the society of which he is a member, a fixed and

---

[18]By the phrases "stable society" and "orderly system of values" I am not referring to the specific historical situation of seventeenth-century Spain (which was as politically turbulent as any other era). I am referring, rather, to the seventeenth-century world view in which men believed in the natural order of society as a reflection of the natural order of the universe, and in both orders as ordained by Divinity (the famous microcosm-macrocosm relationship).

unvarying outline, and Cervantes seizes upon the recurring essentials of this outline to summarize Quixote's conduct in the past and the present.[19]

Because the stable society cultivates the habitual, the quintessential, and the general, Cervantes is also able to ignore the sensuous surface details of Quixote's physical appearance. Like the description of the hero's daily conduct, the description of his face and form is brief, illustrative, and typological: "This gentleman of ours was close on to fifty, of a robust constitution but with little flesh on his bones and a face that was lean and gaunt." This is really as much as Cervantes ever tells us about Quixote's anatomy. We never learn anything about the color of his hair or eyes, the texture of his skin, the precise shape of his hands, nose, or mouth. Don Quixote is intensely felt and intensely understood, but he is never really seen (just as we feel and understand, but never really see, Pamela, Julien Sorel, Elizabeth Bennett, Eugene Onegin, and Tom Jones. It is here, however, that the early nineteenth-century masters—Balzac, Gogol, Dickens—depart from Cervantes. Their characters and settings are seen.). What is true of the Don is true, too, of Sancho and all the major characters in the novel. It is true, also, of the locations in which these characters appear: the farms, the inns, the country estates, the roads, the mountains, the forests, the little villages, and the

---

[19]This pattern of behavior would also pertain to the future had not Cervantes, in the third paragraph, revealed a new trait in Quixote's character. This trait is as habitual and recurrent as any of his other traits, but, unlike them, the new characteristic does not refer to Quixote's social condition. It refers, rather, to the condition of his spirit: he "was in the habit of reading books of chivalry with such pleasure and devotion as to lead him almost wholly to forget the life of a hunter and even the administration of his estate." This is the first indication we have received of those chivalric and romantic tendencies that shortly begin to dictate all the motions of the hero's soul. It is this habit that individualizes Quixote within his social typology; that differentiates him from the other members of his class (with whom, however, he is identified in all other ways). It is also this habit that ultimately urges him to abdicate his role as hidalgo for a new role as knight-errant. Quixote, however, never ceases to be a hidalgo. For all his friends and neighbors, it is his social typology that takes precedence in defining his essential identity: he is always Alonso Quejana, a hidalgo gone berserk. In his own eyes, on the other hand, his spiritual typology takes precedence: he is Don Quixote, who has given up his wordly possessions in behalf of a knightly quest. Throughout the novel, the continual tension between his public status and his inner being, between his social and spiritual typologies, gives complexity and vitality to his character.

great cities—all are evoked with the same classical economy: two or three carefully chosen details suggest the setting as a generalized whole.

The truth about Don Quixote is not to be found in his appearance but rather in his essential being, and Cervantes chooses just those physical details, and not one detail more, that illustrate the shape of that being: Quixote is "lean" and "gaunt" not simply because his diet is spare but because his temperament is ascetic and idealizing and abhors the fleshly realities. The detailed picture of Don Quixote's physical appearance that every modern reader is familiar with is not the result of any visual description provided by Cervantes. Rather, that picture is the result of the efforts of painters, illustrators, and filmmakers, like Doré, Daumier, Dali, and G. W. Pabst, who apparently have all imitated one another's visual fantasies with remarkable unanimity.

We should never think, on the other hand, that the sensory experience is unimportant for Cervantes; on the contrary, it is a necessary aspect of the total reality as Cervantes conceives it and is duly recorded throughout the novel. What distinguishes a writer like Cervantes from his post-Flaubertian counterpart is a different conception of what the *primary* and *essential* reality consists of, and how it is to be found. For Cervantes this reality is never to be found through the five sense modalities: rather, the essential reality is to be found through the mind and consists of what the mind comprehends—and this comprehension is always of a moral and intellectual experience, a conceptual rather than a sensuous reality. It is the mind's comprehension of a conceptual reality that becomes the focal point of the author's deepest insights. Details from the sensuous experience are then brought into play wherever they can be made to clarify, embroider, and illustrate the nature of these insights. In this way the concrete particulars function in the narrative as a kind of algebraic code or sensuous shorthand that immediately evokes the author's conceptual apprehension of any given character, setting, or event. Too many concrete particulars would merely blur or distort, or even contradict, the essential clarity and shape of the concept. And it is the concept that matters above all, that may conceivably, depending upon the author, be held separate and distinct from the particulars that are usually called upon to evoke it (in much of the French fiction of the seventeenth and eighteenth centuries—

particularly in the famous "white" novels of Mme. de LaFayette and Choderlos de Laclos—the sensuous shorthand disappears altogether, as the narrative consists almost exclusively of X-ray analyses of the thoughts, feelings, and moral dilemmas of the characters).

It is obvious, then, that we cannot read the pre-Flaubertian novel without simultaneously encountering the characteristic posture of Renaissance and eighteenth-century thought. Although we note the emergence of the novel form in these two centuries as something new, we also note a depiction of reality in this newly emerged form that derives largely from a classical (that is, Greco-Roman) epistemology. For Cervantes and his successors, there were still two kinds of perception and two kinds of reality to be perceived. These two kinds of reality were separate and distinct from each other, and, in the determination of truth, one reality clearly took precedence over the other.[20] There was, on the one hand, the world of nature as it appears to the senses: a world caught within the temporal flux and characterized by things in continual motion (function, process, things in their so-called secondary qualities).[21] Because things in this world moved, they changed. Because they changed they were admitted, in the final sense, to be unknowable. On the other hand, behind this process of continual change there was thought to exist a substratum of unchanging structure (substance, being, concept, things in their so-called primary qualities) that could be apprehended through the mind.[22] This structure was thought to exist apart from the conditions of the temporal flux and therefore was thought to be unchanging—and thus ultimately knowable.

This structural reality was synonymous with truth, and it is this reality that Cervantes always has in his mind whenever he refers to the "truth," as he so often does in *Don Quixote*. We can understand, then, why Don Quixote's real name (Quejada, Quesada, Quesana, Quejana, Quejano?) means little to the author as long as he does "not depart one iota from the truth." The

---

[20]In spite of the great differences separating the intellectual atmospheres of these two centuries, the distinctions between the subsequent rankings of different kinds of knowledge and different orders of being were characteristic of both. See R. G. Collingwood, *The Idea of Nature* (New York, 1960), pp. 6-7.

[21]Ibid., p. 11.

[22]Ibid.

"truth" is separate and distinct from the particular facts of an ever-changing external reality, a world of shifting, impermanent, and often ambiguous appearances, where Don Quixote might turn up one moment as a conventional hidalgo, the next as a reader of books of chivalry who neglects his estate, still the next as a knight-errant who abandons his estate altogether, and finally, at the end of the novel, as a conventional hidalgo once again. This secondary and inconstant level of reality, although faithfully rendered, never distracts Cervantes from the primary and constant reality that lies behind it. Thus, whether hidalgo or knight-errant, whether victorious or defeated, Don Quixote emerges through all his changing circumstances in his essential, unchanging "structure"; that is, as a noble, eloquent, courageous being, who even in moments of complete despair (as at the end of the novel when he rejects knight-errantry) is never allowed to appear cynical, vulgar, or commonplace. It is this same concentration on a timeless and unchanging reality that enables Cervantes to reveal not only the essential structure of each character's identity in a formal exposition apart from the continuing narrative but also the essential structure of each component of the narrative itself—each landscape, interior, each phase of the action—in clear, hard relief like an arrangement of bones beneath the skin.

Flaubert and Concretized Form

Innovation in any given novel is at once the product of history and its victim. What is new and what is old in any literary procedure largely depends on from which end of the historical continuum the procedure is observed. Looking back at *Don Quixote* from the present, we are naturally impressed by its high degree of conceptualization. Reversing the perspective, however, and looking at *Don Quixote* in comparison to the literature of the ancient past—in comparison, for instance, to the very lean and generalized narratives of Theocritus and Xenophon—we are equally impressed by its high degree of materialization.[23] From

---

[23]These are the terms, of course, in which the "rise of the novel" is usually discussed. See, for instance, Ian Watt, "Realism and the Novel Form," *The Rise of the Novel: Studies in Defoe, Richardson, and Fielding* (Berkeley and Los Angeles, 1962), pp. 9-34.

Concretized Form

the shepherd idylls of the second and third centuries to the naturalist novels at the end of the nineteenth, we can view the evolution of prose fiction as a demonstration of the slow progressive submergence and near dissolution of general classifications, permanent structures, and typologies of character in an ocean of sensuous fact and material process. What Cervantes had called truth becomes inseparable at the end of the nineteenth century from what, for Cervantes, was clearly not truth; that is, the transitory and impermanent, the chameleonic specificities of the physical world.

Unlike Cervantes, Flaubert does not live in a stable society. Darwin and the physical sciences have routed the God that once gave metaphysical resonance to natural fact and ultimate value to the beliefs and traditions of an earlier community. Although the removal of the Deity begins as an idea in the Enlightenment (where Newtonian physics reduces God to a hypothetical first cause), the full effects of this idea are not perceived until we encounter the fiction of the nineteenth century. (Robinson Crusoe still finds God's presence in every particular of his desert island. Jane Austen's society, in the main, is just as stable and hierarchic as Cervantes's.)[24]

It is the presence of the Deity that finally ratifies the moral and social structure of the stable society as fixed and invariable. It is this same presence that permits a novelist, such as Cervantes or Fielding, working in such a society to apprehend the moral and social structure of each fictional character and event as equally fixed and invariable, as structure existing prior to a world of sensory experience that may or may not confirm it. Flaubert and his contemporaries, however, do not live in such a society, and they must, of course, learn to live and work in the only society available to them: one that is skeptical in religious matters, unstable in social structure, and uncertain and relativistic in moral

---

[24]The information in this paragraph is based on Northrop Frye's general remarks regarding this matter: "The modern movement, properly speaking, began when Darwin finally shattered the old teleological conception of nature as reflecting an intelligent purpose" (*The Modern Century* [New York, 1969], pp. 109-10). See also J. Hillis Miller, *The Disappearance of God: Five Nineteenth Century Writers* (New York, 1965), pp. 1-16. Miller describes the "Godless" condition as the "spiritual situation for many western writers during the last one hundred and fifty years" (p. 2).

values. It is here, then, in the nineteenth century, that these new novelists—the realists, the naturalists, as well as some of their immediate predecessors (such as Balzac)—clutch at a new Deity (positivism and the methods of the physical scientist) and a new truth (direct observation and the experience of the senses). "Art," writes Flaubert, "must rise above personal emotions and nervous susceptibilities. It is time to endow it with the pitiless method, with the exactness of the physical sciences."[25]

Flaubert aspires to the methodology of the physical scientist not because he is cold and unfeeling (as some critics would have us believe) but, on the contrary, because he is anxious and uncertain.[26] Flaubert strives to be "pitiless" and "exact" because he lives in an unstable society where there appears increasingly less to be "pitiless" and "exact" about. He must visualize every element of his narrative precisely because it is the visual that can no longer be taken for granted. He must *see* his characters, for if he does not see them he can no longer be certain that they are there at all. Whether his thought now originates in the mind or in the eye, it must always express itself through what can be seen with clarity and exactitude (you must always "have your model constantly posing in front of you"). Where an earlier novelist could simply *tell* his story, Flaubert must now *prove* it moment by moment, must provide a continuing demonstration of the palpable certainty of his characters and events.[27]

---

[25]Flaubert to Mademoiselle Leroyer de Chantepie (1857), *Letters,* pp. 195-96.

[26]As he is here, to Louise Colet (1852): "Meanwhile we are in a shadowy corridor, groping in the dark. We all lack a basis—literati and scribblers that we are. What's the good of all this? Is our chatter the answer to any need?" (ibid., p. 131).

[27]This view is supported by Martin Turnell: "The classic novelist did not bother to describe physical appearances because it was unnecessary. The individual was a concrete reality who was inescapably there, living in a world which was morally, socially, and physically circumscribed. There was not the slightest danger of his losing his identity, vanishing into the crowd, or dwindling into a speck on 'the vast horizon' as he does in Zola. If the Realists and the Naturalists set out to immortalize his features, it was because it was the only way of being sure or recognizing him again and because there was often nothing behind the face, or nothing but the blind instinctual urges which were breaking down and which seemed to be in imminent danger of collapse. That is why they clung so desperately to scientific determinism" (*The Art of French Fiction* [New York, 1959], pp. 25-26).

Erich Heller remarks on the simliar attitude of Flaubert's friend Ivan Turgenev:

Concretized Form

In order to accomplish this demonstration, Flaubert crystallizes the literary form that becomes characteristic not only of him but of the many novelists who followed him and learned to live in societies even less stable than his own. Flaubert's literary form now renders experience through scale, proportion, perspective, color and line, behavioral postures and gestures, plastic shapes and materialized actions. To read *Madame Bovary* after *Don Quixote* is to experience an extraordinary and startling change in literary climate because Flaubert's heroine, unlike Cervantes's hero, is seen before she is known. She is known finally *as* she is seen, by the way she is seen; and because of this, Flaubert is, as it were, never through seeing her, can never see enough of her. She is seen, indeed, even before she is named:

> A young woman wearing a blue merino dress with three flounces came to the door of the house to greet Monsieur Bovary, and she ushered him into the kitchen, where a big open fire was blazing. Around its edges the farm hands' breakfast was bubbling in small pots of assorted sizes. Damp clothes were drying inside the vast chimney-opening. The fire shovel, the tongs, and the nose of the bellows, all of colossal proportions, shone like polished steel; and along the walls hung a lavish array of kitchen utensils, glimmering in the bright light of the fire and in the first rays of the sun that were now beginning to come in through the window panes.[28]

Flaubert introduces his heroine amid a welter of inanimate objects and environmental detail. She materializes before us, a nameless, animate, female form in costume surrounded by kitchen furnishings and metallic bric-a-brac. The action does not stop for this "young woman" as it stops for Don Quixote; time and space never cease to exist for her as they do for the hero of the pre-Flaubertian narrative. Our eyes perceive this "young woman" and the space through which she moves and by which she

---

"Turgenev once confessed that he felt always a little lost when asked to speak his own mind on this or that question, and deprived of the chance of hiding behind the exchanges of imaginary characters: 'Then it always seems to me that one might just as well and with equal right assert the opposite of what I am saying. But if I talk about a red nose or fair hair, well, then the hair is fair and the nose is red, and no amount of reflection will reflect it away' " (quoted in "Literature and Political Responsibility," *Commentary*, July 1971, p. 53).

[28]Gustave Flaubert, *Madame Bovary* (New York: Random House, 1957), trans. Francis Steegmuller, pp. 16-17. Subsequent references to this edition will appear in text.

is all but engulfed long before we come to know and understand her character. Two paragraphs later, in a kind of literary double take, the reader realizes that this "young woman," whose emergence has been so casual and oblique, is, in fact, "Mademoiselle Emma," the same Emma whose name appears in the title of the novel. And the reader—if he is a reader of modern fiction—is not at all surprised to discover Emma in just this way; he is not at all unsettled by Flaubert's radical displacement of novelistic decorum. Emma, after all, is only one in an almost endless series of modern characters who are seen before they are named, who appear first as this man or that woman and only later as Dick Diver or Horace Benbow or Molly Bloom. Flaubert can work in this manner because he knows—as Fitzgerald, Faulkner, and Joyce know—that character cannot precede action, that action shapes, modulates, and embodies character, and that to hold character apart from, and prior to, action as a self-sufficient entity is to perform a supreme act of confidence for which the uncertainties of modern experience will no longer make allowance.[29]

The concretized novel, then, does not have that timeless dimension of expositional analysis (the structural analogue for eternity) where we got to know a character like Don Quixote all at once. In place of exposition, concretized fiction offers exposition through action and presents a highly particularized space-time drama (the structural analogue for human experience) where we can only get to know a character like Emma Bovary gradually, as she unfolds, evolves, modulates, and emerges before us in time and through space, aspect by aspect, moment by moment.

As a member of a stable, circumscribed, God-oriented society, Cervantes can envisage each character whole and all at once and thus can focus his energies on what makes the character what he is at all times and in all places, in spite of the fact that what the character is may or may not coincide with what he does, says, and feels at a specific time and place: in other words, Cervantes can

---

[29]"In Greece and the Middle Ages it was believed that *operari sequitur esse*—actions follow, and derive from, being. The nineteenth century may be said to have established the opposite principle: *esse sequitur operari*—the being of a thing is nothing else than the sum total of its actions and functions" (José Ortega y Gasset, "Notes on the Novel," *The Dehumanization of Art: And Other Writings on Art and Culture* [New York, 1958], p. 62).

Concretized Form

separate human nature (that is, being, structure, essence), if need be, from human behavior (appearance, human action in the space-time continuum). For this reason Cervantes has the confidence to talk about his character in a generalized way, to summarize his behavior over long periods of time, and to focus on those aspects of his behavior that reveal his character in its typical, habitual, and quintessential forms.

As the member of a skeptical, unstable, man-oriented society, Flaubert envisages character as the function of an evolutionary process and cannot separate the essential nature of character from its particular manifestations in a moment-to-moment, ongoing continuum of human behavior. For this reason Flaubert presents character, not as a whole, but through details, and not all at once, but only when the moment-to-moment continuum makes such presentation necessary and inevitable. That usually means one aspect now and another later, or one aspect in combination with another, or one aspect appearing in many contexts, but each time in a different form. Because these contexts are rendered with such extraordinary specificity, each existential situation now stresses those qualities of human behavior that reveal character not in its typical, habitual, and quintessential forms but rather in forms that are unique, circumstantial, and transitory.

When, for example, Charles Bovary meets Emma for the first time at Les Berteaux, he attends to her father's leg:

> For splints, they sent someone to bring a bundle of laths from the carriage shed. Charles selected one, cut it into lengths and smoothed it down with a piece of broken window glass, while the maidservant tore sheets for bandages and Mademoiselle Emma tried to sew some pads. She was a long time finding her workbox, and her father showed his impatience. She made no reply; but as she sewed she kept pricking her fingers and raising them to her mouth to suck. [P. 17]

We know that Don Quixote "always" has a lance in the rack and a stew with more beef than mutton in it. Does Emma always keep "pricking her fingers and raising them to her mouth to suck"? At this point in the narrative we cannot say, nor will Flaubert tell us. The gesture, however, does reveal something about her—a femininity, a sensuality, and a childish charm—which fascinates Charles. Different manifestations of these qualities appear later in the novel when Charles observes Emma drinking liquor from a glass and notes how "the tip of her tongue came out from between her small teeth and began daintily to lick the bottom of the glass" (p. 25). Innumberable little gestures of this kind link up with each other to form a feature (that is, a trait) of Emma's character, while gestures of other kinds link up with one another to form other features. In this manner, then, working gradually and empirically through a careful selection and disposition of observed postures, gestures, and feelings, Flaubert constructs a pattern of behavior for Emma.

Flaubert, unlike Cervantes, permits the narrative action to expose everything that we need to know about the characters. He himself remains silent, unwilling to appropriate any element of this action for his own voice. If one is a member of an unstable society where values are no longer fixed and invariable, one knows finally that one's personal truth may be only a partial truth and that when one speaks, one may be only speaking for oneself. Flaubert, then, acts out of a kind of literary ventriloquism, the effects of which are still to be found in contemporary fiction. He projects a voice that does not belong to any of his characters, or to himself, or to that special self authors often invent for purposes of storytelling (a mask, or a persona). He projects instead a voice that—at least in its general intention—is not meant to indicate any human sound at all; it is meant, rather, to be the sound of a documentation, the sound of the action revealing itself *by* itself—flat, neutral, unvaried, fixed on its object, "pitiless" in its unrelenting progression from point to point in the narrative. This is one of the crucial ways in which Flaubert differs from earlier visualizers like Balzac, Dickens, and Gogol, who still speak in overtly mediating voices.

Can any voice that speaks in a human language separate itself from a human personality? Strictly speaking, it cannot. But Flaubert, in projecting this new voice, is not speaking strictly but is actually educating his reader to accept the terms of a new literary convention: the sound of a voice that is not meant to be heard, the sound, as it were, of the author-not-being-there; a voice that actually informs the reader that this is the way the action must go when the author himself is no longer present to run it. In a sense the modern reader has never stopped hearing the sound of this voice because it has appeared in countless

Concretized Form 23

modern novels in a variety of textures and accents. (It appears, for instance, in many stories by Joyce—like "The Sisters," "Counterparts," and most notably "Ivy Day in the Committee Room"—and certain sections of *Ulysses*, like "The Wandering Rocks."[30] It also appears in the work of such diverse figures as Kafka, Camus, Dos Passos, Graham Greene, John O'Hara, Michel Butor, and Alain Robbe-Grillet.)

The impersonalized voice is one narrative device that deflects the reader's attention from the author's personality to the action itself. Another is the unmediated action, or, more precisely, an action that has been mediated not through the author but through one of his characters who is himself involved in the action. In the above passages, for example, we seem to see Emma not through Flaubert but through Charles; just as later in the novel we seem to see Charles himself, as well as other characters, through Emma. The subjectivity of the character's experience tends to increase in direct proportion to the self-effacement of the author. (In order to keep himself out of the story, Flaubert will sometimes allow one scene to comment on another by juxtaposing the scenes and developing them in counterpoint, as in the famous Agricultural Fair sequence, where the sentimental dialogue between Emma and Rudolphe is interspersed with the judges' speeches concerning pigs and manure.)

Thus, the novel of concretized form usually promotes experience at the expense of reflection; we tend to live through a concretized action before we are able to think about it. Since there is no author present in the narrative to take us above the action, we tend to experience the action the way the characters themselves experience it, and that is with varying degrees of unreflecting immersion in a living moment. Any reflection, of course, will only remind us that someone has invented every moment of this action and that an action unmediated by its author is as fully unattainable—and therefore as much a literary convention—as that of an impersonalized voice.

The ultimate purpose, however, of both devices is to enable Flaubert to construct a narrative form that will appear to be

[30]But not in such stories as "Araby," "Clay," or "The Dead," or in sections of *Ulysses* like "Scylla and Charybdis," where the voices of the characters often insinuate themselves into the voice of the narrator.

self-sufficient, self-justifying, and autotelic; a form that will seem to exist independent of both its maker and its audience, like an organism of parthenogenetic growth; a self-regarding narrative event severed from its origins and seemingly indifferent to its effects. "What seems to me the highest and most difficult achievement of art," he writes, "is not to make us laugh or cry, or to rouse our lust or our anger, but to do as nature does—that is, fill us with wonderment. The most beautiful works have indeed this quality. They are serene in aspect, incomprehensible."[31]

We cannot separate the story of Don Quixote from the particularized personality of the author who directly mediates the narrative and is therefore a part of that narrative, a dramatic ingredient *in* it. Nor can we separate this story from the audience; without its assumed presence the act of mediation would not take place, and it, therefore, is also a dramatic ingredient in the narrative. The pre-Flaubertian novel, then, functions as a kind of group project, an ongoing intercommunal nexus with author as active sender, audience as passive receiver, and the work itself as the larger context that includes both author and audience.

Flaubert, as we have seen, does not conceive of his work as a context but rather as a kind of absolute text remote from human appropriations, a supernal thing in nature, "serene in aspect, incomprehensible." Nor does he conceive of the author as an active presence in the narrative but rather, as a reluctant concession to human necessity, as an "exact" and "pitiless" tone that is present only to the extent that it cannot be entirely absent. Flaubert also demands a new kind of audience, active rather than passive, an audience that must now learn to move toward, seek out, and grapple with the remote and autonomous narrative form. The prerequisites for membership in a pre-Flaubertian audience were essentially literacy and receptivity: the ability to read and the willingness to do so. Flaubert, however, in addition to literacy and receptivity, now demands from his audience an active intelligence, an intensive and analytic involvement in the narrative. The new reader must not only be able to read but to interpret as well.

In practical terms this new relationship between reader and text means that Flaubert's audience must finally learn to think

---

[31]Flaubert to Louise Colet (1853), *Letters,* pp. 160-61.

Concretized Form

through its eyes. The words that convey the concretized narrative, for the most part, refer the reader to objects in the external world that he can see as he reads along; that is, the words have been chosen to make him grasp the subject largely by means of visual images. These images, however, have not been chosen at random. The images embody concepts and the author has chosen them, in fact, to be understood as visualized concepts. Flaubert writes: "Just as you cannot remove from a physical body the qualities that constitute it—color, extension solidity—without reducing it to a hollow abstraction, without destroying it, so you cannot remove the form from the Idea, because the Idea only exists by virtue of its form."[32]

Thus, Flaubert does not have to tell us that Emma is "beautiful" or that Charles is "impressed," for these are notions we can experience for ourselves as we observe Emma through Charles:

> The room was chilly, and she shivered as she ate. Charles noticed that her lips were full, and that she had the habit of biting them in moments of silence.
>
> Her neck rose out of the low fold of a white collar. The two black sweeps of her hair, pulled down from a fine center part that followed the curve of her skull, were so sleek that each seemed to be one piece. Covering all but the very tips of her ears, it was gathered at the back into a large chignon, and toward the temples it waved a bit—a detail that the country doctor observed for the first time in his life. Her skin was rosy over her cheekbones. A pair of shell-rimmed eyeglasses, like a man's, was tucked between two buttons of her bodice. [P. 18]

Nor does Flaubert have to explain the nature of Charles's feeling for Emma or Emma's awareness of this feeling when the concretized form permits him instead to construct a little choreography of sexual interest, contact, and hesitation:

> When Charles came back downstairs after going up to take leave of Monsieur Rouault, he found her standing with her forehead pressed against the windowpane, looking out at the garden, where the beanpoles had been thrown down by the wind. She turned around.
> "Are you looking for something?" she asked.
> "For my riding crop," he said.
> And he began to rummage on the bed, behind doors, under chairs. It had fallen on the floor between the grainbags and the wall.

[32]Flaubert to Louise Colet (1846), ibid., p. 74.

Mademoiselle Emma caught sight of it and reached for it, bending down across the sacks. Charles hurried over politely, and as he, too, stretched out his arm he felt his body in slight contact with the girl's back, bent there beneath him. She stood up, blushing crimson, and glanced at him over her shoulder as she handed him his crop. [Pp. 18-19]

We know that Emma blushes not only from exertion but also from her awareness of the moment of physical intimacy that has passed between her and Charles; and that she boldly nourishes this intimacy by remaining in position and passing the crop over her shoulder, glancing at Charles as he hovers close behind her. Even Charles, naive as he is, is not entirely unaware of what has happened, for while Flaubert does not tell us his feelings, he calmly reports in the next sentence that "instead of returning to Les Berteaux three days later, as he had promised, he went back the very next day, then twice a week regularly, not to mention unscheduled calls he made from time to time, as though by chance" (P. 19). This sentence, of course, indicates to the reader that Charles has fallen in love with Emma, even though Flaubert himself never mentions this fact and even though this fact is the "point" of the entire sequence of narrative action. Five paragraphs later he finally allows Charles's wife (the first Madame Bovary) to reflect and thus make the point for him: "So that's why he [Charles] brightens up when he goes there! That's why he wears his new waistcoat, even in the rain! Ah! So she's at the bottom of it!" (pp. 20-21).

Because the visual images are numerous and succeed one another on the page in a kind of unbroken visual stream, without pause for authorial comment or reflection, we tend to see the images in concretized fiction slightly faster than our minds can grasp their significance or their precise relation to one another. (This is true not only of Flaubert's fiction but also, for example, of Chekhov's, Babel's, Hemingway's, and, of course, Joyce's.) Because of this mental delay, we also tend to see the images not once but twice: first in their immediate visual otherness; then, by a kind of spontaneous and coordinating mental reflex, we see them again, but this time in their continuity and coherence. We see Emma suck her fingers; we see Emma bite her full lips; we see Charles touch Emma; we see Charles return to the farm: we see *how* this relationship happens before we fully know *what* it is that we see. Our second view is always an act of understanding; we immediately see the images as ordered images; we grasp the "Idea" embodied in their arrangement which the author has put there for us to find; the "Idea" which gathers the images—even as it is embodied by them—into art.

The way we finally come to understand the concretized sequences of Flaubert is very much like the way we come to understand the impressionist painting of the late nineteenth century: we learn to respond to both by an act of "stepping back." We learn to understand, not *as* we experience, but always the moment after we experience; after the infinite number of observed details (the impressionist *tache*) coalesce in the mind and the "Idea" embodied in their arrangement locks into place. We learn to experience "near"—then, a moment after, understand "far."

This new way of reading, I suggest, brings about nothing less than a new stage in the evolution of the reader's consciousness, a new development in the reader's capacity for literary understanding. Flaubert's reader must not only accustom himself to read words that refer continually to things that he can see, but he must now make an added effort, just as he would in life, to grasp the meaning expressed by the things themselves. In brief, he must learn to read a verbal language that embodies a seemingly unmediated visual language. And it is the understanding of this silent language that constitutes the primary experience, I think, in the reading of late nineteenth-century prose fiction, an experience, of course, that every twentieth-century reader who has learned how to watch a film or a television set can take for granted as part of his upbringing in a visual culture.

Chapter II
The Oval of Vision

AFTER THE EXAMPLE of Flaubert, the characteristic effort of the post-Flaubertians becomes the creation of a narrative action that can be seen. The intensive visualization in concretized form provides a common denominator for a substantial body of the fiction produced in the last hundred years and establishes a link between the concretized art of Flaubert and that of such moderns as Conrad, Joyce, Faulkner, Hemingway, Dos Passos, Nabokov, and Robert-Grillet.

This chapter examines this new form as the transmitter of an *action that is seen* and analyzes the way in which space is visualized in different kinds of post-Flaubertian fiction and the attitudes of mind and feeling that lie behind such visualization. I will trace the development of the visual field through a variety of late nineteenth- and early twentieth-century writers and attempt to show how the novelists subsequent to Flaubert depart from him just as they draw upon him, how the fiction of one literary generation differs from the fiction of another.

Flaubert and the Camera Eye

In order to appreciate this development, however, we must first understand Flaubert's special way of seeing. At this point I am going to return to *Madame Bovary* and examine Flaubert's characteristic method of visual composition:

One day he arrived about three o'clock. Everyone was in the fields. He went into the kitchen, and at first didn't see Emma. The shutters were closed; the sun, streaming in between the slats, patterned the floor with long thin stripes that broke off at the corners of the furniture and quivered on the ceiling. On the table, flies were climbing up the sides of glasses that had recently been used, and buzzing as they struggled to keep from drowning in the cider at the bottom. The light coming down

The Oval of Vision 29

the chimney turned the soot on the fireback to velvet and gave a bluish cast to the cold ashes. Between the window and the hearth Emma sat sewing; her shoulders were bare, beaded with little drops of sweat. [P. 25]

In this passage Flaubert sees each object in the scene one after the other; that is to say, one object at a time. Each object seems to emerge from its context with remarkable clarity and precision: it is seen as a thing separate and distinct, existing in and of itself and like no other thing. Flaubert is thus sparing in his use of metaphor and simile. This passage, in fact, contains none. The shutters are one thing; the light through the slats another; the table, a third; and so on. Emma, too, is a separate "thing."

Flaubert also works close to the physical surface of the object he is describing. It is characteristic of him to render those qualities of an object that one could discover for himself, not only by looking at it, but also by holding it in his hands and by moving his hands over its surface. That is why Flaubert will often render the line and shape of a thing, as in the sunlight with "long thin stripes" (this rendering of line and shape seems to give his objects a self-bounded quality, an edge); or the texture of a thing, like the soot on the fireback turning to "velvet"; or the qualities of a thing that are tactile as well as visual ("her shoulders were bare, beaded with little drops of sweat."). It is no wonder that Flaubert found the experience of seeing so "voluptuous," or that the publishers of *Madame Bovary* were brought to trial. Had any other novelist before Flaubert ever taken his reader so "close" to the body of a woman?

Furthermore, we not only see one object after another, but we also see one object next to another; that is, we see how the object lies in relation to other objects. We perceive its position in space and thus get a sense of the space itself, the space that surrounds the object. We not only see the light "streaming in between the slats" as a distinct thing, but we also see how it "patterned the floor" and how it "broke off at the corners of furniture"; and how, finally, it "quivered on the ceiling." We not only see Emma with her bare shoulders as distinct from the other objects in the room, but we also see her "between the window and the hearth"; that is *placed in a spatial context*. In this manner the room seems to fill up, as it were, and ultimately realize itself not as a collection of objects but as an architectural fact, a visualized container with a dimension of planned space.

Flaubert observes these objects in a specific spatial position because that is the way they appear at a specific moment. Moreover, Flaubert, in effect, does not observe these objects at all, for the author is not present in his concretized situation: instead, he allows Charles Bovary to observe them at the moment of his entry into the room. We see the room the way Charles sees it as his eye moves from one side of it to the other; from the closed shutters, to the light on the floor and on the ceiling, to the table, to the chimney—and then finally to Emma herself. (We see everything in the room *before* Emma because we are told that Charles "at first didn't see Emma.")

In this passage, as in all of Flaubert's visualizations, we always feel the presence of two factors operating simultaneously: a seen object and a seer; that is to say, an object that is rendered as seen at a specific point in space ("next to" something, "above" something, and the like) and at a specific moment in time (the moment when someone is looking at it); and an observer who resides at a specific point in space that is other than, at a distance—near or far—from, the space he observes. The observer, however, need not always be a specific character in the narrative. In a number of occasions he may be the narrator himself, who will then describe the event with the eye of a neutral spectator and will occupy, like any other character, a fixed and limited space within the scene. When, for instance, Leon seduces Emma inside a moving carriage with drawn curtains, Flaubert renounces the privileged position of the omnipresent novelist and describes the whole journey from outside the vehicle, as if he himself were an observer stationed at various points along the route followed by the carriage.

But whether he "hides" behind his character or behind a neutral narrator, Flaubert will characteristically seek to replace, wherever possible, the voice and presence of a godlike, omniscient novelist with the *seeing eye of a man*.[1] In this manner Flaubert

---

[1] One should only add, however, that certain tendencies in Flaubert criticism have moved in a direction opposite to my own and to that of most American analysis of *Madame Bovary*. French criticism in particular has stressed the subjective side of *Madame Bovary* and the way in which Flaubert allows his consciousness—if not the sound of his voice—to enter into the reveries of Emma

defines visual perspective itself as the fundamental means of presentation in a concretized narrative form. Visual perspective informs the reader that this is the way a specific situation allows a specific eye to view it; that any understanding of a situation is always limited by the way the eye chooses to see it, by the position of the eye in relation to its object; that truth itself now depends as much upon the angle of vision as upon the object of vision.

Flaubert's way of seeing in the above passage reminds me of the cinema, and there are countless other passages in Flaubert that also evoke the art of the filmmaker. I am not the first to say this of Flaubert; others have said it before me.[2] But what these others often neglect to add is what they mean when they say it. What, then, do we mean precisely when we say that Flaubert's manner of vision is like a filmmaker's? How can any novelist be like a filmmaker?

It was, I believe, Béla Balázs, the Hungarian film theoretician, who first called attention to the unalterable nature of the image in film:

Every picture shows us not only a piece of reality, but a point of view as well.... The physiognomy of every object in a film picture is a composite of two physiognomies—one is that of the object, its very own, which is quite independent of the spectator—and another physiognomy, determined by the viewpoint of the spectator and the perspective of the picture. In the shot the two merge into so close a unity that only a very practised eye is capable of distinguishing these two components in the picture itself.

Balázs described the film image that represents the object as "the subjectivity of the object," and what he meant by this was that

---

and into certain metaphorical patterns that recur throughout the novel. As Paul De Man states, "It is clear that a fully inclusive study of *Madame Bovary* would have to combine the French study of metaphors with the American study of narrative structure in the novel" (Introduction, *Madame Bovary*, Norton Critical Edition, ed. and trans. Paul De Man [New York, 1965], p. xiii). For the "French study" see Charles du Bos, "On the 'Inner Environment' in the work of Flaubert"; Georges Poulet, "The Circle and the Center: Reality and *Madame Bovary*"; and Jean Pierre Richard, "Love and Memory in *Madame Bovary*," all in ibid., pp. 360-71, 392-407, and 426-38, respectively.

[2]See Martin Turnell, *The Novel in France* (New York, 1958), p. 285, or Harry Levin, *The Gates of Horn: A Study of Five French Realists* (New York, 1966), p. 261.

you could not see the object in a film without at the same time being aware of the way you were seeing it.[3] Balázs, then, helps us to understand the double-sided and paradoxical epistemology of the camera. On the one hand, the camera is an objective medium, for it can neither think nor feel, and surely no other art in our time has provided us with more objective information about the surface of physical reality than the art of the camera. On the other hand, the camera is a subjective medium, for it cannot show us any object without at the time revealing its own physical position—its angle and distance from the object—as part of what is shown. This means that the images produced by the motion picture camera will only allow us to experience the object through a series of perspectives; that the ontology of the image itself will never allow for an apprehension of the object as a whole. In this sense no other art is less equipped to present a godlike and omniscient view of human experience than the cinema, and no other art form, therefore, represents a more accurate embodiment of a modernist and relativist metaphysics than cinematographic form.[4]

---

[3]*Theory of the Film: Character and Growth of a New Art* (New York, 1970), pp. 89-91.

[4]A view supported by Magny: "In a movie, every scene is of necessity photographed from a certain point of view, and this point of view is part of it, inseparable from its essence; it cannot be eliminated to give up a 'pure' vision, a vision of someone who would not have a point of view" (*Age of the American Novel*, p. 88). When my remarks on this matter appeared in print ("Flaubert to Joyce: Evolution of a Cinematographic Form"), David Lodge found them to be "an acceptable account of 'cinematographic form' from the artist's point of view, as a creative process," but unacceptable from "the audience's or spectator's point of view, as an artistic process. . . . As experienced viewers of films we tend to take the camera eye for granted and to accept the 'truth' of what it shows us even though its perspective is never that of ordinary human vision" ("Thomas Hardy and Cinematographic Form," *Novel*, 7 [Spring 1974], 247-48). A strange statement from a professedly "experienced viewer." Wasn't it precisely the *in*experienced viewer who ducked his head whenever the train came at the camera? And isn't it precisely the "experienced viewer" who knows—or should know—better? Certainly Professor Lodge knows better (otherwise his "truth" would appear without quotation marks). Aside from the fact that the experience of the "experienced viewer" is anybody's guess, I find Professor Lodge's assertion somewhat naive (and a little depressing), for while it is doubtless honest, it is not *critical* (reflective, analytic). Of course any viewer of narrative film may take the configurations of light on the screen "for real" just as any reader of "realistic" fiction may take the words on the page "for real"—but whose fault is that? Any viewer or reader may react in this manner, for he is not obliged to think about his reaction, not obliged,

Balázs, then, also helps us to understand the art of Flaubert, as well as that of any practitioner of concretized form, as essentially a perspectivist's art. The novelist who would present human experience by means of this form must also learn, as part of this effort, to apprehend human experience with an eye that sees like a camera, to render the meaning of the seen object itself as inseparable from the seer's position in time and space.

It is important to remember that this special kind of visualization—visualization through perspective—is not synonymous with literary visualization in general, which appears of course to some degree in the literature of every era. Nor should one forget that while visual perspective may be the defining characteristic of narrative form in the nineteenth century, one can also find isolated examples of visual perspective in any number of random and unrelated literary figures throughout history. I have found such examples, for instance, in the work of Dante and Ovid, just as the Russian film director Sergei Eisenstein found similar examples in the poetry of Milton and the writings of such a nonliterary artist as Leonardo.[5] It is only in the fiction of the nineteenth century, however, that visual perspective moves to the center of a coherent and fully articulated literary form, which then becomes the common mode of apprehending experience for a whole generation of literary artists.

Still, there are those nineteenth-century novelists who employ visual perspective but do not renounce the narrator's privileged position of omniscience and omnipresence. What of Balzac and Dickens? In the interests of clarity, it is essential to distinguish between visualization in a fully concretized form and visualization in the work of Flaubert's immediate predecessors. There is much to see in the novels of Balzac and Dickens, but why are the visual effects in these novels so ambiguous? Here, for instance, is Balzac:

The front of the boardinghouse overlooks a little garden, so that the building stands at right angles with the Rue Neuve-Sainte-Geneviève,

---

in this instance, to remind himself that his response is demonstrably uninstructed. And all this means is that any viewer or reader is not obliged to be a critic, that is, a member of the audience who imposes upon himself the obligation to think, to be critical.

[5]Sergei Eisenstein, *Film Form and the Film Sense*, ed. and trans. Jay Leyda (New York, 1957), pp. 25-36, 57-64.

from which you can see the whole width of it. Along the front of the house, separating it from the garden, there runs a pebbled channel, six feet wide, beyond which there is a graveled pathway bordered with geraniums, oleanders, and pomegranate trees, planted in large pots, of blue and white crockery. The entrance to this pathway is made through a small door surmounted with a placard on which is inscribed: THE VAUQUER HOUSE, and underneath: FAMILY BOARDINGHOUSE FOR LADIES AND GENTLEMEN. During the daytime a latticed door, furnished with a jangling bell, allows you to see at the other end of the path, on the wall opposite the street, an arch painted by some local artist to imitate green marble.[6]

This is only the beginning of Balzac's famous description of the Maison Vauquer (*Père Goriot,* 1835) which proceeds in this manner for many pages, and I have never met anyone who could follow all the spatial relations of this boardinghouse at each point in the description. The problem, however, is not that Balzac does not provide us with enough visual information. If anything, he provides us with too much information, and *that* is the problem. Balzac seems to be everywhere at once. In the first sentence, for example, he seems to be both at the front of the house and at the side of it (that is, "the whole width of it") virtually within the same instant. In the second sentence he is inside the garden at the front of the house. In the third he is outside the garden in front of a "small door," which in the fourth sentence changes "during the daytime" into a "latticed door" which then enables us to see the painted arch on the "wall opposite the street."

A camera could reproduce all of Balzac's perspectives, but it could reproduce only one perspective at a time. (It would be almost impossible for the camera to manage succinctly the doubleview in sentence one.) Within each perspective, moreover, there would also be much less spatial confusion because the camera would make us aware of where we were standing in relation to whatever we were looking at. To see in this manner would be to approximate the eye of a man who was present within the scene. Balzac, however, does not see with the eye of a man, but with the eye of a god that imagines itself as both physically present in the scene and, at the same time, out of and above it. This eye is both everywhere and nowhere and will, therefore, only intermittently incorporate spatial and temporal

---

[6]Honoré de Balzac, *Père Goriot,* trans. Jane Mino Sedgwick (New York, 1963), p. 5.

The Oval of Vision 35

limitations into its vision. Balzac holds all visual perspectives simultaneously in his mind and does not choose to worry about a purely human order of ocular apprehension. With superb confidence he disperses a jumble of angles and distances that seem to fall before our eyes all at once like raindrops.

In contrast to Balzac the visualizations of Dickens present us with much less spatial confusion, for Dickens adheres more closely to the movements of an eye that is fully present at every given scene, and thus an eye that has been fully coordinated to the movements of its object. One can, for example, sense this presence and coordination in the scene in which the Artful Dodger introduces Oliver Twist to Fagin (*Oliver Twist*, 1838):

He threw open the door of a back-room, and drew Oliver in after him.

The walls and ceiling of the room were perfectly black with age and dirt. There was a deal table before the fire: upon which were a candle, stuck in a ginger-beer bottle, two or three pewter pots, a loaf and butter, and a plate. In a frying-pan, which was on the fire, and which was secured to the mantelshelf by a string, some sausages were cooking; and standing over them, with a toasting-fork in his hand, was a very old shrivelled Jew, whose villainous-looking and repulsive face was obscured by a quantity of matted red hair. He was dressed in a greasy flannel gown, with his throat bare; and seemed to be dividing his attention between the frying-pan and a clothes-horse, over which a great number of silk handkerchiefs were hanging. Several rough beds made of old sacks were huddled side by side on the floor. Seated round the table were four or five boys, none older than the Dodger, smoking long clay pipes, and drinking spirits with the air of middle-aged men. These all crowded about their associate as he whispered a few words to the Jew; and then turned round and grinned at Oliver. So did the Jew himself, toasting-fork in hand.

"This is him, Fagin," said Jack Dawkins; "my friend, Oliver Twist."[7]

Dickens's treatment of what Oliver sees in Fagin's den is very similar to Flaubert's treatment of what Charles sees as he enters the room in the Rouault farmhouse. Dickens, like Flaubert, reveals the scene by means of a searching eye, and Eisenstein and others have been right to single out Dickens as an early practitioner of the cinematographer's art.[8] I would add, however, that

---

[7]Charles Dickens, *Oliver Twist* (New York, 1962), p. 57.

[8]Eisenstein, "Dickens, Griffith, and the Film Today," *Film Form*, pp. 195-255; and see Dorothy Van Ghent, "The Dickens World: A View from Todger's," *Sewanee Review*, 58 (1950), 419-38.

Dickens emerges in the history of the development of concretized form not as a fully conscious exponent of this form but rather as a transitional figure between a pre- and a post-Flaubertian manner of presentation.

Dickens is a transitional figure because in most of his visualizations, as in the one above, there are characteristically not one but two eyes present. The first belongs to the character, the second to the narrator himself. While the second eye sometimes sees conjointly with the first (as in the opening sentence, and then again at the end of the paragraph when the boys turn to Oliver), the second often sees apart from, and beyond, the first, as well as in an order of apprehension of which the first would hardly be capable. It is the narrator, not the character, that reveals this interior to us in the manner of a great stage dramatist. Oliver has neither the artistry nor, at this moment, the composure for this kind of presentation. First we see the set (the wall and the ceiling), then the props (the table, the pots, the plate), then the objects that lead us to the main character ("frying-pan" and "toasting-fork"), and finally, at the climax, we see Fagin himself. At this moment Oliver, unlike the narrator, cannot see Fagin's face, nor presumably can anyone else in the room, for Fagin is facing the fire. Nor can Oliver yet say of this face, as does the narrator, that it was "villainous-looking and repulsive." This is the sort of comment that would never appear in a visualization by Flaubert. A thoroughly concretized art does not make comments nor, we need hardly add, does the camera.

This is the sort of comment, however, that marks Dickens as a member of a pre-Flaubertian generation of novelists, a bolder, freer, less self-conscious generation than the one that replaced it, a generation less reluctant to separate what it knew to be true from what it saw to exist. Dickens—like Balzac, Cooper, Gogol, Thackeray, and George Eliot—imposes his point of view upon the world as unimpeachable testimony, and Fagin's "villainous-looking and repulsive" face thrusts itself upon us with the force of a visualized ultimatum. The materiality of the Dickensian object is thus imbued with moral and emotional urgencies that transfigure matter, that indeed virtually transfigure Fagin, with his "red hair," "toasting-fork" and the "fire" into a red devil with pitchfork and the flames of hell.[9] Without these transfiguring urgen-

---

[9] Lauriat Lane, "The Devil in *Oliver Twist*," *Dickensian*, 52 (1956), 132-36.

The Oval of Vision 37

cies, the materiality of the Flaubertian object seems, by contrast, to be flat, opaque, and inert. The point here is not that Dickens is less cinematographic than Flaubert (this is a quibble), but that he has less patience with the perspectivist's stance, that he is, finally, less modern.

But one must add an important qualification to the cinematic effects in both Dickens and Flaubert: when these writers—as in the passages above—describe a scene, they characteristically arrange the objects within the spectator's field of vision as if the objects themselves were present on a stage at the theater. Their space is characteristically theater space in that all the objects that need to be seen are simultaneously present and gathered together within a single framework, a field of vision bounded, so to speak, by the pillars of a mental proscenium. These staged objects are thus seen continuously and as wholes—as at the theater—with none of their parts hidden or even momentarily blocked off from the view of the spectator. In Flaubert, the character sees exactly what he needs to see, just as whatever needs to be seen in Dickens is seen by the narrator himself. Thus, in the work of both writers, the reader characteristically experiences an open visual field (though perhaps less so in Dickens, who is, in all matters of technique, more flexible and less consistent than Flaubert). In the light of this, it is only fitting that Flaubert's most celebrated set piece should take place on the stage of the opera house in Rouen, where Emma watches, and Flaubert visualizes, a complete performance of *Lucia di Lammermoor* from the first balcony.

Film space is more fluid and varied than theater space and characteristically presents a partialized space with parts of the object severed from the whole by the frame of the camera. It has never been any problem for the camera to reproduce the stage image (which is roughly equivalent to a medium full shot). The cinema, however, only began to distinguish itself from a "filmed theater" and to define a unique space the moment that it began to break up a unified stage image into a series of partialized views.[10] The innovating achievement of D. W. Griffith and his successors

---

[10] André Malraux describes the prototypical film space in terms similar to mine in "Sketch for a Psychology of the Moving Pictures," in *Reflections on Art*, ed. Susanne K. Langer (Baltimore, 1958), pp. 320-21. But my statements here are to be taken as facts of history rather than as judgments of the medium. There are actually so many different ways to use space in film that it would be worse than dogmatic to imply that the use of partialized space is substantially "superior" to

was to educate the audience to follow a narrative line through a sequence of truncated images—torsos cut off at the waists, disembodied hands and heads, fragments of rooms and landscapes. In this way film space, in contrast to theatre space, became projective space as the audience learned to add to the film image with its mind what it could not see with its eye.

So, then: the use of perspective in the novels of Flaubert and Dickens reminds us of the use of perspective in the film—but we must add that their treatment of space, their arrangement of what is seen within the perspective, often reminds us of the treatment of space in the theater as well; or, to sustain the cinematic analogy, reminds us of the spatial arrangements and angles of vision found in those films most heavily influenced by the practices of the stage (such as the films of Chaplin, Renoir, Cukor, and the early work of Marcel Carné).[11] In its most extreme form this kind of cinema actually derives its spatial aesthetic from the earliest treatments of film space found in the work of Lumière, Méliès, and Edwin S. Porter. These men experimented in the new medium at the turn of the century (for the most part, before the arrival of D. W. Griffith in 1908) and in their films tried to reproduce the unities of spatial design—of scale, of movement—ordinarily attained within the proscenium arch of the stage. They gathered together all the components of any given scene—the scenery, the actors, and the props—within the frame of a single camera angle and recorded the interaction of these components continuously, often without a change of angle throughout the entire scene. The superiority of the stage image was unhesitat-

---

the use of theater space, and still worse that the former is "intrinsic to the medium" while the latter is not. Film as such is a hybrid form, and film space as such is a hypothetical zone of variables and potentialities and perhaps can best be understood in and through, but not apart from, its specific usages: the "intrinsic" nature of film space is the theoretical form of a way of seeing incarnate in human vision.

[11]I do not think it is accidental that Jean Renoir has drawn upon the French fiction of the late nineteenth century—the literary scenography of his beloved *la belle époque*—for inspiration in so many of his important films: *Nana*, 1926, and *La Bête Humaine*, 1938 (both from novels by Zola); *Madame Bovary*, 1934 (from Flaubert); *Une Partie de Campagne*, 1936 (from the short story by Guy de Maupassant); *The Diary of a Chambermaid*, 1946 (from the novel of Octave Mirabeau); *Le Carrosse D'or*, 1952 (from a play by Prosper Mérimée).

ingly accepted for social as well as aesthetic reasons. The new medium was attempting to assimilate the prestige associated with a centuries-old tradition of theater.[12] The French art historian Pierre Francastel describes this theatrical framing and coordination of space by the term *scenographic*, and uses it to characterize the dominant mode of spatial organization in four centuries of painting from the early Renaissance to the middle of the nineteenth century.[13] I think that scenography was also the dominant mode of spatial organization for Flaubert and for those novelists who followed his manner of visual composition. The major scenographers in the late nineteenth century—to name five from an international cross section—were Turgenev, Zola, Hardy, Moore, and William Dean Howells. And one of the innovating achievements of the twentieth-century novelist—of Conrad, of Joyce—was, as we shall see, the destruction of the scenographic image.

The Development of Interior Form: Zola, Lawrence, Woolf

As I have already implied, Flaubert's manner of vision establishes the essential prerequisite for the apprehension of objects in a concretized narrative form: visual perspective. By focusing on the different ways in which different writers employ visual perspective, we will find it possible to trace two distinct and characteristic lines of development in late nineteenth- and early twentieth-century fiction. In the first line the emphasis of the novelist will move away from the object and toward the eye of the observer and will ultimately result in the virtual dissolution of the object itself; in the second line the novelist will continue to focus on the object, maintaining a counterpoise between object and observer, as did Flaubert; but now, unlike Flaubert, will apprehend the object neither continuously nor as a whole, but only intermittently and as a fragment. Both trends will tend finally to diminish the status of the object as a total and self-sufficient presence: the first, by locking us into the mind of the beholder; the second, by

[12]Jacobs, *Rise of the American Film*, pp. 60-61.
[13]"The Destruction of a Plastic Space," in *Art History: An Anthology of Modern Criticism*, ed. Wylie Sypher (New York, 1963), p. 382.

mediating the object through the singular distortions of an eye that partializes the visual field in the characteristic manner of the motion picture camera. Each trend will shape a profile clearly discernible as one of the two faces of the novel in the first quarter of this century.

No discussion of the modern novel can ignore the importance of the first trend, which represents a movement *away* from concretized form, from cinematic effects, and thus from visual perspective itself. Each stage in the development of this trend is marked by an increasing diminishment of the object's material presence and an ever-deepening penetration into the inner life of the seer (who may function in the narrative as either a character or an imposing authorial presence). The final stage of this development results in the creation of a new and thoroughly interiorized literary form.

We can begin to detect the earliest manifestations of this trend in the work of Zola, one of the major novelists in the post-Flaubertian tradition who works within the conventions of a concretized form but at the same time clearly wishes to break free of them:

A long tremor ran through the crowd while the bell announced that the horses were on the track. In order to see better, Nana stood up on the seat of her landau, trampling the bouquets of forget-me-nots and roses. She glanced around the immense horizon. At this final moment of excitement the track was empty, closed by gray barriers, with policemen standing at every other post. The strip of grass, muddy in front of her, grew greener as it stretched away, until it finally turned into a bright, velvety carpet in the distance. Then, when she lowered her eyes, she saw the field swarming with people standing on tiptoe or perched on carriages, raised and stirred by a wave of passion. Horses were neighing, tent flaps were fluttering in the wind, riders were urging their mounts through the people on foot rushing to lean against the barriers. When she looked at the stands on the other side of the track, the faces seemed smaller, the heads formed a motley mass that filled the passages, tiers, and balconies with dark profiles outlined against the sky. And she saw the surrounding plain beyond. Past the ivy-covered mill to her right, there were shady meadows; in front of her, all the way to the Seine, which was flowing at the foot of the hill, the intersecting roads were lined with waiting carriages; then, in the direction of Boulogne, to her left, the landscape widened again, opening into the bluish, faraway expanse of Meudon, crossed by a road lined with paulownias, whose pink, leafless

The Oval of Vision

tops made a strip of bright color. People were still arriving, looking like a long procession of ants as they moved along the thin ribbon of a road that stretched across the fields. Far away, toward Paris, the non-paying spectators formed a line of dark, moving points beneath the trees at the edge of the Bois. Suddenly a surge of gaiety swept through the hundred thousand people covering the field like a host of scurrying insects beneath the vast sky. The sun, which had been hidden for the past quarter of an hour, reappeared and poured out a flood of light. Everything sparkled again. The women's parasols were like countless golden shields above the crowd. The sun was greeted with applause and laughter; arms reached up to push away the clouds.[14]

It is not difficult to surmise, even from a single passage (*Nana*, 1880), that Zola, like Flaubert, is an artist from whom not even the smallest particle of the material environment could ever remain a secret. Here the contents of Nana's vision are laid out before us with the scope, draftsmanship, and spatial majesty of the cartographer whose craft has been elevated to a fine art. Zola is another novelist, like Flaubert, who consistently and at almost every point reminds us of a filmmaker; the observer's angle of vision is firmly positioned in space (standing "on the seat of her landau" behind and above the crowd) at a specific moment (just before the appearance of the jockeys at the beginning of the race); and we follow the movements of the observer's eye and the exact order in which this eye perceives the objects arranged before it.

But even here the object has already begun to lose its solidity of shape and contour. The whole of the scene seems to be covered by a fine haze, a delicate shimmer that seems to blur the outline of the objects even as they are enumerated and placed before us, and seems also to impart a quality of agitation to them even as they stand in place (in contrast to Flaubert, who can make his objects seem to stand in place even when they are active).

How can we account for these effects? Unlike Flaubert, Zola is a connoisseur of mass posture and panoramic swarmings and characteristically does not see a thing as one thing, but rather as part of a group (usually composed of identical members, a species: horses neighing, tent flaps fluttering, dark profiles, heads that form a "motley mass"). He tends to merge one thing

[14]Emile Zola, *Nana*, trans. Lowell Blair (New York, 1964), pp. 318-19.

into a mass of similar things and to differentiate one mass from another, not by its line or shape—thus his masses do not seem to have an edge, as do the objects of Flaubert—but primarily by *qualities of the atmosphere,* by varying textures and densities of light, odor, and sound. In the passage quoted, for example, masses are distinguished from one another essentially by color and shading—green, gray, pink, blue, gold, flickering points of light and darkness.

It is characteristic of Flaubert to thrust the eye of the reader, as it were, near the object he is describing and to enumerate those qualities that inhere in the object itself: texture, volume, contour, and shape. It is characteristic of Zola, in the manner of the impressionist painters whom he admired,[15] to shift the emphasis of his visualization away from those qualities that inhere in the object itself to those qualities that are largely determined by the receiving apparatus of the observer. (Color, for instance, is not a property of the object itself. The experience of color is subjective.)[16] The objects in Flaubert's visualizations seem to take on a weight, an integrity, an implacable corporeality. The objects in Zola's tend to diminish in gravity and tangibility in deference to—in the words of Ortega y Gasset—"the hollow space" that interposes itself between the surface of the object and the eye of the observer.[17] In view of this, it is perhaps no accident that Zola's racetrack should remind us of Degas's *At the Races* (1872), as well as the other compositions of those impressionist painters whose experiments in oblique perspective were influenced by camera angles in photography.[18]

As is always the case with Zola, it is difficult here for the reader to determine whether the frenzy that invigorates the description belongs to the crowds that are being described or to the author that is describing them. One always feels that at some point in his mise-en-scène, the varying thrusts of his masses intoxicate Zola

---

[15]Emile Zola, "Mon Salon," in *From the Classicists to the Impressionists: A Documentary History of Art and Architecture in the Nineteenth Century,* ed. Elizabeth Gilmore Holt (New York, 1966), pp. 371-88.

[16]William Johnson, "Coming to Terms with Color," in *The Movies as Medium,* ed. Lewis Jacobs (New York, 1970), p. 216.

[17]José Ortega y Gasset, "Point of View in the Arts," *Dehumanization of Art,* p. 172.

[18]The influence of the camera on such painters as Degas and Bazille is discussed by Wylie Sypher in *Rococo to Cubism,* pp. 184-85.

to the point where he characteristically discharges furies of observation to keep pace with all their movements, at each moment and at all points within the spatial field. The climax of such observation is usually reached at that moment when Zola is able to encapsulate the entire visual field in a single summary observation, at that moment when all the masses of things are finally perceived as one vast thing. In the passage quoted that moment is reached in the second paragraph, when the "hundred thousand people covering the field" are perceived in an aerial perspective that encompasses all of them as a single whole.

It is here that Zola fully reveals himself as an artist who characteristically aspires to the omniscient vision of the epic poet; an artist in whom great spaces and swelling masses unleash an inflationary passion to oversee, to "get above"; who in order to realize his deepest impulse must leap beyond the limited angle of vision of his single observer and thus beyond the ordinary conventions of concretized form. It is doubtful whether Nana's position in space allows her access to the bird's-eye vision of the final paragraph. It is more appropriately the vision of the author himself. Zola never actually approaches the "total perspectives" of a pre-Flaubertian like Balzac, but there are many passages in his work where it is clear that his willingness to submit to the requirements of a perspectivist's art does not equal his passion to *oversee* the material environment, to have it beneath him as his conquest.

The novels of D. H. Lawrence extend the tendency toward authorial presence even further, and here the observing character often disappears altogether. Where Zola attempts to "cover" the physical world, Lawrence attempts to merge with it; where Zola attempts to maintain a limited perspective and then to go beyond it, Lawrence often ignores the concept of perspective entirely, so that as a result the interior life of the seer often becomes virtually indistinguishable from the interior life of the seen. When Lawrence does this, he too moves beyond the basic assumptions of a concretized form:

The first to run across the lawn was the little Italian, small and like a cat, her white legs twinkling as she went, ducking slightly her head, that was tied in a gold silk kerchief. She tripped through the gate and down the grass, and stood, like a tiny figure of ivory and bronze, at the water's edge, having dropped off her towelling, watching the swans, which came up in surprise. Then out ran Miss Bradley, like a large, soft plum in her dark-blue suit. Then Gerald came, a scarlet silk kerchief round his loins, his towels over his arms. He seemed to flaunt himself a little in the sun, lingering and laughing, strolling easily, looking white but natural in his nakedness. Then came Sir Joshua, in an overcoat, and lastly Hermione, striding with stiff grace from out of a great mantle of purple silk, her head tied up in purple and gold. Handsome was her stiff, long body, her straight-stepping white legs, there was a static magnificence about her as she let the cloak float loosely away from her striding. She crossed the lawn like some strange memory, and passed slowly and statelily towards the water.

There were three ponds, in terraces descending the valley, large and smooth and beautiful, lying in the sun. The water ran over a little stone wall, over small rocks, splashing down from one pond to the level below. The swans had gone out on to the opposite bank, the reeds smelled sweet, a faint breeze touched the skin.[19]

These bathers (*Women in Love*, 1920) are not perceived by any character in the novel, and because of this we do not feel that anyone stands at an imagined point in an imagined space of a graphically articulated environment. Thus, Lawrence never becomes for us one of those novelists who visualize scenes in the manner of a filmmaker. The bathers, rather, are perceived directly by the author himself (or, more precisely, that self as represented by a special vocal contrivance that tells the story), whose presence becomes an imposing and participating factor in the visualization. Consequently, unlike Flaubert or Zola, Lawrence's characteristic treatment of a specific spatial and temporal arrangement appears to be casual and intermittent, an emotional response to time and space rather than an empirical rendering of them. Time is often collapsed or distended largely on the basis of the author's intuitive feeling for the emotional density of a particular moment. The spatial relationships within a particular environment also seem magically to remold themselves from one instant to the next; space seems to come and go, swell and recede, in a state of perpetual ferment and transformation. It is never clear, for instance, in the above passage where the bathers are coming from when they suddenly appear one by one on the lawn; or where that spatially strange and unaccounted-for gate lies in relation to the water's edge (near or far?); or where the three

---

[19]*Women in Love* (New York, 1964), p. 93.

The Oval of Vision

ponds lie in relation to the lawn and the gate; or exactly which of the three ponds is signified by the water's edge; or how much time elapses between the appearance of each bather. Does enough time elapse for each to reach the water's edge, as is implied in the description of the first bather, or does each follow the other as quickly as the rest of the description seems to indicate?

These are questions that do not expect answers—nor are they posed as derogations of Lawrence's marvelous visualization. The superb welding of emotional fact to bodily motion as well as the dazzling, almost hallucinatory rush of color and metaphor tend to reduce most questions to nit-picking. Spatial and temporal elasticity are simply the primary facts of a literary domain in which chronology and environment are forever subject to oscillations in human desire and biological force. Here feeling contours time; the thrust of human personality seems, by turns, both to devour and regurgitate space. For Lawrence the psychic center (that is, the core, the whatness, the "allotropic condition") of the human being, and finally of all living things—an animal, a flower, a landscape—represents ultimate and implacable value; time and space do not.[20]

There can be no observation of any object, no seeing of it, without an initial separation from it, without an initial settlement of the necessary distance, near or far, between the seer and the seen. Distance is the essential postulate of the camera's stance and that of all artists in any medium who choose to observe the way a thing presents itself to the eye. In Lawrence, however, this necessary distance is bridged by the author's presence; the mediating observer is dismissed in order that the author might

---

[20]Lawrence's famous phrase occurs in a letter to Edward Garnett (1914), *Selected Letters of D. H. Lawrence*, ed. Diana Trilling (New York, 1961), p. 80. It hardly needs to be demonstrated that by 1920 the properties of a concretized narrative had become standardized to the point where one did not have to be a student of Flaubert (as Lawrence certainly was not) to embody some of the strategic qualities of the form. But in spite of the fact that he often arranges his action in the form of dramatized scenes and usually reveals character through situational behavior, Lawrence is not really an exponent of the new form. The dominant ontological tone of the post-Flaubertian literary atmosphere is that action precedes character, and everywhere Lawrence's fiction reveals nothing but the reverse of this assumption.

participate directly through his narrative voice in the living center of the object. To see, for Lawrence, would mean to stand apart, and to stand apart would result in a violation of the tenacious rapport Lawrence seeks to establish between himself and each of his imagined beings. Any visualization from without follows from and is dependent not upon distance but upon the author's initial identification with the interior life of his materials.

What is true of the author's relation to his characters is equally true of the characters' relation to one another and the animated universe of which each is a part. This universe is wonderfully close and compact and vibrates with forces that are metamorphic as well as anthropomorphic. Each component of Lawrence's universe is characteristically perceived in varying proportions of both fusion and emergence, both for what it is in itself and for how it interpenetrates with something that is other than itself; that is why the language of metaphor is central to the author's vocabulary. The little Italian with "legs twinkling," "ducking slightly her head," is very much in her own order of being, yet at the same time is also "small and like a cat." Miss Bradley is separated from the other bathers by her "large, soft" self and by her "dark-blue suit," yet also, by virtue of this distinction, seems to merge with the volume and color of a plum. The author perceives the identity of each object as fluid and continuous with a living context of other objects—as isolate yet conjoined.

Because they are first perceived from within and rendered as such, Lawrence's objects rarely possess the precisely imagined shape, scale, volume, and material individuality of Flaubert's; nor do they nearly approximate the atmospheric density of Zola's; nor, above all, do they ever rival the renderings of either in corporeality and tangibility. What they reveal, instead, and perhaps to a degree unequaled by any other modern fictionalist, are the qualities of an overwhelming psychic presence, an extremity of spiritual form; radiance as opposed to contour, buoyancy as opposed to weight, intensity as opposed to visibility, and kinetic flash as opposed to fixed posture.

Thus, Lawrence will rarely describe, qualify, or modulate his object with reference to its objective, measurable, or strictly quantitative aspects. His attributions of adjectives, adverbs, and particularly verbs rarely represent qualities that are empirically demonstrable; rather, they represent aspects of the object's spiritual style and force, the author's moral and poetic interpretations of the particular inner life with which he has identified himself. In the above passage, for instance, the bulk of Lawrence's verbal energy expends itself in describing the way his characters seem to move: motion is the result of spiritual force energizing the external form that embodies it. Consequently, the bathers *twinkle, duck, trip, run, linger, stroll, stride, pass,* and the like; one body goes "small and like a cat, her white legs twinkling as she went"; another strides stiffly, with "a static magnificence about her...like some strange memory." Velocity here is entirely a matter of the spirit; the way an object seems to move represents a concrete investiture of the way its psychic form urges it to go. Motion, of course, is also the primary distinction between a living object and a dead one, and Lawrence's universe is singularly devoid of inanimate objects. Even when at rest his creations sustain the possibility of activity by a kind of contained vitalism, an internal quivering-in-place, a standing still like that of Henry Miller's famous hummingbird.

And what of the object's material properties? What is left, then, for the senses to apprehend? What was noted of Zola becomes even more pronounced in Lawrence: the material gravity of the object continues to evaporate in favor of the object's reflections and refractions as sifted out by the receiving faculties of the author-observer; that is, the object's sensuous surface is now reduced almost entirely to scintillations of color. And even this, in Lawrence, seems less dependent upon empirical observation than upon the author's feeling for the interior heat of another being. Color, for Lawrence, like body motion, is primarily the outward expression of what lies within: it is the visible afterglow that spiritual force leaves in the wake of its passage through time and space (for instance, it is emotionally proper for Hermione to be regal in "purple and gold," as it is for Gerald to be sensual and "white" with "a scarlet silk kerchief round his loins").

When we come to the fiction of Virginia Woolf, we find the process of the object's dematerialization virtually complete. Lawrence moves toward the exterior in order to get inside the object. Woolf withdraws from the exterior in order to go deeper into the self. Both writers go beyond concretized form by attempting to interiorize either the seen (Lawrence) or the seer (Woolf). In Virginia Woolf's fiction the author, to all appearances, again retires and the mediating character seems to reenter the narrative, but now what is mediated matters less than the process of mediation itself:

> Nonsense, nonsense! she cried to herself, pushing through the swing doors of Mulberry's the florists.
> She advanced, light, tall, very upright, to be greeted at once by button-faced Miss Pym, whose hands were always bright red, as if they had been stood in cold water with the flowers.
> There were flowers: delphiniums, sweet peas, bunches of lilac; and carnations, masses of carnations. There were roses; there were irises. Ah yes—so she breathed in the earthy garden sweet smell as she stood talking to Miss Pym who owed her help, and thought her kind, for kind she had been years ago; very kind, but she looked older, this year, turning her head from side to side among the irises and roses and nodding tufts of lilac with her eyes half closed, snuffing in, after the street uproar, the delicious scent, the exquisite coolness. And then, opening her eyes, how fresh like frilled linen clean from a laundry laid in wicker trays the roses looked; and dark and prim the red carnations, holding their heads up; and all the sweet peas spreading in their bowls, tinged violet, snow white, pale—as if it were the evening and girls in muslin frocks came out to pick sweet peas and roses after the superb summer's day, with its almost blue-black sky, its delphiniums, its carnations, its arum lilies was over; and it was the moment between six and seven when every flower—roses, carnations, irises, lilac—glows; white, violet, red, deep orange; every flower seems to burn by itself, softly, purely in the misty beds; and how she loved the grey-white moths spinning in and out, over the cherry pie, over the evening primroses!
> And as she began to go with Miss Pym fron jar to jar, choosing, nonsense, nonsense, she said to herself, more and more gently, as if this beauty, this scent, this colour, and Miss Pym liking her, trusting her, were a wave which she let flow over her and surmount that hatred, that monster, surmount it all; and it lifted her up and up when—oh! a pistol shot in the street outside![21]

We realize almost at once that the return of the mediating character (*Mrs. Dalloway*, 1925) constitutes a fact that is actually less illuminating and more ambiguous than one might have originally supposed. Certainly we are once again looking at something with someone who obviously represents a fictional presence that is other than the author's. But if someone is indeed

[21]*Mrs. Dalloway* (New York, 1953), pp. 17-19.

The Oval of Vision

looking, it must also be admitted that relatively little is ever really seen (relative, that is, to the authors we have been examining). The reader finds himself locked into the desperate and characteristic circumstances of Virginia Woolf's literary ambience; that is, of vision without focus, of experiencing the act of perception without a concentrated engagement of the object perceived. The general effect of these circumstances is of participation in a protracted drama of the self's abandonment to its own ruminations, of the perceiver forever remote from, and lost to, the world.

In what sense is the object looked at but never really seen? What has happened to the object? In the simplest terms, the object cannot be seen, for it is no longer described. Every description to some degree entails an enumerative rendering of the object in terms of its parts, and such a rendering, by its very existence, becomes a kind of testimonial to the object's incorrigible presence, a validation of the object as no other thing except that thing which it is. Virginia Woolf attempts no such rendering; instead of describing the object, she names it, and by substituting a name for a description determines the object's new status: no longer an integral presence composed of its parts, the object now becomes an *item*. The quoted passage is full of items: "roses, carnations, irises, lilac." Sometimes these items are associated with certain epithets: "dark and prim the red carnations...the sweet peas spreading in their bowls, tinged violet, snow white, pale." But "red carnations" no more vivifies the object than do any other of the more conventional epithet-noun associations, such as "blue sky" or "green grass." Eventually the epithets themselves are itemized: "white, violet, red, deep orange" (that "deep" becomes particularly gratuitous in this context).

An object becomes an item when it has been stripped of everything but the common noun that determines its name. The author tags the object with its name not because she is incapable of rendering it more fully but because the bare name is her way of indicating what is left of the object at the moment of its entry into a receiving consciousness; at the minimal point, the zero-degree of its individuality and corporeal gravity; at that moment when it submits to its assumption by consciousness and under the aspect of consciousness reduces to a glancing sensation, a pinpoint of sense-datum from "out there." On the printed page this object appears as an item; and this, then, is Virginia Woolf's signal to the reader that the object has become, in her own words, an "atom."[22] The process of atomization applies not only to objects per se but to observed character and behavior as well, to every component within the mediating observer's field of consciousness. Each appears in its minimalized form, the verbal analogue of an atom.

As might be expected, the author also makes no attempt to create the verbal illusion of spatial solidity and arrangement. We are informed that Mrs. Dalloway enters the florist's shop and moves about from point to point within its confines, but the spatial design of the shop itself remains invisible. The effect is the very reverse of moving through tangible and continuous space. The shop, rather, seems to have exploded into any number of discrete sensory units, and these units now seem to flow through the observer's field of consciousness as aggregations of flotsam (that is, items are arranged in lists, catalogues of brief observation and sensory notation). The effect, indeed, is that of space liquified and its contents now swimming about the beholder. The narrative voice seems to modulate just short of breathlessness, hard pressed to keep pace with the flood of external sensation. Perception becomes edgy, full of risk-taking: each subject-object encounter contains the threat of inundation, of consciousness besieged and barely holding firm this side of psychic dissolution.

Virginia Woolf obtains these effects of spatial liquification not by perceiving the spatial relations of one object to another, as did Zola and Flaubert (who in this manner achieved the verbal illusion of solid and continuous space), but by noting the seemingly random order in which the objects strike the consciousness of the observer. One follows another like notes of music, each taking its place as part of a linear entry into consciousness. In this way space seems to stream by, each sensory component arranged according to its position in a temporal flow ("roses, carnations, irises").

No one component attains importance by itself. What matters, rather, is essentially the general concatenation of components,

---

[22]"Let us record the atoms as they fall upon the mind in the order in which they fall, let us trace the pattern, however disconnected and incoherent in appearance, which each sight or incident scores upon the consciousness" (*The Common Reader* [*First Series*] [New York, 1953], pp. 154-55).

The Oval of Vision

the sensory pileup that helps to generate a feeling, attitude, or memory in the mind of the beholder. It is of course the dramatization of these feelings, memories, and attitudes that comprises Virginia Woolf's great and abiding subject. Her interest in the physical world begins at that point where the ordering of matter is assimilated and all but dissolved by a temporal ordering of meditation and desire; that point, so to speak, where matter liquifies into feeling.

For instance, in the first paragraph quoted, Mrs. Dalloway enters the shop full of hate and out of sorts with herself for allowing this feeling to possess her so completely. By the end of the last paragraph—just before her reverie is interrupted by a shot from the street—she is already carried off on a "wave" of memory and emotion that enables her to "surmount that hatred, that monster, surmount it all." The subject of the long intervening paragraph, and the dramatic center of the passage, concerns itself with everything that helps Mrs. Dalloway get from one state of mind to another, from bad feeling in the present to a pleasant memory of the past; the next, and last, paragraph dramatizes the diminishment of the former feeling in the light of the latter memory. In rendering this delicate sequence of emotional transition, all the sensory units from the outside (the flowers, the smells, the colors, the comfortable presence of Miss Pym herself) are brought into play as accumulating catalysts that help to effect the internal changes in Mrs. Dalloway's sensibility. The material world is rendered at every point not on its own terms but in the light of this rich, various, endlessly shifting sensibility.

But, finally, even the rendering of this internal drama is less stable and consistent than the foregoing analysis might imply. How close does any reader ever get to even the mental life of one of Virginia Woolf's characters before encountering Virginia Woolf herself? I stated earlier that the author was to all appearances absent from the novel. But any careful reading of any passage of Virginia Woolf's fiction will convince us, I think, that this absence is only nominal. We note, for instance, that Mrs. Dalloway's perspective is not consistently maintained; that in one moment we will have Mrs. Dalloway's view of Miss Pym ("she stood talking to Miss Pym"); and in another, Miss Pym's view of Mrs. Dalloway ("but she looked older, this year"); and then, on occasion, the author's view of both women ("She advanced, light, tall, very upright, to be greeted at once by the button-faced Miss Pym"). Yet in spite of these shifts in perspective, there seems to be no concomitant shift in the tone of the narration. The manner of expression in all of these passages seems to be exactly the same.

Between the reader and the characters—indeed, between the reader and the entire narrative experience—a delicate but idiosyncratic tone insistently interposes itself. It is the tone that the knowing reader always associates with the fiction of Virginia Woolf, the tone that indicates the voice of the author telling her story. This is the voice that the author often intentionally confuses with the interior voice of her characters, the voice that utters the words that a particular character might utter had he or she the capacity to articulate the facts of his or her consciousness. But this rich and puzzling effect loses its force as soon as it becomes apparent that all the characters utter the same words in the same way, that the voice the author elects for each character at each point in the narrative is fundamentally the same voice.

We quickly come to generalize the common qualities of this voice apart from the character about whom it is speaking. We come to recognize it by its elegant and almost breathless ejaculations ("Ah yes...how she loved the grey-white moths spinning in and out, over the cherry pie, over the evening primroses!"); by its graceful and lyrical inversions ("Miss Pym...thought her kind, for kind she had been years ago"); by its refinements of precious sensibility ("the delicious scent, the exquisite coolness") and featherweight perception ("girls in muslin frocks came out to pick sweet peas and roses after the superb summer's day"); by its speed, wit, and nervousness; and by its compound of hectic observation and upper-class chat. While at first we may think that this voice exists to substantiate the mental stance of the characters, we ultimately come to realize, I think, that the mental stance of the characters exists primarily to substantiate this voice; that this voice is ultimately more consistent and recognizable, more finally and weightily present than any other aspect of Virginia Woolf's fiction.

The evolution of prose fiction from Flaubert to Virginia Woolf establishes a line of novelistic development—that is, a line determined by the seen objects' increasing dematerialization—which continues into the present day. Zola's attempt to oversee and subjugate literary space finds its parallel in the work of those casual and impatient exponents of concretized form like Norris, Dreiser, Tolstoy, and those Soviet writers working in Tolstoy's shadow, Sholokhov and Solzhenitsyn. Lawrence's effort to fuse with, and emerge from, literary space has its counterparts in the quasi-apocalyptic incantations of D'Annunzio, Céline, Henry Miller, and Jack Kerouac. It is, however, the fully interiorized form of Virginia Woolf that perhaps best characterizes the dominant tendencies in this line of post-Flaubertian development. Variants of interior form can be found in the highly dematerialized narratives of Kafka, Broch, Musil, and Svevo; in the novels of sensibility by Dorothy Richardson, Elizabeth Bowen, and Henry Green; and even in the otherworldly monologues of Borges, Beckett, and Rudolph Wurlitzer.

The contrast between concretized form and interior form also provides us with a definitive profile of subject-object depictions in the post-Flaubertian novel. From a fiction that cultivates a literary texture of sensuous surface, spatial density, plastic and tangible quantity, we now turn to a fiction that cultivates a literary texture of bottomless interiority, temporal elasticity, and weightless and transient feeling. From a fiction that presents time as chronology by emphasizing the body's behavior and relationship in space, we now shift to a fiction that presents time as duration by emphasizing the mind's behavior and relationship in past, present, and fantasy; from a fiction that distinguishes itself by precise and accurate renderings of the material life of the seen, we now move to a fiction that distinguishes itself by precise and accurate renderings of the emotive life of the seer; and from a fiction where the narrative voice has become neutral and uninflected in order to present the object of depiction with a minimum of authorial mediation, we now confront a fiction where the narrative voice becomes increasingly personal and self-reflexive in order to stress that the true object of any depiction is, in fact, the depictor himself.

The Development of Cinematographic Form: James, Conrad, Joyce

The second line of development in the post-Flaubertian novel leads us again to the special epistemology of the cinema and to the central subject of this discussion: cinematographic form. This form, unlike interior form, does not represent a restructuring of the basic typology of concretized form; on the contrary, cinematographic form represents a historical offspring, a new and important outgrowth of the parent form.

The cinematized narrative stems from the achievement of Flaubert and adheres closely to his relatively balanced view of the subject-object encounter. Because of this, it also adheres closely to a perspectivist's approach to experience. This form, however, introduces two important changes into the original manner of presentation. First, a partialized treatment of space replaces the scenography of the nineteenth-century novel; second, a passive, affectless way of seeing enters into the visualization of the post-Flaubertian novelist.

Earlier I spoke of the camera as a medium of presentation that was both subjective and objective, and throughout the previous discussion, I have stressed the subjective side of this instrument (the seer's position in space, and so on). In the following discussion, however, it will be necessary to take a more balanced and complex view of the camera and speak of its subjective and objective qualities together. I will do this whenever I speak of the passive and affectless eye, a way of seeing that in the hands of modernists like Joyce and Conrad becomes a technique for separating the seer from his visual field.

I am going to examine these developments and the consolidation of this form in the work of three authors: Henry James, Conrad, and Joyce. Both Conrad and Joyce are unequivocal heirs of the Flaubertian legacy. James's credentials are perhaps questionable; however, his treatment of the eye and of literary space defines James, as we shall see, as a necessary figure in the context of these developments, the beginnings of which can be observed here:

Adjusting her respirations and attaching, under dropped lashes, all her thought to a smartness of frock and frill for which she could reflect that she had not appealed in vain to a loyalty in Susan Ash triumphant over the nice things their feverish flight had left behind, Maisie spent on a bench in the garden of the hotel the half-hour before dinner, that mysterious ceremony of the *table d'hôte* for which she had prepared with a punctuality of flutter. Sir Claude, beside her, was occupied with a

The Oval of Vision 55

cigarette and the afternoon papers; and though the hotel was full the garden showed the particular void that ensues upon the sound of the dressing-bell. She had almost had time to weary of the human scene; her own humanity at any rate, in the shape of a smutch on her scanty skirt, had held her so long that as soon as she raised her eyes they rested on a high fair drapery by which smutches were put to shame and which had glided towards her over the grass without her noting its rustle. She followed up its stiff sheen—up and from the ground, where it had stopped—till at the end of a considerable journey her impression felt the shock of the fixed face which, surmounting it, seemed to offer the climax of the dressed condition. "Why mamma!" she cried the next instant—cried in a tone that, as she sprang to her feet, brought Sir Claude to his own beside her and gave her ladyship, a few yards off, the advantage of their momentary confusion. Poor Maisie's was immense; her mother's drop had the effect of one of the iron shutters that, in evening walks with Susan Ash, she had seen suddenly, at the touch of a spring, rattle down over shining shop-fronts. The light of foreign travel was darkened at a stroke; she had a horrible sense that they were caught; and for the first time of her life in Ida's presence she so far translated an impulse into an invidious act as to clutch straight at the hand of her responsible confederate. It didn't help her that he appeared at first equally hushed with horror; a minute during which, in the empty garden, with its long shadows on the lawn, its blue sea over the hedge and its startled peace in the air, both her elders remained as stiff as tall tumblers filled to the brim and held straight for fear of a spill.[23]

In James (*What Maisie Knew*, 1897), as in Flaubert, we note the effort to attempt a balanced distribution of emphasis in the rendering of what is looked at, who is looking, and what the looker makes of what she sees. This passage engages equally the three basic components of any conventional interaction between subject and object: an actor (Maisie), an action (Maisie's discovery of Ida's presence by raising her eyes), and a reaction (the subsequent complex of disappointment, guilt, and confusion beginning at almost midpoint in the paragraph with "poor Maisie's was immense"). It can hardly be denied, however, that the entire field of vision, throughout the sequence, remains dim and exceedingly remote.

The passage is an example of James's famous late manner, where the seen objects are dematerialized by the detached and

[23]*What Maisie Knew* (New York, 1954), pp. 167-68.

considered appropriations of a critical intellect and where James translates the object into a function of analytic discourse and speculation. The object is distanced and dematerialized so that it might become an appropriate object for contemplation. James's purpose, then, becomes not so much to see the object as to understand it in its fully untrammeled moral and causal significance. "A high fair drapery" does not do very much for the material specificities of Ida's dress, but it does help to conjure up the idea of Ida's grand and gilded materialism.

To effect this translation of matter into discourse, James sifts his visual field through an elaborate verbal display of abstraction, generalization, and literary grandiloquence. He also creates a special resonance through the repeated deployment of many elegant and sometimes bookish circumlocutions ("a smartness of frock and frill," "her responsible confederate," "a high fair drapery by which smutches were put to shame,"). The general effect of these phrases is to create the literary equivalent of an abstracted gaze or a glazed expression.

But we must not judge this effect too quickly. The author knows exactly what he is about: just when we think that the wandering clauses of moralized nuance, generalized analysis, and circumlocutory observation are about to lead us off into a kind of verbal fog of fine discrimination—too fine to really matter—just at this point there is a marvelous tightening of the dramatist's grip. James comes down hard on the point. The general dimness is balanced and opposed by a sudden sharpening of focus, as if the narrator had, without warning or explanation, suddenly pressed his attention, if not his eye, hard upon the object. We sense this sudden sharpness of narrative attention in Maisie's passionate outburst, "Why mamma!" and in that remarkable fear-and-trembling simile, so vivid and pointed, when "both her elders remained as stiff as tall tumblers filled to the brim and held straight for fear of a spill." These two moments are of primary importance in the passage: Maisie's cry and her discovery of Ida represent the climax of the "action" sequence; the simile represents the climax of the "reaction" sequence, the definitive insight into the parents' relationship. Each moment of hard focus here has the effect of climactic revelation.

Each moment also makes the function of the generalized dis-

The Oval of Vision

course come clear. The long sentences of abstract analysis represent forays of intellectual detection that prepare us for and necessitate the moments of discovery; the generalized inquiry, far from being of small matter, actually tightens the spring that the moment of discovery releases. Thus, while the objects within the field of vision may seem remote and deactivated, James's rhetorical strategy for unveiling the mysteries of this field is vigorous and dramatic. The strategy behind his rhetoric is actually the strategy behind most inspector-suspect dialogues in detective fiction: it is the strategy of search and seizure.

What is true of the rhetorical strategy in this passage is equally true of the central observer's (Maisie's) cognitive experience here and throughout the novel. The climax of the dramatic action is usually represented by the observer's seizure of knowledge and certainty, of a culminating insight into the self and the nature of its experience in the world. The dramatic action, however, is usually represented by the search itself, the observer's slow, tentative, often erratic but ineluctable motion from the state of apprehension to the state of comprehension. It is this mental motion, of course, that forms the major part of the dramatic structure of so much of James's fiction. Much of it, and particularly the later work, centers about the process of cognition itself as a dramatic enterprise. The observer's field of vision, then, becomes of absolute importance to this mental activity, for the field of vision is where the process of apprehension begins, where, indeed, the dramatic action itself begins. What Maisie sees is the basis, the only basis—here and throughout the novel—for what Maisie eventually comes to know.

Thus, James pays careful attention to the observer's spatial position, to what the observer sees (however abstractly), and, above all, to how the observer does her seeing; that is, the experience of the eye itself, the *way* in which this eye tracks down its object and takes full possession of its meaning. It is the attempt to be faithful to the life of the eye that makes James an active member of the generation that emulated the literary model first established by Flaubert (and thus very different from almost *any* interior novelist with whom, otherwise, his late manner bears certain obvious affinities).

Now, much of the visualization in James's fiction (particularly in the early and middle periods) is organized along scenographic lines; that is, the objects within any given spatial field are seen continuously and as wholes as if on stage at the theater. But in his late fiction James begins to visualize many of his climactic sequences in a substantially new way that not only separates him from the other late nineteenth-century realists and naturalists but actually defines him as the precursor of a new kind of visual form.[24]

What is remarkable about the passage quoted is that James makes no attempt to engage the objects within Maisie's field of vision either continuously or as wholes but rather charts the upward progress of Maisie's eye as it fastens itself to the successive sections of Ida's dress. Each section adds a new item of information to Maisie's understanding of the dress as a whole (again, as in detective fiction, where logical deductions lead from clue to clue until the mystery is unraveled). At first the dress is simply a large expanse of cloth: "a high fair drapery." Then Maisie's eye follows the "stiff sheen—up and from the ground, where it had stopped." Only when Maisie sees "the fixed face...surmounting it" is the drapery fully understood as a dress (that is, "the fixed face" becomes the "climax of the *dressed* condition"). And only in the next and climactic sentence ("Why Mamma!") are the face and the dress understood as parts of Ida, a living whole that has now become distinctly more than the sum of its parts.

The whole sequence, then, is rendered not scenographically but cinematographically; not through the stationary arch of a proscenium but rather through the frame of a moving camera in a series of *partialized* views as the lens pans upward from the bottom of its object to the top, each aspect of the object momentarily severed from the whole by the camera frame. By contrast, the ordinary human eye can encompass its object in an instant, but James transforms Maisie's eye into a camera by unnaturally slowing its movement upwards. James wants to emphasize the strangeness and impenetrability of the objects in Maisie's visual field (for example, Ida becomes an "it") and thus evolves a visual

---

[24] I have in mind most notably Strether's discovery of Chad Newsome and Madame de Vionnet in the climactic sequence of *The Ambassadors*. Here Strether's object (the couple in the boat) is tracked down, like Maisie's tracking of Ida, in successive stages of increasing visual and mental revelation.

The Oval of Vision 59

technique perfectly congruent with the motions of a mind that is trying to solve a mystery.

While James seems to discover film space only late in life, Joseph Conrad seems to have made frequent use of it throughout his literary career:

> I directed my glass to the house. There were no signs of life, but there were the ruined roof, the long mud wall peeping above the grass, with three little square window-holes, no two of the same size; all this brought within reach of my hand, as it were. And then I made a brusque movement, and one of the remaining posts of that vanished fence leaped up in the field of my glass. You remember I told you I had been struck at the distance by certain attempts at ornamentation, rather remarkable in the ruinous aspect of the place. Now I had suddenly a nearer view, and its first result was to make me throw my head back as if before a blow. Then I went carefully from post to post with my glass, and I saw my mistake. These round knobs were not ornamental but symbolic; they were expressive and puzzling, striking and disturbing—food for thought and also for vultures if there had been any looking down from the sky; but at all events for such ants as were industrious enough to ascend the pole. They would have been even more impressive, those heads on the stakes, if their faces had not been turned to the house. Only one, the first I had made out, was facing my way. I was not so shocked as you may think. The start back I had given was really nothing but a movement of surprise. I had expected to see a knob of wood there, you know. I returned deliberately to the first I had seen—and there it was, black, dried, sunken, with closed eyelids—a head that seemed to sleep at the top of that pole, and, with the shrunken dry lips showing a narrow white line of the teeth, was smiling too, smiling continuously at some endless and jocose dream of that eternal slumber.[25]

Though significantly contemporaneous with James's late period, this passage comes from one of Conrad's relatively early works (*Heart of Darkness*, 1899). The passage reveals, however, a somewhat exaggerated and aggresive display of camera vision of which many more sedate and subtle examples could be found in almost any one of Conrad's novels, novellas, and short stories. Conrad, of course, is one of *our* novelists, a member of the new literary faction that continued to develop on this side of the dividing line between the centuries, and one of the remarkable

---

[25]*Heart of Darkness*, Norton Critical Edition, ed. Robert Kimbrough (New York, 1963), p. 58.

features that distinguishes his "new" work from the "old" work is the cultivation of a literary space analogous to the usual treatment of space in the cinema.

Like so much modern fiction, however, the passage bears the obvious remnants of the Flaubertian legacy and the legacy of an entire literary era permeated by the results of analytic, objectivistic, and positivistic thinking. Like the earlier practitioners of concretized form, Conrad duly notes the peculiarities of the observer's position in space (his "glass," previously identified as "binoculars," now observes the shoreline of a Congo village from the safety of his riverboat). He also notes the contour and shape of the seen objects, qualities residing in the objects themselves and not in the mind of the observer ("the *long* mud wall," "*square* window-holes," "*round* knobs," "a *narrow white line* of the teeth"). With a "scientific" eye he renders the objects in terms of precise measure and quantity ("*three little* square window-holes," "*no two of the same size*," "*one* of the remaining posts," "from *post* to *post*") and reveals their proximity in space, thus creating a sense of the surrounding space itself ("the long mud wall peeping *above* the grass," "went carefully *from* post *to* post," "if their faces had not been *turned to* the house," "the first...was *facing my way*"). In this manner, the typical Conradian object takes on a fullness, a thickness, and a gravitational density that is reminiscent of the treatment of objects in Flaubert.

But like James, and not at all like Flaubert, Conrad makes no attempt to arrange the space within the observer's perspective as a single continuous unobstructed field; instead, he literally decomposes his field into an arrangement of successive views. But here, unlike James, Conrad does not make one view flow logically into the next: rather, the visual fragments are now ordered in a relatively discontinuous sequence. Thus, the rhythm of the observer's—and the reader's—apprehension of the scene becomes abrupt, quirky, stop-and-go; at first Marlowe sees the house, but cannot see the posts, for they do not appear within the "ovular field of [his] glass"; then, with a "brusque movement," he cuts to the first post; he is shocked; next, he begins to track "carefully from post to post"; next, he realizes the full import of what he has initially seen; he cuts back "deliberately to the first" post; he stops; he describes in detail (close-up) the head at the top of the pole.

The Oval of Vision 61

The visual excitement in this scene derives in large part from the stopping-starting-sliding-back-tracking motions of the glass. Expectation increases with each successive view until the final close-up of the shrunken head—as the glass finally comes to rest at the end of the paragraph—provides a release that is satisfyingly horrible. But the excitement also derives in almost equal measure from the strange, almost hallucinatory way in which the visual information impresses itself upon the eye. Something peculiar, almost unnatural happens, for example, when the observer comments that the seen objects were "all...brought within reach of my hand, as it were"; and even more remarkable—indeed, surreal—is the comment that the first post "*leaped* up in the field of my glass."

Now both of these statements are provocative not only because they embody remarkably observant notations but because the eye that observes these phenomena is no longer thinking about what it sees. This eye—like Maisie's before it makes its discoveries—suddenly seems to have gone numb before the incomprehensible otherness of its visual field. It is an eye that seems to have momentarily separated itself from a mind. Can the observer actually touch these distant objects with his hand? Do stationary fence posts take life and leap up in any field of vision? Not exactly. But that is exactly the way these objects will appear to an eye that refuses to think about or feel for what it sees and is content *only to see*—that, and nothing more. In other words, fence posts will leap in the observer's field of vision when he learns to see, as Conrad does here, with an eye that is without affect; that is, a camera eye precisely.[26]

Thus far, we note that Conrad's rendering of the object itself is impressively solid and objective but that his manner of apprehending it is full of abrupt and violent disjunctions, as well as provocative and brilliant optical maneuvers. Why is all of this cinematic razzle-dazzle necessary? Conrad works this way—here and throughout his fiction—because he wishes to create a visual field and a manner of apprehension commensurate with a context of mystery, physical adventure, and moral enigma. The observer

---

[26]This distinction between the camera eye and the human eye takes its point of departure from Rudolf Arnheim's important discussion in *Film as Art* (Berkeley and Los Angeles, 1964), pp. 8-34.

throughout the sequence assumes an emotional posture of unalleviated awe and astonishment (the characteristic posture of many of Conrad's paradoxically tough-minded observers). This posture is the necessary complement of the aggressive visualization, of the shrunken heads that seem to leap up, and of the ocular motions that are so jarring and attenuated. Conrad continually manipulates space and visual form to express a mind that is in a perpetual state of agitated amazement before its visual field. This effort is supported by a purely verbal texture saturated with the language of cliff-hanger fiction and the magazine yarn: the observer's head is thrown back "as if before a blow"; he experiences the customary "start back" and the traditional "movement of surprise"; terrible things are introduced by a well-worn verbal drum roll: "and there it was." Objects not only *leap up* and *vanish*, but they are also *puzzling, strange, disturbing, bizarre,* and so on.

The result of these efforts is that Conrad seems to be trying to deracinate a spatial field that has already been rendered as solid, tangible, fully materialized, and distinctly earthbound. Conrad seeks to compel his objects into contexts beyond their own material presences: that is why he characteristically discharges so many epithets per noun and why so many of these epithets are characteristically vague. But if it has any effect at all, a stream of enigmatic qualifiers straining toward something unnameable and ineffable probably convinces many readers of just how resistant to mystification these objects really are. Can the "sunken skull...with the shrunken dry lips showing a narrow white line of the teeth" actually support—indeed, have anything much at all to do with—the "endless and jocose dream of that eternal slumber"? Perhaps it does—for some readers at least.[27]

It is clear that where James seeks to solve a mystery in a relatively nonsensuous, unparticularized environment, Conrad seeks to create one in a field that is fully sensuous and highly particularized. James, however, sees each object under the aspect of the observer's analytic intelligence so that in this regard the

---

[27] I have no doubt that my skeptical view here is in the minority; yet it is similar to the one held by Marvin Mudrick when he says that Conrad "is liable to drift into the mooning or glooming that for some critics passes as Conrad's 'philosophy' " ("The Originality of Conrad," *Hudson Review*, II [1958-59], 545-53).

mental act of comprehension seems to follow upon, and all but swallow, as it were, the visual act of apprehension. In Conrad, on the other hand, these two acts often seem to be, if not exactly at odds with each other, not exactly confluent either. What Conrad sees and what Conrad knows about what he sees often represent two different levels of cognition that do not always mix easily. The objects are eminently and brilliantly present, yet the very fullness of their presence often renders them reluctant to speculation.

At the very least, Conrad's work at times betrays the unconcealed exertions of a novelist pressing hard to bridge the gap between a puzzled subject and a highly intractable object. In Joyce, however, the subject does make connection, with its object though of a special sort; yet, oddly, the object itself, in the very manner of its presentation, continues to remain impervious to full comprehension:

Stephen, an elbow rested on the jagged granite, leaned his palm against his brow and gazed at the fraying edge of his shiny black coat-sleeve. Pain, that was not yet the pain of love, fretted his heart. Silently, in a dream she had come to him after her death, her wasted body within its loose brown grave-clothes giving off an odour of wax and rosewood, her breath, that had bent upon him, mute, reproachful, a faint odour of wetted ashes. Across the threadbare cuffedge he saw the sea hailed as a great sweet mother by the wellfed voice beside him. The ring of bay and skyline held a dull green mass of liquid. A bowl of white china had stood beside her deathbed holding the green sluggish bile which she had torn up from her rotting liver by fits of loud groaning vomiting. [*Ulysses*, p. 5]

Of all the novelists we have examined, it is perhaps Joyce who in the conscientiousness and precision of his workmanship, as well as in the conversation of his language and the finish of his phrasing, reveals the closest kinship with Flaubert. Joyce, like Flaubert, can also make an object seem to stand apart from the total visual field in startling, hard-edged relief. He can also see this object as one object like no other, and at the same time press his eye remarkably near its surface. That is to say, both Joyce and Flaubert respect the integrity of the seen object and lavish their verbal energies upon its material intricacies to give it palpable presence apart from the presence of the observer. We note, for instance, in Joyce, that Flaubertian feeling for the controlling line and shape of a thing, thus demarcating its separateness from everything other than itself (the "fraying *edge*" of the coatsleeve, "the threadbare *cuffedge*," "the *ring* of bay"). Joyce, like Flaubert, also renders an object in terms of texture and tactility ("the *jagged* granite," "*threadbare* cuffedge," the "*shiny* black coatsleeve," "the green *sluggish* bile") as well as volume and density ("a *bowl* of white china," "a dull green *mass* of liquid"). Even in a comparison with Conrad, who will often seem heavy, thick, and loquacious, Joyce, in the Flaubertian manner, is always crisp, hard, and concentrated.

Yet it is perhaps in this matter of concentration that the differences between Joyce and Flaubert begin to appear. While they are alike in their verbal concision, it is the economy of Joyce's *visual* notation, his apprehension of the object within the most constricted of ocular frames, that not only distinguishes him from the French master but from any one of his (Joyce's) predecessors. The realists and the naturalists characteristically saw a large spatial field within a wide angle of vision. In Joyce the spatial field has diminished, the angle of vision narrowed, and because of this he must learn to see fewer objects within the new, contracted space more intensively than ever before. Where Flaubert saw "wider," Joyce must now see "harder" and "deeper."

Joyce's visual brevity actually represents a new stage in the development of the cinematographic tendencies already noted in late James and Conrad. In *Ulysses* the observed truncations and obstructions are more heightened and attenuated than they have ever been in James or Conrad, and in the very extremity of their presentation we recognize the characteristic formal procedure of Joyce's modernism: it is the method of fractured and cellular narration and description, of rendering wholes by their parts. Thus, we view Stephen only in terms of his palm, his elbow, and his brow; his coatsleeve and his cuffedge. The deathbed of his mother is represented only by the "bowl of white china" with its contents of "green sluggish bile." In this manner all of Joyce's apprehensions take on the character of visual aphorisms, a new kind of observational shorthand that severs everything from the seen object save only for an expressive fragment that now replaces and represents the missing whole. Here Joyce's method of narration perfects the literary equivalent of a tightly framed close-up.

The dividing line, then, between Flaubert and his late nineteenth-century followers, on the one hand, and the modernist tendencies represented by late James, Conrad, and Joyce, on the other, is the dividing line between a unified, unobstructed, continuous field of vision and a blocked, truncated, and discontinuous field; between a large single vista and a multiplicity of peepholes; between scenography and cinematography.

The new fragmented space of the modern novel indicates that we are now closer to the thoughts and feelings of the observer than we have ever been in the Flaubertian novel. The discontinuous field becomes the external counterpart of an internal process, the world as seen through the abrupt and alogical agitations of a living mind. At the same time, however, the discontinuous field also attests to the uncertainty and discord between one dissociated fragment and another in both the inner and outer worlds, and thus to the ultimate unknowableness of the seen fragment (unknowable because incomplete). Indeed, the epistemology of the camera eye, as we shall see, renders the seen fragment more unknowable than ever.

We can experience the disturbing effects of camera focus in what is perhaps the single most remarkable note of optics in the passage above: "Across the threadbare cuffedge he saw the sea." Stephen's eye, in other words, not only apprehends the sea but also, cutting across his oval of vision, his own cuffedge. Here, of course, we confront an angle of vision that anyone familiar with film would probably wish to put forward as one of the prototypical gestures of movie optics: the diagonal bisection of space (another instance of the truncated and obstructed field), an angle of vision that even the least committed moviegoer would probably associate with the medium of film and perhaps no other medium. It is virtually impossible to reproduce anything like this angle in the theater, and it is almost never reminiscent of the point of view in painting, except in those specific compositions also influenced by film. Yet it is an angle that is characteristic of Joyce's way of seeing and, in spite of his great familiarity with the movies, probably derives, as we have seen, as much from a novelistic tradition of ocular self-consciousness and explorations in cognition as it does from the cinema. (Joyce's relation to the cinema, as well as that of other writers, is discussed fully in chapter 3.)

But why do I insist on the extraordinary nature of this particular detail of visual apprehension? What is so remarkable about a literary rendering of a particular way of seeing that imitates one of the conventional postures of the camera? An analogy may be helpful. Stephen's eyes here are like the eyes of a man who stands before a painting and is asked to describe everything that he sees. This man proceeds to describe everything that is in the painting and then, just when we think he is about to stop—indeed, should stop—he does not stop but continues to describe the frame surrounding the painting; and then the wall space surrounding the frame; and then the point where the wall meets the ceiling; and then the point where the wall meets the floor; and then the floor space between the wall and the tip of his shoe; and so on until he has met the initial request naively, literally, exactly, and has described not just the painting but *everything* that he sees. When Stephen sees both his cuffedge and the sea within the same oval of vision, he, like this man, is attempting to reproduce the oval of vision in its entirety. Neither Stephen nor this man, however, is seeing in the way the human eye ordinarily sees, but rather in the way that it would see if it had momentarily separated its oval of vision from the entire process of the inner life that lies behind it.

As we know, we do not see only with the eye, but with the mind as well. We see what we desire to see, what the mind allows us to see; or, more precisely, what both mind and eye conspire to see. I want to view the sea, but my palm is against my brow. Thus while my oval of vision may reflect both the sea and part of my forearm, my mind will automatically cut out of my field whatever is not congruent with the focus of my thought. I will view both sea *and* forearm only when and if I want to see everything that I am seeing, as opposed to everything that I want to see.

The camera, unlike the human eye, is unselective. It is, in a manner of speaking, an eye that has been severed from a brain: a dumb eye. Once it has been placed in position the camera will see everything that can be seen within its frame. It cannot pick or choose like the human eye, however unconsciously the eye may perform this function; nor can it be "fascinated," or "inattentive," or "obsessive," or "absentminded." It can only see whatever is to be seen—the accidental as well as the necessary, the ephemeral as well as the essential, the "cuffedge" as well as "the sea," both held and coordinated, without distinction, in a single field of vision.

The literary cultivation of a passive and affectless oval of vision is another way in which we can distinguish the cinematographic form of the twentieth century from the concretized form of the late nineteenth, another way in which we can distinguish Joyce

The Oval of Vision

from Flaubert. This manner of vision tells us that the modern novelist—such as Joyce, Conrad, Faulkner, and, in our own time, Nabokov and Robbe-Grillet—has brought us farther away from the seen object—without losing sight of this object—and closer to the eye of the subject, and therefore closer to the subject himself, than any other novelist before him. In this way the fundamental subject-object paradox of the camera's epistemology now embodies itself in the ocular situation of the observer: he stands dumb before visual experience, but it is *his* visual experience before which he stands. Analogies between the cinema and visual form in modern fiction begin to emerge precisely at that moment when one recognizes that their initial point of intersection represents nothing less than a shared method of cognition.

The passive, affectless eye is also a characteristic of the Joycean observer throughout most of his work. While the cameralike vision brings the reader very close to the experience of the observer's eye, this vision also indicates something very special about the nature of the observer's sensibility and his relationship to the world in which he participates: it indicates that whatever the special circumstances, whoever the participating observer, and however intimate this observer may become with whatever the field of vision may contain, the seen object itself will always remain slightly other than, and slightly apart from, the life of the observer. To see in the manner of the camera is to recognize finally that whatever life is within you is yours and that whatever is contained within the oval of vision is not yours, bears no impress of that life within you, no impress of your thought, your feelings. The object is only seen, and because only seen, ineradicably distanced, for nothing can be seen without distance.

I am not only talking about optics now. I am also talking about a very special kind of estrangement that manifests itself in Joyce's characteristic coldness of vision, a kind of spiritual separateness that begins with a passive, affectless eye and will never permit the observer total rapport with his visual field. I am talking, as it were, about a kind of ocular loneliness. Thus, the impossibility of a complete and permanent human relationship, and the finality of "the soul's incurable loneliness,"[28] one of Joyce's major themes, finds its point of origin in the estranged psychic structure

---

[28]James Joyce, *Dubliners* (New York: Viking Press, 1958), p. 111. Subsequent references to this edition will appear in text.

of an observer whose manner of vision becomes the very measure of his own estrangement. The Joycean prototype of human relationships, incomplete, tenuous, partialized, all but broken—Gabriel and Gretta Conroy, Stephen and Bloom, Bloom and Molly—finds its home in a spatial environment that is also rendered as blocked, fragmented, and incarcerated.

To be sure, the Joycean observer habitually symbolizes and mythologizes his field of vision, reading the seen objects according to his shifting moods. Thus, in the passage above the fraying edge of Stephen's coatsleeve becomes an aspect of his "pain," and the sea itself, at Mulligan's suggestion, is associated with Stephen's dead mother. It is important for Stephen to symbolize objects in this manner, for that is the only way he can coordinate what is in his mind with what he sees before him; but even here, in presenting the act of symbolic association, Joyce keeps the objects themselves slightly apart from Stephen's interpretation of them. Joyce's rendering makes it clear that the only objective connections between the seen objects in Stephen's oval of vision and the personal objects in Stephen's mind are based almost entirely upon material, mechanistic, and essentially nonhuman similarities. "The ring of [the] bay" is associated by its shape with the "bowl of white china," just as the "green mass of liquid" is associated by its texture and tonality with the "green sluggish bile." Thus, Stephen goes from one object to another, not by any comprehensive grasp of, or participation in, the object's "being" or essence, but simply by a primarily visual apprehension of its graphic and material surface. Stephen's readings, though of absolute importance to *him*, remain private and idiosyncratic, while the object in and of itself remains, in a sense, equally private and idiosyncratic, aloof from any single observer's appropriation of it (thus, Joyce will often have any number of observers offer different views on the same object). The object not only remains impervious to mortal assumption but probably to mortal life as well. Even Stephen seems to realize this as he observes the "fragments" along the Sandymount strand: "See now. There all the time without you; and ever shall be, world without end" (*Ulysses*, p. 37).

Part Two

Film and the Modern Novel

Chapter III
Joyce and Company

HERE I WISH to discuss cinematographic form at some length, for this is the form employed by Joyce and many of his most gifted contemporaries, not only in literature but in the other arts as well. This form has in fact been employed so pervasively during the first quarter of this century as to constitute a period, or modern, style.

Cinematographic form, like the modernist movement in literature, begins to emerge in the second half of the previous century, but only establishes itself, along with the movement, as a cohesive and consolidated stylistic posture in the first quarter of the twentieth century. Beyond this point, however, and into the period where the modernist movement is often said to have begun to dissipate its energies, cinematographic form continues to endure;[1] perhaps no longer with the same consolidation and cohesion, but with so widespread a proliferation of its tendencies into and beyond the second quarter of this century that these tendencies may be said to forge irradicable links between the novelists of Joyce's generation and the major novelists of today, the novelists by whose work we define the current literary situation.

Joyce and the Cinema

Throughout this discussion I have been describing this form and the changes that have occurred within it in terms borrowed from the photographic arts, both from photography and cinematog-

---

[1] Harry Levin, "What Was Modernism?," in *Varieties of Literary Experience*, ed. Stanley Burnshaw (New York, 1962), pp. 315-16.

raphy.[2] And since I am going to continue using these terms—but now in specific and immediate relation to James Joyce and other modernists—I think it advisable to establish at this point exactly what I have in mind whenever I speak of Joyce in conjunction with filmmakers and the photographic arts. What did film actually mean to Joyce in his lifetime? And in what sense is it justifiable to talk about film in relation to his work? These matters are worth examining, for in many respects I think that Joyce's relation to the cinema is typical of the relation maintained by many modern artists, literary and otherwise.

In reference to the first question, I am not going to claim, for instance, as did one film critic, that "James Joyce was movie crazy."[3] This, as it stands, is simply a journalistic extravagance in support of which the Joyce biography and his correspondence provide very meager evidence. Joyce obviously *liked* the movies—indeed, started liking them a good bit before it became fashionable to do so—seemed to attend them with a fair degree of

---

[2]Throughout this discussion I assume an affinity between film and photography. I also assume this affinity to be simple and obvious: that is to say, whenever one looks at a film one is also looking at a photograph. In this sense film and photography are linked, and more than one film theoretician has sought to extrapolate the nature and function of the motion picture from its "parent" form. See especially André Bazin, *What is Cinema?* (Berkeley and Los Angeles, 1967), pp. 9-16, 23-40, Siegfried Kracauer, *Theory of Film* (New York, 1960), pp. 3-23, and Stanley Cavell, *The World Viewed: Reflections on the Ontology of Film* (New York, 1973), pp. 23-25. Still, it should be pointed out that to assume an affinity between two things is not, at the same time, to assume an identity between them, and nowhere in this discussion do I assume—or even mean to suggest—such an identity between these two art forms. It is obvious that one or two of the literary visualizations previously cited (e.g., Flaubert's description of Emma) could have been recreated by either the still camera or the motion picture camera. Most of the visualizations (e.g., Zola's, James's, Conrad's), however, could have been accurately recreated only by the latter since they are specifically concerned with the eye's movement (as opposed to its arrest) and thus with the life of the seen object as it exists in time (since all movement implies passage through time as well as space). Apart from its aural component, film departs from photography in its sovereign power to establish or suggest a temporal continuum. So, again: whenever one looks at a film one is also looking at a photograph, but usually of a special kind—a photograph of a duration. The obvious exception to this would be the use of stop-motion photography in a film—see my discussion (The Ontology of the Camera) pp. 82–89..

[3]"Not the Best, Not the Worst," *Time*, 31 Mar. 1967, p. 92.

regularity throughout his life, and once in 1907, while in Rome and in particularly low spirits, was even capable of writing about them in the following manner:

> I have come to the conclusion that it is about time I made up my mind whether I am to become a writer or a patient Cousins. I foresee that I shall have to do other work as well but to continue as I am at present would certainly mean my mental extinction. It is months since I have written a line and even reading tires me. The interest I took in socialism and the rest has left me. I have gradually slid down until I have ceased to take any interest in any subject. I look at God and his theatre through the eyes of my fellow clerks so that nothing surprises, moves, excites or disgusts me. Nothing of my former mind seems to have remained except a heightened sensitiveness which satisfies itself in the sixty-miles-an-hour pathos of some cinematograph or before some crude Italian gazette-picture.[4]

Here, given Joyce's melancholy, the movies seem to function for him as a kind of emotional court of last resort, but this alone is hardly enough evidence to qualify Joyce as a film aesthete or, for that matter, a buff, or in any case certainly not as the man who, as popular opinion seems to have it, was "movie crazy." From time to time in the letters we find mention of the fact that he is about to attend a film or that he has come back from one, but never do we find more than a passing comment on the particular nature and quality of these films or any others. Perhaps his correspondents were not interested in this sort of comment; perhaps Joyce himself was not.

There is, of course, the rather curious matter of Joyce's brief and ill-fated venture in the management of Dublin's first movie theater. This happened in 1909 and marks one of the three occasions when Joyce returned to Ireland after his decisive break with it in 1904. Since it was the film enterprise specifically—setting up the theater and overseeing its operation—that brought him back to Dublin, it is altogether too easy to misinterpret the actual object of his enthusiasm. But according to Professor Ellmann's account of it, Joyce's motive in the affair seems to have been neither cultural nor aesthetic, but primarily financial.[5] His attitude to-

---

[4]Joyce to Stanislaus Joyce (1907), *The Letters of James Joyce*, ed. Richard Ellmann (London, 1966), II, 217.
[5]Ellmann, *James Joyce*, pp. 310-14, 320-22.

ward the whole undertaking seems to have been determined not so much by a desire to bring the pleasures of the new medium to a cinematically innocent Dublin, and still less by any particular passion for the medium itself, but primarily by a drive—one that was never again to surface so blatantly—to become very rich very quickly and free himself from his many economic worries. The enterprise failed within a few months after he returned to Trieste, and Joyce never attempted it, or anything even remotely like it, again. The fact that the cinema happened to be the agency through which Joyce could exercise his profit motive cannot, I think, represent much more than a curious and misleading contingency: he simply and reasonably must have judged that other Dubliners would pay to enjoy what one Dubliner had already paid to enjoy—and he was wrong.

Finally, there are the innumerable references to the cinema that appear in one linguistic transformation after another throughout the pages of *Finnegans Wake*. In this work, Joyce's least visualized narrative, we find, as we find in no other, linguistic collages comprising the vocabulary of vision, photography, and cinematography; film history, film gossip, film technique, and film terminology; the names of movie stars and film directors. One of the episodes (pp. 558-90) is even presented in the form of a film script. But that these matters should appear in such an encyclopedic study of the contemporary scene and the popular culture as *Finnegans Wake* should surprise no one, for the book is liberally sprinkled with references not only to film but to all the media and *all* the arts, popular, serious, and esoteric; literature, painting, opera, theater, vaudeville, radio, television, magazines, and newspapers. Here Joyce's interest in the cinema is equaled by his interest in practically everything else. His curiosity in film may have been real enough, but it was never the curiosity of a specialist. Joyce was only movie conscious, never movie crazy.

I also find it hard to agree with another film critic when she states that "Joyce wrote *Ulysses* in the form of a movie and that is probably why so many people, including Joyce himself, thought it should be made into one."[6] When Joyce wrote *Ulysses* many people did indeed think it should be made into a movie. Among them were Stuart Gilbert and the poet Louis Zukovsky, who

---

[6]Pauline Kael, *Kiss Kiss Bang Bang* (Boston, 1968), p. 169.

Joyce and Company

actually worked up screen treatments and submitted them to Joyce. But Joyce himself remained skeptical in the matter and held off film producers throughout the later years of his life. Once in 1932, when Warner Brothers had misguidedly announced that it would film *Ulysses*, Paul Léon, acting on Joyce's authorization, hastily wrote to the proper authorities that Joyce was "in principle opposed to the filming of *Ulysses*" and that he took "the literary point of view" and was "therefore opposed to the filming as irrealizable."[7] But Joyce, in spite of this "principle" and his "literary point of view," was obviously not unmoved by Warner Brothers' interest in the book and, according to Ellmann, allowed Léon "to keep the matter going."[8]

There had also been the famous interview of 1930 with Sergei Eisenstein, who had always been interested in preparing *Ulysses* for the screen. During their meeting in Joyce's apartment, Joyce read aloud passages from *Ulysses*, expressed a desire to see Eisenstein's films *Potemkin* and *October*, and seemed to be as generally impressed with Eisenstein as was Eisenstein with him. Later Joyce told Eugene Jolas that if *Ulysses* was ever to be made into a movie only Eisenstein or the German director Walter Ruttmann could do the job.[9]

So while Joyce himself did not seem to think that *Ulysses* could be made into a movie, he was obviously willing enough to listen to the arguments of those people who thought otherwise, willing enough "to keep the matter going." He seems to have been waiting for the right script and the right director to show him that the job could be done. He must have suspected, I think, that the "literary point of view" was not the only point of view one could take in the matter.

But if Joyce was reluctant to admit that his book could be made into a film, would he have been equally reluctant to admit that film had been influential in the making of his book? Do we have the right to claim that Joyce's art was consciously influenced by the art of the film? Though it is indeed tempting to do so, I do not

---

[7]Paul Léon to Ralph Pinker (1932), *Letters*, ed. Ellmann, III, 88-89.
[8]Ellmann, *James Joyce*, p. 666.
[9]Marie Seton, *Sergei M. Eisenstein* (New York, 1960), p. 149. Joyce might have seen Ruttmann's famous film *Berlin, Symphony of a City* (1927), in which the feeling for the tone, rhythm, spatial arrangement, and variety of urban incident and detail is not dissimilar to Joyce's anatomy of Dublin in *Ulysses*.

think that we can make any such claim, and there is substantial evidence in Joyce's very early work to support this contention. I am thinking in particular of the passage in *My Brother's Keeper* where Stanislaus describes his brother's first attempts at prose fiction (unfortunately lost to us):

> But more indicative of the trend of his thoughts were the sketches that he began to write while still at school and while we were still living at Windsor Terrace. He called them *Silhouettes* from the first sketch, and though I remember only two of them there may have been a few more. *Silhouettes*, like the first three stories of *Dubliners*, was written in the first person singular, and described a row of mean little houses along which the narrator passes after nightfall. His attention is attracted by two figures in violent agitation on a lowered window-blind illuminated from within, the burly figure of a man, staggering and threatening with upraised fist, and the smaller sharp-faced figure of a nagging woman. A blow is struck and the light goes out. The narrator waits to see if anything happens afterwards. Yes, the window-blind is illuminated again dimly, by a candle no doubt, and the woman's sharp profile appears accompanied by two small heads, just above the window-ledge, of children wakened by the noise. The woman's finger is pointed in warning. She is saying, "Don't waken Pa."[10]

If Stanislaus remembers this scene correctly—and the specificity of the vivid detail seems to indicate that he does—then the passage must have been written sometime between 1893 and 1898, when the Joyce family, according to Stanislaus, was living at Windsor Terrace and when Joyce himself must have been no younger than eleven and no older than sixteen. It is almost certain that young Joyce could have had no knowledge of the cinema since at the time there was almost certainly no cinema in Dublin.[11] And yet in its optical invention and treatment of time and space, the passage is presented in a mode that could only be

---

[10]Stanislaus Joyce, *My Brother's Keeper*, ed. Richard Ellmann (New York, 1964), p. 90.

[11]Dublin might have had a film show by 1898 as did some large international cities (like Shanghai). This is possible but not probable, for two reasons: (a) around 1898 any large international city would not be comparable to Dublin, a very small community notoriously resistant to change and novelty (see the writings of Joyce); and (b) more certain, if Joyce himself attempted to establish Dublin's first movie theater in 1909, where could he possibly have seen a film in the period 1893-98? (At a traveling film show perhaps, but that brings us back to [a].)

described as cinematographic. In fact, it is as striking a visual rendering as any to be found in late nineteenth-century fiction. We note here all the characteristics of the literary equivalents of camera vision and cinematic form as they have been defined thus far (specifically, the subjective nature of the seen object and the fragmentation of the visual field); and we are impressed by the observer's limited position in space; the appearance of the observed objects themselves as determined by the individuality of this position; the extraordinary temporal elision between the two phases of the action; and the equally extraordinary notation of how the heads themselves appear in profile cut off from the rest of the body by the "window-ledge." Moreover, we feel the sense of estrangement that pervades the entire scene, the estrangement we have already noted as characteristic of Joyce's mode of vision in particular and, as we shall see, of this form of modernism in general. We sense this quality especially in the oblique separation between the observer and the event and in the remote and enigmatic quality of the event itself, which is presented almost entirely in terms of opaque visual surfaces existing in and of themselves, virtually beyond human assessment or understanding.

All of this is to be found in the remarkable and very early "silhouette," whose date of composition tells us that Joyce was not only not influenced by the cinema but that he was cinematographic in his literary procedure before the cinema; that he was, in fact, at a very early age, developing and perfecting the cinematographic variety of concretized form, that mode of fiction that had been evolving, as we have seen, in the work of his predecessors and contemporaries previous to, and quite apart from, the invention of the motion picture camera.

Moreover, even after the introduction of movies into the European scene, one is amazed to find in almost any one of the remarkable stories in *Dubliners,* composed between 1904 and 1907, innumerable angles of vision and sequences of literary montage far more bold and original than any of the naive and primitive executions offered by the "cinematograph" during this period. And I think we feel the procedural discrepancy between the cinema and Joyce's fiction just as acutely when we read *Portrait of the Artist as a Young Man,* and especially *Ulysses.* These books, composed when the cinema was already exercising a very rich and expressive vocabulary, reveal passage upon passage of cinematographic form that appear even today not only more sophisticated than many of the characteristic film practices of the silent era (with the possible exception of Soviet practices), but just as ingenious as the best of our current film practices. (Let me stress that the issue here is procedural innovation, not art.)

While certain movie critics may feel that Joyce wrote *Ulysses* in the form of a movie, my own feeling is that very few movies ever attain the complexity of movie procedure that we find in many episodes of *Ulysses*. This is certainly true in the case of the very flat, pedestrian, and "uncinematic" film that was recently based upon it (*Ulysses*, 1967). But the fact that a bad film has been made from *Ulysses* does not mean that a good film could not have been made from it, nor does it mean, if such a film had indeed been made, that Joyce's book would have been, by virtue of this fact, any more or less cinematographic than it already is. Good movies and cinematographic novels really do not have that much to do with one another. There is really no literary fiction so inflexible that it cannot be made into some sort of movie. Whether this film has any merit has less to do, I think, with the original literary fiction than with the imagination and intelligence of the people behind and in front of the camera. A bad film has been made from *Ulysses* while *Ulysses* itself puts me in mind of the contention held by the great French film critic André Bazin: "The way things are," he argued, "it would seem as if the cinema was fifty years behind the novel."[12]

If we conclude, then, that the movies themselves probably did not have any direct influence upon the development of Joyce's literary methods—methods that had obviously evolved out of his own personal cast of mind and temperament as well as out of a whole tradition of concretized novelistic activity—can we also conclude that the medium of film has had nothing at all to do with Joyce or his work? I think we would be mistaken to reach such a conclusion, and here again it is Joyce himself who provides the most revealing information concerning his own literary habits:

Letter just received. What I have told you about rooms is painfully correct. I don't know why we were given notice by the landlady nor do I know whether it was the reason you suggest. I don't know anything

[12]"In Defense of Mixed Cinema," *What is Cinema?* p. 63.

except that I suppose I ought to cease grumbling and take up the white man's burden. Do you imagine you are corresponding with the indifferential calculus that you object to my vituperation on Italy and Rome. What the hell else would I do? If you had to traipse about a city, accompanied by a plaintive woman with infant (also plaintive), run up stairs, ring a bell, "Chi c'e?" "Camera!" "Chi c'e?" "Camera!" No go: room too small or too dear: won't have children, single man only, no kitchen. "Arrivederla!" Down again. Rush off: give a lesson for 9½ d, rush back to bank, etc., etc. Am sending MS to John Long by same post. Didn't change anything. No pen, no ink, no table, no room, no time, no quiet, no inclination. Never mind, it will be back in a week or so. Only I stuck in "bloody" before the late lamented. How I should enjoy a night on Venetian waters with Miss Farchi's romance and reality. The Italian imagination is like a cinematograph, observe the style of my letter.[13]

When Joyce refers to his style here as cinematographic, he is referring to the way he can describe a kaleidoscope of incident with speed and economy, leaping from point to point in the narrative with a minimum of spatial and temporal connectives: just like the "cinematograph." And much later in life there is also the occasion when he refers to his dreams as "Cinema Nights," and then again, after an eye operation, writes to Harriet Shaw Weaver that "whenever I am obliged to lie with my eyes closed I see a cinematograph going on and on and it brings back to my mind things I had almost forgotten."[14]

We should note, then, that in all these examples, Joyce looks to the film because the new medium provides him with new words to describe certain things which are happening in his mind and in his writing, and that he draws upon this medium not as a source of emulation but rather as a mode of precise analogy to define mental and stylistic postures that in all probability had developed independently of it. Clearly it is not the content or quality of any particular film that promotes his interest, but rather it is the formal constitutents of the medium itself; the intensities and the elisions, the seamless flow and the jumpy kinetics; the whole range and variety of this new and exciting syntactical temper. It is

[13]Joyce to Stanislaus Joyce (1906), *Letters*, ed. Ellmann, II, 202.
[14]Joyce to Harriet Shaw Weaver (1924), *Letters*, ed. Ellmann, III, 112; Joyce to Harriet Shaw Weaver (1924), *The Letters of James Joyce*, ed. Stuart Gilbert (New York, 1957), p. 216.

this, then, that stimulates him to allude to film form when describing his own habits of mind and craft.

Thus, while having little or no manipulative influence on his art, a sense of the way film works helps Joyce to define and clarify, and ultimately corroborate, what might otherwise, without this sense, appear to be less precise and more discouragingly private and idiosyncratic. Joyce simply and revealingly discovered in the cinema a source of correspondence for his own imaginative projections, and in this instance, as in so many others, Joyce's response can serve as a touchstone, a central gathering force for some of the prototypical intellectual currents of his literary era—and ours.[15] It is, I think, one of the inescapable facts of the literary life in this century that the modern novelist often comes to his craft with at least a semiconscious recognition that his own narrative art form can proceed to take formal and textural shapes that find their precise correspondents in another and newer narrative art form, namely, film form.

When I refer to film as a narrative art form, I do not mean to define the "intrinsic nature" of this medium (whatever that might be). I simply mean to describe the majority of films that have been made in the past seventy years. During this time film has largely devoted itself to the art—and the business—of storytelling. It should also be remembered, however, that film has cultivated other modes besides the narrative, such as dramatic modes in the filmed play; poetic and nondiscursive modes in the experimental, or underground, film; and modes of journalistic analysis and essay in the documentary film. But whenever a novelist has become aware of the film as narrative, it has usually produced in his own narrative art any one or more of the four following results:

1. The literary form develops, as a whole or in part, in conscious and professed imitation of the photographic art forms.

---

[15]As one might judge from this discussion of Joyce alone, the *specific* impact of the emerging cinema on each of Joyce's literary contemporaries would be a broad and complicated subject, but it is one that lies beyond the scope of this study. My own remarks here simply mean to suggest the range of problems that one might encounter in examining a single representative figure. Other figures would doubtless present other problems. A fully documented history of the reaction of various modern writers, both pre- and post-Joycean, to the advent of film needs to be written.

Joyce and Company

Here we find the work of those novelists who, in one way or another, have admitted or self-consciously demonstrated (in such phrases as "camera eye") the influence of film form upon their own literary operation: Aldous Huxley, John Dos Possos, Graham Greene, James Agee, Wright Morris, Vladimir Nabokov, William Burroughs, Alain Robbe-Grillet, and others.

2. The literary form develops, as a whole or in part, as an analogue to the photographic art forms, but never in conscious imitation of them. Here the stimulus in the creative act rarely derives from a cinematographic source, but nevertheless some or all of the literary effects produced by such an act, regardless of the source, find their correspondents in film form. This relation to film, in many instances semiconscious and oblique, is perhaps the one most representative of the modern novel. We note here the work of those novelists who can be considered modern practitioners of concretized form and who in all probability derived stimulus and reaffirmation from a continuing tradition of concretized novelistic endeavor: Joseph Conrad, James Joyce, Wyndham Lewis, Ernest Hemingway, F. Scott Fitzgerald, William Faulkner, Dashiell Hammett, David Jones, Evelyn Waugh, Nathanael West, John Steinbeck, Raymond Chandler, Jean-Paul Sartre, André Malraux, Albert Camus, Malcolm Lowry, Ken Kesey, Flannery O'Connor, and many others.

3. The novelist applies his craft directly to the film form. Here we find those novelists who have actually participated in the creation of one or more films, usually in the capacity of screenwriter for their own novels or those of others. Significantly, many of the names here also appear in categories (1) or (2): Aldous Huxley, Ernest Hemingway, John Dos Possos, F. Scott Fitzgerald, William Faulkner, Dashiell Hammett, Nathanael West, John Steinbeck, Raymond Chandler, Graham Greene, Jean-Paul Sartre, André Malraux, James Agee, Vladimir Nabokov, Samuel Beckett, Jean Genet, and many others.

4. The artist defines himself as a cultural hybrid, as both man of letters and filmmaker, operates within each medium impartially and without condescension, and finds in each an outlet for his deepest creative concerns: Jean Cocteau, Jean-Pierre Melville, Alain Robbe-Grillet, Curzio Malaparte, Norman Mailer, Susan Sontag, and others.

We know that Joyce did not participate in the creation of any film and that he is perhaps the last modern literary figure that we would ever think to define as a cultural hybrid. We tend to think of Joyce, as we think of Flaubert, as an artist whose devotion to his chosen medium was almost absolute. Yet Joyce did create a body of writing, and one novel in particular, that is more lavish and intricate in its embodiment of cinematographic procedure than the writing of any other modern novelist. In this sense, we will find it useful to examine Joyce as a kind of centrifugal force in modernist literature, and to demonstrate how the attitudes and procedural habits embodied in his own writing reappear, develop, and modulate in the writing of others.

The Ontology of the Camera

I have traced the emergence of a cinematographic form from *Madame Bovary* to *Ulysses* largely in terms of two changes that occur in the depiction of the external world: (1) a change in emphasis from the object seen to the seer seeing (that is, a literal depiction of the observed field as it appears in the image on the retina); and (2) a change in the presentation of the field of vision itself, from a continuous, open, and unobstructed presentation to one that is discontinuous, fragmented, and incarcerated.

In the following discussion of modern fiction, I shall examine other characteristics of this form, but it cannot be stressed too strongly at the outset that *all* of the components of a cinematized narrative derive specifically from what I have called a passive, affectless way of seeing which in itself represents the effects of a broken circuit between the seer and the contents of his visual landscape; that is, a sense that the visible world is something other than, remote from, and resistant to, the human mind.

When I speak of passive vision, then, I am actually describing what Albert Camus in *The Myth of Sisyphus* also described—and in terms not so very different from my own—as "the divorce between man and his life, between the actor and his setting." Here Camus delineated the situation that gives shape to the outlines of a modern consciousness, that consciousness which conceives of the self as an exile, as it were, in its own house. Stripped of religious sanctions and the securities of a common value system, the modern increasingly comes to perceive the visible world as "deprived of illusions and illuminations," as a kind of lunar specimen where the images presented to his eyes seem not only to withhold their meaning but ultimately do not even seem to have, in their very teleology, a meaning to withhold: they no longer exist to be known, but to be described.[16]

Many of the early moderns—like Joyce, Proust, and Faulkner—make attempts, or at least partial attempts, to bridge the gap between the seer and the seen, and through the use of symbol and myth, try to "know" as well as to "describe." In certain kinds of recent fiction, however, the novelist has been content only to describe (as in the fiction of Robbe-Grillet) or neither to know nor to describe (as in the fiction of Beckett) but to ruminate on the linguistic impossibilities of doing either. In almost all instances, however, the particular kind of literary form we will be examining, and the neutrality of vision that resides at its center, will take its point of departure from the prototypically modern split between the human mind and the contents within its oval of vision.

Throughout the previous discussion I have been comparing the qualities associated with this kind of vision to those qualities associated with the photographic image; that is, I have been concerned with the epistemology of the camera. And as a way of summarizing the previous discussion and introducing the new one, I am going to draw upon Marcel Proust's fascinating remarks on camera vision that appear in one of those long prose cadenzas from *Guermantes Way*. Here the narrator enters the room where his grandmother sits, and observes her in a strange and unprecedented way:

> I was in the room, or rather I was not yet in the room since she was not aware of my presence, and, like a woman whom one surprises at a piece of work which she will lay aside if anyone comes in, she had abandoned herself to a train of thoughts which she had never allowed to be visible by me. Of myself—thanks to that privilege which does not last but which one enjoys during the brief moment of return, the faculty of being a spectator, so to speak, of one's own absence—there was present only the witness, the observer, with a hat and travelling coat, the stranger who does not belong to the house, the photographer who has called to take a photograph of places which one will never see again. The process that mechanically occurred in my eyes when I caught sight of my grandmother was indeed a photograph. We never see the people who are dear

---

[16]*The Myth of Sisyphus and Other Essays* (New York, 1958), p. 6.

to us save in the animated system, the perpetual motion of our incessant love for them, which before allowing the images that their faces present to reach us catches them in its vortex, flings them back upon the idea that we have always had of them, makes them adhere to it, coincide with it. How, since into the forehead, the cheeks of my grandmother I had been accustomed to read all the most delicate, the most permanent qualities of her mind; how, since every casual glance is an act of necromancy, each fact that we love a mirror of the past, how could I have failed to overlook what in her had become dulled and changed, seeing that in the most trivial spectacles of our daily life, our eye, charged with thought, neglects, as would a classical tragedy, every image that does not assist the action of the play and retains only those that may help to make its purpose intelligible. But if, in place of our eye, it should be a purely material object, a photographic plate, that has watched the action, then what we shall see, in the courtyard of the Institute, for example, will be, instead of the dignified emergence of an Academician who is going to hail a cab, his staggering gait, his precautions to avoid tumbling upon his back, the parabola of his fall, as though he were drunk, or the ground frozen over. So is it when some casual sport of chance prevents our intelligent and pious affection from coming forward in time to hide from our eyes what they ought never to behold, when it is forestalled by our eyes, and they, arising first in the field and having it to themselves, set to work mechanically, like films, and show us, in place of the loved friend who has long ago ceased to exist but whose death our affection has always hitherto kept concealed from us, the new person whom a hundred times daily that affection has clothed with a dear and cheating likeness. And, as a sick man who for long has not looked at his own reflection, and has kept his memory of the face that he never sees refreshed from the ideal image of himself that he carries in his mind, recoils on catching sight in the glass, in the midst of an arid waste of cheek, of the sloping red structure of a nose as huge as one of the pyramids of Egypt, I, for whom my grandmother was still myself, I who had never seen her save in my own soul, always at the same place in the past, through the transparent sheets of contiguous, overlapping memories, suddenly in our drawing-room which formed part of a new world, that of time, that in which dwell the strangers of whom we say "He's begun to age a good deal," for the first time and for a moment only, since she vanished at once, I saw, sitting on the sofa, beneath the lamp, red-faced, heavy and common, sick, lost in thought, following the lines of a book with eyes that seemed hardly sane, a dejected old woman whom I did not know.[17]

[17]*The Guermantes Way, Remembrance of Things Past,* trans. C. K. Scott-Moncrieff (New York: Random House, 1934), I, 814-15.

What Proust gives us here can and should represent the equivalent of an epigraph to any proper understanding of visualization in the modern novel. The passage contrasts two kinds of vision: the ordinary human kind, which participates in the apprehension of its object, as against the kind that seemingly does not—the vision of the photographic plate with its cold, blank, and indifferent gaze, which startles and ultimately disheartens Proust, and—we might add—in opposition to which, in an effort of awesome confutation and transcendence, he had erected the entire edifice of his artistic enterprise, *Remembrance of Things Past*.

It is the vision of the human eye, full of "intelligent and pious affection" that is compared to the eye of the lover, that is inseparable from the mind and imagination of the perceiver and apprehends its object in a condition "charged with thought," memories, and past associations; that flings the images presented by the object "back upon the idea that we have always had of them," retaining only those images that help make the purpose of the object "intelligible," that reflect only its permanent structure and qualities. On the other hand, the vision of the camera eye is compared to the vision of the witness, "the stranger who does not belong to the house"; an isolated and alienated presence who reveals to us something we have never seen before, something, Proust tells us, "we ought never to behold"—a common, dull, heavy world of images seen under the aspect of time and chance, and apparently very different from those ideal images of the world we usually carry in the mind.

It is significant, I think, that Proust does not consider the camera in its subjective capacities, as an instrument of creative and expressive possibility, or even as a simple means of conveying any of the attitudes, artistic or otherwise, of its operator, the cameraman himself. Instead, he interprets the camera as virtually a "dumb eye," and he reminds us of something we are likely to forget nowadays when we think of the still camera in terms of a Walker Evans or a Cartier-Bresson, or of the motion picture camera in terms of any number of great filmmakers. Proust reaffirms the first and oldest function of the camera as a semiautotelic device that mechanically records and reproduces whatever is present within its field of vision. By contrast, the artist's brush and the writer's pen are objects of almost total implementation, and function as virtually nonmediating extensions of the artist's mind and imagination, adding little or nothing to the original conception or to his finished creation. The camera, however, is both instrument and machine, specifically, a recording machine, and once placed in position and pressed into operation, functions like any other machine: that is, it can perform its service in place of its operator and is not dependent upon his presence for whatever it has been asked to do.

Unless he is a cartoonist or draws directly on the negative, the filmmaker and the photographer do not ordinarily have the same degree of personal and absolute control over each millimeter of space within the camera frame that, for instance, a painter will have over the area of his canvas. The painter or the writer fills his space *sequentially,* as it were, stroke by stroke, word by word, and thus exercises almost total control over each "point" at each moment of the creative process. The camera, on the other hand, fills its space *synchronously,* all at once and as a whole with the flick of its shutter. So while the ordinary filmmaker or cameraman may prepare his subject— manipulate or arrange whatever is in front of the lens—and prepare the camera—select position, lens, emulsion, and the like—he cannot control the creative process point by point, for this process is not entirely under his control, and is, at least partially, undertaken within the camera itself at the moment it begins to operate.

The difference, then, between the camera arts and the other arts—painting, literature, music—begins with the relative ability or inability of the individual artist to impose his presence at each stage of the creative process. No matter how objectively any artist attempts to render his subject in words or paint, he will always incorporate, as part of this rendition, a part of himself. The same attempt through the medium of the photographic arts will yield as part of the rendition not only something of the artist himself but also something of the *necessitarian structure* of the camera mechanism and the photographic image.[18]

Now Proust obviously feels that these structures represent

[18] My sense of the way the camera works has been inspired by André Bazin's brilliant essay "The Ontology of the Photographic Image," *What is Cinema?* pp. 9-16. "For the first time, between the originating object and its reproduction there intervenes only the instrumentality of a nonliving agent. For the first time an image of the world is formed automatically, without the creative intervention of man" (p. 13).

something unique, that they accustom us to kinds of visual experience not yet provided by either the human eye or the other arts. What functions, then, does the camera most readily and naturally perform that the other arts must strain their materials—and even exceed their limitations—to approximate? And what kinds of images does it teach us how to see, images that the ordinary human eye either neglected or was not physically structured to apprehend until the photographic habit itself was appropriated by human consciousness? Based on Proust's highly figurative and suggestive description, I am going to explore four characteristics that are not only essential to any understanding of camera and film manners but equally essential to any understanding of analogous visual procedures in the modern novel—indeed, essential to those procedures that in turn help to define the cinematographic nature as well as the modernity of the narrative form.[19]

The Adventitious. Time and chance often provide the photograph with random and unforeseen details of personality and situation apart from, and often in spite of, the photographer's original intentions. Moreover, the still camera's natural tendency is to fix the provisional and accidental moment as if it were final and immutable; thus, the photograph characteristically reveals not the "dignified emergence of an Academician" but rather "his staggering gait, his precautions to avoid tumbling upon his back." Perhaps more than any other instrument of perception, it is the camera, both the motion picture camera as well as the still camera—for the former always has the capacity to *emulate* the latter (though stopmotion is definitive of the latter and only one of the former's many effects)—that time and again reveals its affinity for the specificities of the single isolated instant; the moment separated from a continuum of past and future moments that alone confers shape and significance upon it. When this moment is thus stripped of its context, it assumes the character of an unrelatable and inexplicable fortuity. In the following discussion, I am going to explore the cultivation of the adventitious detail in descriptions of posture and gesture in the modern novel.

---

[19]My first two categories are based on Siegfried Kracauer's discussion of photography in *Theory of Film,* pp. 3-23.

Anatomization. The camera simply conveys more detailed information about how animated things and beings look when they move through time and space than perhaps any other artistic or mechanical invention. A series of photographs not only can reveal the seemingly adventitious gestures and postures of the Academician but also suggests the "parabola of his fall." The motion picture camera, of course, with its almost infinite range of speeds—from stop to slow to accelerated motion, and virtually anything in between—can perform even more detailed and surgical analyses. The camera places a new and concentrated attentiveness upon the infinite number of phases that constitute the shape of any single action and thus brings to human consciousness a new accretion of process images and an increased awareness of process itself. I shall discuss this new anatomical transcription of reality in relation to the descriptions of physical action in the modern novel.

Depthlessness. The camera emphasizes "the sloping red structure of a nose as huge as one of the pyramids of Egypt." Since the photographic image depicts its subject only in terms of its physical surface, it tends to stress the subject's purely structural, geometric, and material properties. Furthermore, the camera eye tends to de-emphasize and flatten out the depth of field that the human eye ordinarily perceives; to foreground and thus equalize everything in the visual field—people, objects, and surrounding environment—on the same flat, two-dimensional plane. When I describe the diverse qualities of character and depictions of inanimate objects in the modern novel, I shall refer to the depthlessness of the photographic image.

Montage. The foregoing three categories represent expansions of what Proust tells us about the photographic image and the characteristic uses of the still camera. The present category will examine an aspect of the camera that Proust does not speak of: the characteristic uses of the motion picture camera as such, and specifically its use in that part of the filmmaking process known as editing, the arrangement of photographed perspectives (images, shots) in sequence according to a predetermined concept. I am going to refer to this process to describe certain treatments of temporal and spatial continuity in modern literary narration.

I shall be applying the concepts in each of these categories to a number of modern writers. It should be emphasized at the outset that these categories are not mutually exclusive and that, except where noted, any writer who appears in one category could also appear in any of the others. In each instance I have tried to place the writer in the category that best expresses the dominant formal and intellectual qualities in his work. Note, however, that each category represents a different facet of the same literary form, and it is this form that is shared by all.

Chapter IV
The Adventitious Detail

WHEN I USE THE TERM *adventitious* to describe something that happens in a visualized narrative, I am referring either to the postures or gestures of a character or an object that neither signify nor connect with anything else in the narrative context beyond their own phenomenal appearances. The adventitious detail usually takes the form of an accident, the causes of which are not readily apparent; an accident that is seemingly without a narrative function and cannot be easily related to any pattern of artistic inevitability. It is, of course, a relative term and depends for its effects primarily on our sense of its opposite, that is, our sense of the necessary and the inevitable as we have experienced them, not only in life, but, even more crucially, in the traditional practices of narrative fiction.

Surely there is no need for this term in Homer's famous scene where Odysseus' nurse suddenly recognizes her master by the scar on his thigh and in her surprise drops her basin. This gesture would indeed be purely circumstantial were not its cause readily transparent to the reader, (the nurse has not seen Odysseus for twenty years, had given him up for dead, and so on) as is the dramatic significance of the effect itself (he has not been forgotten: will the nurse now give him away to the others?). What is true of this use of the adventitious in the *Odyssey* is equally true of its use in *Don Quixote* where the barber's basin is first lost and then later reclaimed by its owner, and in *Tom Jones* where the late night confusions at the inn at Upton seem to make all the major characters contiguous with one another. These events that seem to occur by chance are, in fact, *necessary* accidents, necessary to the characters, plots, and themes of the narratives in which they occur; each accident is thus caught up, as it were, in a structural and ideational schema of artistic fatality.

In *Madame Bovary*, however, we confront a diversity of postures, gestures, and incidental detail less overtly related to patterns of structural necessity and thus more overtly circumstantial.

The Adventitious Detail 91

When, for instance (in the scene previously analyzed), Charles Bovary misplaces his riding crop and Emma finds it for him, the entire incident seems to be one of those moments that "just happen." No explanation is given for the loss of the object; it is simply missing and Charles and Emma hunt for it. When Emma retrieves it, however, and in so doing comes into contact with Charles's body, the explanation for the entire incident becomes clear: the missing crop quite literally brings the characters together, transforms a superficial relationship into an intimate one, and advances the plot one step further. The cause of the incident may be arbitrary—and this fact is significant, for it indicates an aspect of Flaubert's modernity—but the effect of the incident is a necessary part of Flaubert's total artistic design and is, therefore, as functional as Homer's dropped basin.

Yet it can hardly be denied that there are many passages of descriptions of character and setting in virtually everything Flaubert wrote that represent significant departures from a traditionally integrated and strictly purposeful line of action. As part of the concretization of the narrative complex, Flaubert's descriptions begin to take on a motionless, tableaulike self-sufficiency, and the depiction of object and locale proceed to function in a new way in relation to the narrative context.[1]

These descriptive innovations can be observed in any number of post-Flaubertian novelists, but perhaps most succinctly in Joyce: "His eyes moved to the chair over which she had thrown some of her clothes. A petticoat string dangled to the floor. One boot stood upright, its limp upper fallen down: the fellow of it lay upon its side" ("The Dead," *Dubliners*, p. 222). This is a characteristic description from one of Joyce's relatively early works (1907). Even within its context, it is extremely difficult to relate this description to any of the traditional, pre-Flaubertian patterns of literary necessity. Unlike Homer's basin—or, for that matter, Flaubert's riding crop—Joyce's objects are never actually put to use by any of his characters, either at the moment they are being described or at any other moment; nor do they ever interact or unite with the ongoing dynamic of the lives of these characters or

---

[1]The still-life quality of many of Flaubert's descriptions is discussed by Georg Lukács in "Narrate or Describe?," *Writer and Critic and Other Essays* (New York, 1970), pp. 115-16.

the continuous forward movement of what may be called the plot's horizontal action.

Yet in spite of this, Joyce's objects are not without a significant function. Like many of Flaubert's objects, they are vital aspects of an artistic design and relate *vertically*, as it were, to the dramatically necessary resonances of meaning in the mind of the author. They are symbols and function symbolically by gathering up, intensifying, and deepening the dramatic action rather than carrying it forward in the pre-Flaubertian manner. Thus, the symbol in narrative fiction often functions essentially as a regrouping and reinforcing device, a mode of contextual retrenchment. This particular description follows immediately upon a climactic scene of blocked and frustrated sensual passion in which Gabriel Conroy discovers that he has, in effect, been cuckolded by his wife's memory of her dead lover. Upon the conclusion of this scene, the description of the boots and petticoat distills and epitomizes a mood of drooping anticlimax (the dangling string), emotional exhaustion (the fallen boot), and sexual failure ("the limp upper fallen down"). In a similar manner Charles's encounter with Emma represents a moment of sexual awakening, and the description here also takes on a symbolic resonance that belies its supposititious appearance: Charles has indeed "lost" his "riding crop" in a loveless marriage with the first Madame Bovary, and it is Emma who "finds" and "returns" it to him at their first moment of physical contact. Thus, in Joyce and Flaubert the seemingly adventitious aligns itself with a tradition of artistic necessity, but in a new way, by providing an undercurrent of interior resonance beneath the narrative surface.

Still, the visible appearances of the objects themselves in all of Joyce's descriptions are always intriguing—sometimes frustrating—precisely because these appearances seem so thoroughly casual and haphazard. While the description of the boots and petticoat may be in its general intent part of Joyce's symbolic design, the seemingly adventitious posture and arrangement of the objects as such provide them with an individuality and self-sufficiency that sets them in counteropposition not only to the characters but also, and finally, to their own internal value as symbols. It is thoroughly typical of Joyce's descriptive tactics to render objects and settings (and people, too, as we shall see) in the photographic manner, as they appear under the sway

The Adventitious Detail 93

of time and mutability; that is, in the indeterminacy of the moment, in their least guarded, most unpropitious and deliquescent phases. We view the objects, not in their generalized, generic, and pristine forms (as unqualified nouns: *boots, petticoat*), but rather in forms that are immediate, tarnished, and chanceful (*fallen* boots, *dangling* string, upright boot with *limp upper*).

The nightmare of history, human and otherwise, has worked on these objects, lending them a kind of broken melancholy that simultaneously stirs in us a corresponding sense of the fragility and sheer perishability of the life of things in time. Joyce's treatment is similar to those still-life camera studies of Atget, Walker Evans, and Paul Strand—the deserted front of an open-air cafe, an empty city street, an arrangement of rusty farm tools against the side of a barn—where the visible arrangement, character, and fate of the objects seem as hopeless, timebound, and adventitious as Joyce's objects.

Everywhere in Joyce's work, from *Dubliners* through *Finnegans Wake*, we confront the attempt to resolve the dramatic incompatibility between an object's adventitious appearance as part of a chaotic and senseless material flux and its meaningful depths, between the opaque surface of things and their symbolic value. Sometimes a union is achieved between these two, sometimes not. Most often, however, the adventitious and the artistically necessary exist side by side within the same work. As a result we often find critics speaking of two Joyces: a traditional Joyce, a neoclassical temperament with bottomless capacities for transforming senseless contingencies into patterns of artistic consistency, and a radical Joyce with correspondences in dada, pop art, and the like, and with an amused affinity for the adventitious in all its plasmic indeterminacy.[2]

It is this second Joyce, I think, that probably best explains the modernity of a book like *Ulysses*, where the use of adventitious detail attains its fullest expression, and our sense as we read it that no matter how deftly we relate accident to symbol, fact to value, welter to form, there will always remain a large and vibrant

---

[2]The pop art element is discussed by John Gross in *James Joyce*, Modern Masters Series, Vol. 10 (New York, 1970), pp. 52-55; the dada comparison is taken up by Robert Martin Adams in *Surface and Symbol: The Consistency of James Joyce's* Ulysses (New York, 1967), pp. 247-48.

residue of fortuitous detail *within* the artistic design that cannot be fully explained by it, that strains the limits of this design, that makes the book seem to spill over at its seams; that provides it with its unique texture of clutter, congestion, trivia, and the kind of concentrated employment of inexplicable waste energy that we get here:[3]

Striding past Finn's hotel, Cashel Boyle O'Connor Fitzmaurice Tisdall Farrell stared through a fierce eyeglass across the carriages at the head of Mr. E. M. Solomons in the window of the Austro-Hungarian viceconsulate. Deep in Leinster street, by Trinity's postern, a loyal king's man, Hornblower, touched his tallyho cap. As the glossy horses pranced by Merrion square Master Patrick Aloysius Dignam, waiting, saw salutes being given to the gent with the topper and raised also his new black cap with fingers greased by porksteak paper. His collar too sprang up. The viceroy, on his way to inaugurate the Mirus bazaar in aid of funds for Mercer's hospital, drove with his following towards Lower Mount street. He passed a blind stripling opposite Broadbent's. In Lower Mount street a pedestrian in a brown macintosh, eating dry bread, passed swiftly and

---

[3]When the earliest readers of *Ulysses* responded with such anger and dismay to Joyce's eccentric and unprecedented form, did not the cause of this response reside in the very fact that where these readers looked for design, they found only chaos? Where they wanted formal purpose, they got only adventitious detail? Certainly the earliest critics of *Ulysses*—Eliot, Gilbert, and others—demonstrated that those first readers had been careless in their reading, too hasty in their judgments, and that these readers were indeed getting what they were looking for, though they did not know it; and where they saw only formlessness, there was, in fact, system. Until recently subsequent critics and scholars of all of Joyce's work have followed the lead first established by those early scholars and critics of *Ulysses*. In the last ten years or so, however, the trend has reversed itself and the current group of Joyce explicators—Adams, Gross and others—have now come around full circle to agree with those early readers (while not dismissing the early critics either). We know now that the first readers of *Ulysses* were not entirely wrong; that much of what was first read in Joyce's book as bewildering, circumstantial, and indeterminate cannot be legitimately read in any other way; that to recognize what was adventitious in appearance was, in many instances, to recognize what was adventitious in fact; and that to recognize the book in this way was also to recognize the intentions of its author. "Many of the changes that Joyce imposed on the raw materials of his book and some of the selections that he made among them are designed to confuse or blur, rather than to create or emphasize patterns.... A close reading of *Ulysses* thus reveals that the meaningless is deeply interwoven with the meaningful in the texture of the novel" (Adams, *Surface and Symbol*, pp. 244-45). See also Gross's overview of Joyce scholarship in *James Joyce*, pp. 263-70.

unscathed across the viceroy's path. At the Royal Canal bridge, from his hoarding, Mr. Eugene Stratton, his bulb lips agrin, bade all comers welcome to Pembroke township. At Haddington road corner two sanded women halted themselves, an umbrella and a bag in which eleven cockles rolled to view with wonder the lord mayor and lady mayoress without his golden chain. On Northumberland and Landsdowne roads His Excellency acknowledged punctually salutes from rare male walkers, the salute of two small schoolboys at the garden gate of the house said to have been admired by the late queen when visiting the Irish capital with her husband, the prince consort, in 1849, and the salute of Almidano Artifoni's sturdy trousers swallowed by a closing door. [*Ulysses*, pp. 254-55]

The tone and the manner of the entire passage are those of the court stenographer mechanically reproducing a gross and cluttered body of information, both the purposeful and the utterly useless, with equal attributions of value attached to each. This tone and manner reduce everything to the level of the adventitious.

The observed details and expository fact, trailing their subjects in appositional phrasing, are exact, scrupulous, and amusingly irrelevant: Dignam's fingers "greased by porksteak paper"; the man in the macintosh (surely the most intentionally superfluous character in fiction) "eating dry bread"; the lord mayor "without his golden chain"; and the salute of the two schoolboys "at the garden gate of the house said to have been admired by the late queen when visiting the Irish capital," etc., etc. The postures and gestures of the characters themselves are equally inept and inapposite (even certain appropriate gestures, like Hornblower's salute, become meaningless, swallowed up as they are by the stream of overt stupidities): the fierce face of the eccentric Farrell staring off in the "wrong" direction; the gratuitous salute of Dignam's collar; Eugene Stratton's poster smile (a picture of a man, a mute, motionless, strictly visual gag: the grinning nonhuman fits naturally without dissonance into the catalog of the mechanized human); and the contemptuous banality of the fadeout, Artifoni's behind "swallowed" by a closing door.

None of these gestures and notations, to say the very least, are ever brought into a functional relationship with the major characters or the central situations of the novel. And unlike the description of the boots and the petticoat in "The Dead," this description presents no hint of interior depths behind the visible phenomena:

the postures and gestures here are not symbolic. Nor do they have more than a tangential acquaintance with Joyce's mythopoeic schema. Homer's passing reference to the Wandering Rocks in the *Odyssey* hardly illuminates the variety and density of this swarm-life. They are self-reflexive happenings, and in their utter banality reflect Joyce's lifelong preoccupation with the visible reality as an amusing and charming void (*"un bellissimo niente,"* as he called it in later life),[4] and if they constitute a part of any pattern of artistic recurrence, they do so by linking with the other postures, gestures, and notations of a similar nature that are found everywhere throughout *Ulysses*.

These effects are not only gratuitous and self-reflexive, they are also "wrong" and "strange": wrong because they are inappropriate in relation to the requirements of the situation in which they occur; and strange because in a strict sense their full significance can never properly be determined. Each gesture is rendered at the precise instant in which the carriage passes the character and at no other instant either before or after. In this manner the gesture assumes the character of a strict and almost meaningless present with a supposititious past and an undetermined future; for it is only when the isolated gesture takes its place in the arch, as it were, of a continuous activity, in the "before" and the "after" of a temporal continuum, that its sense and purpose begin to emerge.

Joyce never renders visible behavior, animate or inanimate, continuously. Instead, he renders this behavior in a modern and photographic manner: as a discontinuous series of visualized fragments. Sentence by sentence, literally one per character, each figure presents himself in the form of a verbal snapshot—framed typographically by a capital letter at one side and a period at the other—with the continuity and totality of his actions reduced to a single, off-guard and absurd moment, a single phase frozen fast by the literary analogue of the stop-motion camera.

I do not suppose that the peculiar effect of this procedure should surprise anyone. For the past seventy years the modern consciousness has been continually exposed to, and thus shaped

[4] "Adesso Termino. Ho gli occhil stanchi. Da piu di mezzo secolo scrutano nel nulla dove hanno trovato un bellissimo niente" ("Here I conclude. My eyes are tired. For over a half century, they have gazed into nullity where they have found a lovely nothing"). Joyce to George Joyce (1935), *Letters*, ed. Ellmann, III, 359.

The Adventitious Detail

by, endless examples of camera journalism in the newspapers and magazines that direct attention to the stop-motion gesture, that teach us how to recognize and ultimately expect human behavior to present itself in these fragmentary and indeterminate forms. In fact, it can be said with a certain wry justice that the vague, inept, often absurd expressions on the photographed faces of countless dignitaries and celebrities have even helped us to generate an active taste for these visual forms, for this sort of snapshot tells us pretty much what we want to know. We are eager—all too eager perhaps—to give the photo the skeptical and ironic response that it seems to ask of us, and this skepticism and irony, as everyone knows, constitute a large part of precisely what is meant by "thinking in a modern manner."

And in a way reminiscent of the newspaper photo, Joyce also uses the adventitious detail for cynical and humorous purposes. In the above passage the fragmented postures and gestures are, in effect, so many classic sight gags, subdued variants of the pratfall and the pie-in-the-face in which the various expressions of the human body are teased, mocked, and exploited to make us laugh. The stop-motion technique results in a jerky rigidity of human gesture that in itself becomes a precise exemplum of Bergson's famous formula for the comic effect: the imposition of mechanical fixity upon human flexibility (which Joyce emphasized linguistically as well as visually, by repeating virtually the same syntactic formula for each sentence). "The laughable element," argued Bergson, "consists of a certain *mechanical elasticity* just where one would expect to find the wide-awake adaptibility and the living pliableness of a human being." And Bergson goes on to provide concrete descriptive illustrations of this formula that are in their visual elements similar to Joyce's frozen figures.[5]

[5] Henri Bergson, "Laughter," in *Comedy*, ed. Wylie Sypher (New York, 1956), pp. 66-67. "There came on the stage two men, each with an enormous head, bald as a billiard ball. In their hands they carried large sticks which each, in turn, brought down on the other's cranium. Here, again, a certain graduation was observable. After each blow, the bodies seemed to grow heavier and more unyielding, overpowered by an increasing degree of rigidity. Then came the return blow, in each case heavier and more resounding than the last, coming, too, after a longer interval. The skulls gave forth a formidable ring throughout the silent house. At last the two bodies, each quite rigid and as straight as an arrow, slowly bent over towards each other, the sticks came crashing down for the last time on to

Both Joyce and Bergson, however, find even more intriguing correspondences in the pantomime of the American silent film comedian who often, for comic effect, would engineer his arms and legs into hard-line, sharp-angled, machinelike shapes. I am thinking particularly of Keaton, whose body geometry was compared by James Agee to "an automatic gearshift."[6] This was Machine Age humor and all three—novelist, philosopher, and silent clown—helped to shape a moment in the cultural history of the modern sensibility by creating viable comic images of human assimilation into a mechanized and technocratic landscape.

Perhaps one way to summarize the nature of the adventitious in Joyce's descriptions would be to say that Joyce treats the peripheral aspects of human behavior as if they were central. And by using the term *peripheral* I am actually alluding to the remark of the German dramatist Friedrich Hebbel, who, when *he* used it, was responding to a tendency in the new writing that he disliked: "The peripheral blooms everywhere; the mud on Napoleon's boots at the moment of the hero's abdication is as painstakingly portrayed as the spiritual conflict in his face."[7] Often in Joyce's visual treatments, then, the humanly circumstantial and peripheral take precedence over the humanly necessary and central with the consequent diminishment of human grace, dignity, and purposefulness.

Other modern writers use the adventitious detail in a similar manner—for we may say with Hebbel that "the peripheral

---

the two heads with a thud as of enormous mallets falling upon oaken beams, and the pair lay prone upon the ground. At that instant appeared in all its vividness the suggestion that the two artists had gradually driven into the imagination of the spectators: 'We are about to become...we have now become solid wooden dummies' " (ibid., pp. 98-99).

[6]"Comedy's Greatest Era," *Agee on Film: Reviews and Comments* (Boston, 1964), p. 15.

[7]Quoted by Lukács in "Narrate or Describe?" pp. 131-32. Hebbel's remark is reflected, and Joyce's technique adumbrated, everywhere in the work of another post-Flaubertian, Leo Tolstoy, who often employed banal and circumstantial detail to debunk famous historical personnages (including Napoleon) and social dignitaries (e.g., an official's horse cantering out of step during a parade, a distinguished nobleman removing his false teeth after a game of *vint*). This sort of ironic notation became part of Tolstoy's well-known deflationary tactic for rewriting romantic and cliché-ridden situations from the point of view of a naif (also called by Russian critics "making it strange" [*ostrannoe*]). See D. S. Mirsky, *A History of Russian Literature*, ed. Francis G. Whitfield (New York, 1958), p. 263.

The Adventitious Detail

blooms everywhere"—but often with purposes different from Joyce's. Ernest Hemingway, for example, does not use it to attain comic effects, but rather to attain effects that are serious, anguished, and nihilistic:

> They shot the six cabinet ministers at half-past six in the morning against the wall of a hospital. There were pools of water in the courtyard. There were wet dead leaves on the paving of the courtyard. It rained hard. All the shutters of the hospital were nailed shut. One of the ministers was sick with typhoid. Two soldiers carried him downstairs and out into the rain. They tried to hold him up against the wall but he sat down in a puddle of water. The other five stood very quietly against the wall. Finally the officer told the soldiers it was no good trying to make him stand up. When they fired the first volley he was sitting down in the water with his head on his knees.[8]

This passage from Hemingway's early work (1925) is a remarkable example of his famous statement of aesthetic purpose, in which the writer's problem (and his art) is to discover "what the actual things were which produced the emotion that you experienced," and to separate those things and that emotion from the emotion and the things which you did not feel, but "were supposed to feel and had been taught to feel."[9]

The power and the freshness, then, of young Hemingway's artistry, and particularly here in his war vignette, derive from a disparity between what a reader had read, heard, and imagined about a given event and the author's description of it, which would present "the actual things" and "what you truly felt": it was the disparity between what the average reader expected and what Hemingway would actually give him.

One kind of reader, for example, might conceive of war, and even a military execution, in terms of army romance (Hemingway, after all, was debunking an older generation's idealization of war). This reader would expect examples of martial etiquette, flourish, precision, and ritual. But Hemingway's description gives him none of these things. There are no threatening drums, no flags, no files of soldiers marching in double-column lockstep, no blindfolds proferred and then denied. Hemingway's scene is quietly soggy, graceless, and disorderly; the soldiers fumble with the sick man while the others stand quietly against the wall.

[9]Ernest Hemingway, *Death in the Afternoon* (New York, 1960), p. 2.
[8]*In Our Time* (New York, 1958), p. 63.

Another kind of reader, on the other hand, might demand the violent and horrifying aspects of war, which is to say, he might want a different kind of romance: screams, pleas for mercy, maimed limbs and bloody heads. But the vignette gives him none of these things either. Hemingway's vision is more terrible than any scene of exaggerated violence because it is more ordinary. He creates an atmosphere of quietude, empty spaces, and a thoroughly prosaic kind of listlessness (the pools of water, wet dead leaves, the men standing quietly). His selection of detail suggests a final and almost unbearable nullity: the material particularities of the setting, represented by certain sparsely adorned and often repeated substantives, are united by common qualities of flatness, blankness, and stillness; "wet dead leaves," "pools of water"; the three references to the wall, and the pointed notation of the "shutters," "nailed shut" (with almost immediate associations of a coffin); and the "five" who stand "very quietly against the wall."

Joyce's objects evoke a sorrow and a melancholy because they are seen under the aspect of temporal decay, in medias res, some time before the final stages of dissolution. Hemingway's depictions of violent death, however, evoke a despair that is beyond melancholy and sorrow. For his objects have virtually achieved the final and absolute phase of their decline beyond which they can no longer go or be; they are "at the wall" precisely, dead ends: corpses.

Hemingway's choice of detail here derives from an attitude of detachment and massive impassivity. The vision that describes the scene effects a neutrality which, in turn, tells us that the describer is determined not to be interested by anything that he sees, that the distance between the seer and the seen is immense. We are observing, of course, the effects of a camera's vision, and Hemingway is one of the eminent cinematographic artists, not simply because he makes you see, but because he makes you see in a special way—the camera's way. He makes you see everything—the peripheral and the central, the adventitious and the necessary—with an equal proportion of emphasis and therefore on the same plane of value. The dead leaves, the waiting men, the pools of water, the sick soldier, the nailed shutters are all described in the same flat, even tone, each observed with an equality of disinterest and each embodied in sentences of similar length and syntactic arrangement.

But perhaps the most powerful effect of Hemingway's illusion of passive vision, and the masterstroke that also distinguishes him from so many of his imitators, is the depiction of the sick man. Here the describer quietly and flatly observes that this man "sat down in a puddle of water." I find this notation unforgettable and convincing because Hemingway makes us see something that we do not expect, that goes against all our notions of what actually is supposed to happen during violent death. This man makes the "wrong" gesture in exactly the same way Joyce's characters in the "Wandering Rocks" all make the "wrong" gesture, a gesture that seems perfectly irrelevant to the situation in which it occurs. One sits down to write a letter, or one sits down to butter a slice of toast, but one does not sit down to die.

The less fastidious and more conventional imagination would demand that the sick man "keel over" or "crumple" or "collapse." These, however, are the more intense and flagrant expressions that derive from a mental set that conceives of violent death in the time-honored manner, as terrible and *violent*. And precisely because Hemingway knows the time-honored manner, knows, that is, what everyone knows, he rejects this knowledge and presents the scene only in terms of what the eyes exactly see at the moment they are being used; for it is with the eyes alone that you discover "what the actual things were which produced the emotion that you experienced." The sick man's gesture is fresh and powerful precisely because it is so banal, anticlimactic, and thoroughly *adventitious* in relation to our normal (and false) expectations.

This effect is exactly like all of those newspaper photos of wartime violence and disaster where the victim always seems to have the wrong look on his face: boredom, blankness, irritation, surprise, confusion—momentary phenomenal appearances fixed forever by the camera and nothing at all like the ones we expect. After the Second World War the Italian filmmakers cultivated exactly this sort of adventitious and often antidramatic gesture for dramatic purposes, and made it the trademark of the film movement known as neorealism. It was, for example, Vittorio De Sica and Roberto Rossellini who became the true heirs of Hemingway when they incorporated the unstaged indeterminacy and camera neutrality of the newsreel technique into works of film fiction. I remember in particular how Rossellini presented one of the great moments in *Open City* (1945) when the woman played by Anna

Magnani is shot down in the street from a moving truck. In the midst of a sequence of high, almost operatic passion (she is running after her lover, who has been arrested by the Gestapo and is being carried off in the truck), the gunshot is abrupt and dull, and in the middle distance the body of the woman in a dark dress drops quickly to the pavement, looking for an unforgettable instant like a black lump, an indeterminate heap against the overexposed, high-contrast whiteness of the streets and surrounding walls. The look of this gesture in its sudden gracelessness, amorphousness, and adventitious inappropriateness is, in principle, exactly analogous to Hemingway's verbal depiction of the sick man: both effects, literary and cinematic, are typical of a modern visual style that employs the adventitious detail to separate phenomenal appearances from preconceived mental catagories and expectations—from, as Proust would have it, a mind "charged with thought."

It is Jean-Paul Sartre who takes this use of the adventitious to its logical extremity in the following passage from *Nausea* (1938):

When the patronne goes shopping her cousin replaces her at the bar. His name is Adolphe. I began looking at him as I sat down and I have kept on because I cannot turn my head. He is in shirtsleeves, with purple suspenders; he has rolled the sleeves of his shirt above the elbows. The suspenders can hardly be seen against the blue shirt, they are all obliterated, buried in the blue, but it is false humility; in fact, they will not let themselves be forgotten, they annoy me by their sheep-like stubbornness, as if, starting to become purple, they stopped somewhere along the way without giving up their pretentions. You feel like saying, "All right, *become* purple and let's hear no more about it." But now, they stay in suspense, stubborn in their defeat. Sometimes the blue which surrounds them slips over and covers them completely: I stay an instant without seeing them. But it is merely a passing wave, soon the blue pales in places and I see the small island of hesitant purple reappear, grow larger, rejoin and reconstitute the suspenders. Cousin Adolphe has no eyes: his swollen, retracted eyelids open only on a little of the whites. He smiles sleepily; from time to time he snorts, yelps and writhes feebly, like a dreaming dog.

His blue cotton shirt stands out joyfully against a chocolate-coloured wall. That too brings on the Nausea. The Nausea is not inside me: I feel it *out there* in the wall, in the suspenders, everywhere around me. It makes itself one with the cafe, I am the one who is within *it*.[10]

[10]*Nausea*, trans. Lloyd Alexander (New York, 1959), pp. 30-31. Subsequent references to this edition will appear in text.

The Adventitious Detail 103

Unlike the descriptions in Joyce and Hemingway, this is a description only in the nominal sense. Strictly speaking, there are no descriptions in *Nausea:* there are only attempts to describe, projects and prospectuses for description that never accomplish their ends. Each description eventually becomes an agitated meditation on its own impossibility.

Here the narrator attempts to describe Adolphe's purple suspenders (while Adolphe himself is quite peripheral to them) at the moment that they seem to nestle against the fold of the blue shirt. He starts with the color and never really progresses much beyond it; for the "purple" seems to slowly slide off into now one thing and now into another, seems forever slipping off beyond its name. What Roquentin is beginning to learn here is Sartre's sense of the infinitive form of all existence, the absolute nature of people and things as a condition of adventitious Becomings, a continual *to-be-there*. All of Sartre's sensuous depictions attempt to dramatize objects via this condition as a kind of liquid erosion, a spreading-in-place, a slow crawl toward futurity, neither "here" nor "there," for both "here" and "there" are mental fictions imposed upon something that is always *about-to-be;* purple-but-not-purple; blue-but-not-blue-and-yet-not-purple. "They stay in suspense," says Roquentin, and *suspense* is the key word for all of Sartre's depictions. Suspense represents the dramatic form of the imminent, of a Becoming, and the existence of the suspenders, like all aspects of existence, including Adolphe and the narrator himself, are rendered in this form.

The pre-Flaubertian novelist assimilated the adventitious detail into an all-pervading pattern of artistic necessity and thereby absorbed it, removed it, so to speak, from its own quality of adventitiousness. The post-Flaubertian novelist, culminating in the first wave of literary modernism, presents it apart from, but within a pattern of, formal and cosmic necessity; Joyce and Hemingway both confront the adventitious as a single crucial part of a total vision of reality that is composed of many parts. In Joyce, for instance, the surface world of chance and accident often appears within a larger perspective of eternally returning patterns of human experience. In Hemingway the hero characteristically creates and preserves a Stoic code which then helps to anesthetize the self to withstand intrusions from the surrounding void.

But for Sartre—and for many contemporary (that is, post-

Joycean) novelists—the adventitious *is* necessity, and all other aspects of reality are illusions that fade upon confrontation with the adventitious. Adventitiousness, or, as Sartre puts it, "contingency," represents the ultimate reality. ("The essential thing is contingency," says Sartre's hero. "It is the absolute" [p. 176]). And Sartre's great early work, *Nausea,* not only embodies that ultimate reality in its descriptions and narrative procedures, but that reality is also what *Nausea* is about. More precisely, *Nausea* is about one man's, Roquentin's, attempt to dramatize, define, and understand the nature of the adventitious as represented in the narrative action by people, landscape, and things—especially things.

Sartre, unlike Joyce, seeks to describe things, not apart from, but *within* process, as evolving aspects of a universal temporal continuum. Joyce *suggests* this continuum by placing his objects in adventitious and dilapidated positions while the objects themselves are presented as permanent and solid, their forms and outlines clearly delineated. For Sartre permanence and solidity are illusions, false attributions to the object of a necessary being, a self-containment and sufficiency apart from all other objects that it does not actually have. The objects in *Nausea* are characteristically described without reference to form or outline, but almost solely in terms of color, taste, and smell, the most ephemeral, impermanent, and subjective of the senses, for these are the best qualities to represent dramatically the state of suspense, the shifting ambiguities of an object as a thing that is about-to-be. The effect of these color-taste-smell descriptions is to provide the sensuous surface of all Sartre's objects with a viscous yet nervous texture, like plasma, heavy and trembling, as if he were trying to represent objects through the activation of their molecular composition.

If the visual effects in *Nausea* remind us of camera effects—and I think in large measure that they do—they are camera effects of a very special sort. Throughout all of *Nausea* we can find countless examples of cinematographic perspective (angles of partial vision far more dramatic and extreme than the relatively straightforward encounter in the passage above). Yet due to the idiosyncratic nature of Sartre's plasmic descriptions, which represents Roquentin's attempts to be objective about what he sees, these effects remind us of camera practices of the most atypical and subjective kind. The sensuous and visual forms in this novel are most like those moments in film where the director blurs the lens of the camera to indicate drunkenness, dizziness, mental aberrations, and other subjective distortions of reality. Sartre's visual forms are actually distortions of this kind, always making us less aware of what is seen than of who is seeing and how he sees. Sartre, of course, knows this, and Roquentin ultimately comes to know it too, comes to know finally that colors, smells, and tastes are mental constructs, imaginings like form and outline, vain and self-deceiving hypocrisies on the part of the beholder: "Colors, tastes, smells," he learns, "were never real, never truly themselves and nothing but themselves" (pp. 175-76).

And so Roquentin abandons physical description in an attempt to get closer to the object on its own terms, to see it, as it were, from the inside out. But the harder he tries to penetrate the object, the deeper he recedes into the eccentricities of the self. In other words, sensuous delineation gives way to a characteristic stream of Sartrean poetic and figurative comparisons; the purple has a "false humility," a "sheep-like stubbornness"; it is "stubborn in [its] defeat," "a small island"; the blue is a "passing wave," but "pales in places"; Adolphe snorts "like a dreaming dog." Each comparison upon the instant of its utterance seems already to have outlived its usefulness, is already, as it is born, about to be (and indeed is) replaced by another comparison, and another. The typical stream of metaphors, similes, and comparisons represents Roquentin's desperate and agonized efforts to pace the rhythm of his own feeling and insight with that of the object's Becoming as well as his inability to contain the existence of the object within any one comparison.

But if these attempts are doomed to futility and feverish subjectivity, why, then, are they every made at all? Because even though the narrator himself knows that they are illusory, he does not wish, as Robbe-Grillet has argued, to avoid yielding himself to them: "The important thing in his eyes, is, in fact, to yield to it [a suspect intimacy with the world] as much as possible, in order to arrive at self-awareness."[11] Sartre's descriptions, then, actually present the growth of Roquentin's awareness of his own Becoming, of his own existence. The delineation of objects, as provisional, approximate, and ineffectual as they must be, reve-

[11] Alain Robbe-Grillet's important remarks on *Nausea* appear in "Nature, Humanism, Tragedy," *For a New Novel: Essays on Fiction*, trans. Richard Howard (New York, 1965), p. 64.

als again and again (as in the last paragraph) Roquentin's fundamental awareness that these objects have a life apart from him, are living that life, exist. And because he knows this, he comes to the conviction that he also has a life apart from them, is living that life, also exists, and that whatever adventitious process defines their existence also defines his own: "Existence everywhere, infinitely, in excess forever and everywhere; existence—which is limited only by existence" (p. 178).

Nausea is perhaps Sartre's most fateful and influential novel—if not his most characteristic, for he never wrote another one quite like it—and one of the seminal works of French modernism. *Nausea* not only brings the adventitious to a center of philosophical concern, but out of this concern establishes the subsoil from which grows a whole range of novelists—Simon, Butor, Robbe-Grillet, Le Clézio—whose primary concern is to examine the life of the phenomenal world, a world of things, as it exists apart from a mind "charged with thought," that is, apart from all human influence and manipulation.

Recent trends in French fiction represent the somewhat exacerbated culmination of tendencies not only apparent in Sartre but already apparent in the fiction of the first quarter of this century. These literary tendencies reflect, however, only one part of a generalized cultural effort that has increasingly sought to remove man from his privileged position in a world of things and to merge the humanly central with the materially peripheral. In this effort man enters "democratically" into a world of things, and both man and thing occupy an equal position under the overriding rubric of existence.

This equalizing process is readily observable not only in the action painting of Jackson Pollock and in the concrete music of John Cage but, most significantly, in the cinema. In the last twenty-five years, filmmakers as diverse as Michelangelo Antonioni, Jean-Luc Godard, and Robert Altman have all revealed a marked preference for off-center and asymmetrical framing in which the human figure is often pushed to the edge of the visual field. Antonioni in particular, developing tendencies already implicit in the work of De Sica and Rossellini (especially the latter's *Voyage in Italy*, 1953), has made the decentralized camera setup the virtual (and much imitated) hallmark of his compositional method: at the center, a vast and inanimate setting, precise and thrumming (for instance, a chalk white and ash gray sweep of

The Adventitious Detail

boulders against a heavy metal sea, a London park matted in pea-soup green) while off to the side a human figure, small and impassive. In Antonioni's *Blow Up* (1966) method becomes matter as a young photographer attempts to solve (or create?) a mystery by decentralizing a photograph, cropping the human figures out of the frame, and through progressive enlargements drawing a peripheral detail (a handheld gun) to the center. Here the necessary (the human) and the adventitious (the thing) exchange places and the human becomes adjunct to the thing.

In a similar manner, it was André Bazin who insisted that the edges of the motion picture screen never were to be thought of as delimiting boundary lines but rather as provisional markers and that what the screen showed us was to be understood as "part of something prolonged indefinitely into the universe."[12] Bazin's vision of a "centrifugal screen" was fully realized some fifteen years ago in the emergence of the French New Wave, and particularly in the films of Godard and François Truffaut, and in the documentary films of Chris Marker and Jean Rouch (the latter a full-time member, the former only part-time, of the movement that came to be known as cinema verité).

These filmmakers used the frame of the camera to create a loose, open, seemingly uncomposed visual field in which the action would slide amorphously throughout the different planes of each composition. Abrupt and peripatetic camera movements would often insure the exchange of peripheral details at the edges of the frame with central details in the middle (an effect facilitated by prominent use of a shaky handheld camera in which "bits" of reality would shift in and off the edges of the frame). The particular assumptions of the cinema verité group were that the camera must synchronize its movements to the ever-changing movements of existence itself and that the camera must at least create the illusion that it did not know where to find its subject until existence itself provided the opportunity. Thus, the camera must either wait for the subject to reveal itself or must tentatively roam the visual field in search of it.

This approach to reality was best epitomized (and satirized) in one revealing and amusing moment from Truffaut's otherwise negligible film *Stolen Kisses* (1968). Here the lovers leave the frame

[12]Bazin, "Painting and Cinema," *What is Cinema?* p. 166.

of the camera and presumably retire into the bedroom. The camera begins to look for them, climbing over the stairs, across the landing, through the open door of the bedroom, past the discarded clothing of the lovers, only to stop short at—an empty bed. Where are the lovers? The camera has made a mistake and slowly—shamefacedly—backtracks past the objects, withdraws from the room, and continues its search. The discarded clothing and the empty bed, however, are witty and expressive signatures; by comparison the lovers themselves seem rather inconsequential. Truffaut's camera tells us, perhaps unwittingly, that the adventitious and the necessary are really indistinguishable, that the search and the subject are really the same.

Thus, when Jean-Luc Godard asserts, "You can put anything and everything in a film, you *must* put in everything," his statement reflects something more than his own private concerns.[13] Godard's statement could be echoed by the camera concepts of the New Wave, by Bazin's vision of a centrifugal screen, by an Antonioni or a John Cage or a Jackson Pollock—or, as we have seen, by Roquentin, himself.

[13]"One or Two Things," in *Jean-Luc Godard: A Critical Anthology*, ed. Toby Mussman (New York, 1968), p. 280.

Chapter V
The Anatomy of Motion

EARLY IN HIS CAREER Joyce established his characteristic procedure for describing seen objects in motion. Later on, as he developed his art, he also developed this procedure, deepened and intensified it, shaped it in striking ways. But the essential components of the method were already present in the early story "An Encounter" (1905):

> There was nobody but ourselves in the field. When we had lain on the bank for some time without speaking I saw a man approaching from the far end of the field. I watched him lazily as I chewed one of those green stems on which girls tell fortunes. He came along by the bank slowly. He walked with one hand upon his hip and in the other hand he held a stick with which he tapped the turf lightly. He was shabbily dressed in a suit of greenish-black and wore what we used to call a jerry hat with a high crown. He seemed to be fairly old for his moustache was ashen-grey. When he passed at our feet he glanced up at us quickly and then continued his way. We followed him with our eyes and saw that when he had gone on for perhaps fifty paces he turned about and began to retrace his steps. He walked towards us very slowly, always tapping the ground with his stick, so slowly that I thought he was looking for something in the grass. [*Dubliners*, p. 24]

Here the seen object is presented as a moving spectacle that advances inexorably toward the seer, who is presented as a stationary spectator, adding little or nothing to the visual data that his eyes receive. Joyce establishes the position of the eyes in the second sentence and allows the figure to approach without changing this position until the end of the paragraph.

Each sentence adds a new item of visual information to the viewer's knowledge of the moving figure, and at the same time each item literally brings the figure closer to the viewer; as the distance between the figure and the eye decreases, the specificity and intimacy of the observed detail increases proportionately. When the boys first sight the figure in the second sentence, the figure is simply a man; in the third and fourth sentences this man is watched but not described, for he is still too far away to be seen clearly. In the fifth sentence, however, the man is close enough for the boys to discern the general outlines of his form and posture—"one hand upon his hip" and the tapping stick in the other; the sixth describes his suit and hat; while the seventh is the closest of all—"his moustache was ashen-grey." This last sentence has brought him close enough to make the eighth sentence natural and inevitable; he passes the boys, and in the ninth sentence Joyce carefully notes how the boys follow him with their eyes.

We recognize here that Joyce organizes motion in much the same way he organizes space: part by part, phase by phase. This mode of organization holds true not only for those passages where the seen object is moving and the seer is stationary but also for those passages where the seer is in motion and the seen object is static, as in this description from "Two Gallants" (1906):

Lenehan observed them for a few minutes. Then he walked rapidly along beside the chains at some distance and crossed the road obliquely. As he approached Hume Street corner he found the air heavily scented and his eyes made a swift anxious scrutiny of the young woman's appearance. She had her Sunday finery on. Her blue serge skirt was held at the waist by a belt of black leather. The great silver buckle of her belt seemed to depress the centre of her body, catching the light stuff of her white blouse like a clip. She wore a short black jacket with mother-of-pearl buttons and a ragged black boa. The ends of her tulle collarette had been carefully disordered and a big bunch of red flowers was pinned in her bosom stems upwards. Lenehan's eyes noted approvingly her stout short muscular body. Frank rude health glowed in her face, on her fat red cheeks and in her unabashed blue eyes. Her features were blunt. She had broad nostrils, a straggling mouth which lay open in a contented leer, and two projecting front teeth. As he passed Lenehan took off his cap and, after about ten seconds, Corley returned a salute to the air. This he did by raising his hand vaguely and pensively changing the angle of position of his hat. [*Dubliners*, pp. 55-56]

The seer approaches from a distance, and here, too, as in the previous passage, visual information is withheld until the seer is close enough to make an accurate appraisal. The visualization itself actually begins in the fifth sentence with a slow pan upward of the seer's eye, beginning at mid-torso with the "belt of black

The Anatomy of Motion

leather" and concluding with a description of the woman's face and a grotesque close-up of the "two projecting front teeth." The treatment, of course, is similar to Maisie's discovery of her mother, but more vivid and concrete than James, if also a good deal less suspenseful and protracted.

Since the process of apprehension in both passages is sliced, as it were, into a succession of distinct phases, each phase with its own cluster of visual detail, the process of apprehension not only seems to take longer to complete itself than it ordinarily would in our daily visual experience, but the speed and continuity of the motion itself is greatly reduced. This is especially noticeable in the Joyce passage, where the intention is to present a "swift" scrutiny, but the *effect* of the eyes' upward movement is anything but swift.

We should remind ourselves that natural vision can only in rare instances approximate Joyce's pan shot. The ordinary human eye usually apprehends any single object not section by section but rather all at once as a continuous whole. Even when we fasten our gaze on one part of any given object—as we do, for instance, in speaking face to face with a friend—we rarely experience the sensation of apprehending a disembodied fragment: mind and feeling add to the limited visual information on the retina to sustain our sense of the object's continuity and wholeness.

Nor do we often perceive a moving object in the distance the way Stephen Dedalus first perceives a running dog on Sandymount strand: "A point, live dog, grew into sight running across the sweep of sand" (*Ulysses*, p. 45). Here, too, Joyce ignores the ordinary operations of the human eye, which, as psychologists of visual perception inform us, do not usually allow for a "point" to turn into a "live dog," but usually present the objects within the visual field—whether near the eye or far away—with a "constancy of size and shape." The retinal image alone—what I have called the contents on the oval of vision—registers the variables in the size and shape of the object, but the conscious and unconscious motions of the mind add "constancy of size and shape" to this object's appearance on the retina, as well as continuity and depth to the entire visual field. As Rudolf Arnheim reminds us, "It is impossible for most people—excepting those accustomed to drawing and painting, that is, artifically trained—to see according to the image on the retina." But the retinal image, as Arnheim also points out, is of course the kind of image most closely approximated by the eye of the camera.[1]

The "slow" vision, the phase-by-phase apprehension, the piling up of visual detail within the phase—these are the components of the anatomical form of motion description that frequently appear in the cinematized narrative. Like all the other components of the cinematographic form, the components of the anatomized description represent the findings of a "trained" eye, an analytic and self-conscious eye, conscious of what it sees and the way it sees; the kind of eye that teaches us to see those retinal images that we rarely take note of apart from the assumptions, protections, concealments, and transformations of the ordinary human mind. It was precisely this kind of eye that Walter Benjamin had in mind when he described the impact of the camera on modern consciousness.

> Evidently a different nature opens itself to the camera than opens to the naked eye if only because an unconsciously penetrated space is substituted for a space consciously explored by man. Even if one has a general knowledge of the way people walk, one knows nothing of a person's posture during the fractional second of a stride. The act of reaching for a lighter or a spoon is familiar routine, yet we hardly know what really goes on between hand and metal, not to mention how this fluctuates with our moods. Here the camera intervenes with the resources of its lowerings and liftings, its interruptions and isolations, its extensions and accelerations, its enlargements and reductions. The camera introduces us to unconscious optics as does psychoanalysis to unconscious impulses.[2]

Benjamin's "unconscious optics" and "unconsciously penetrated space" find their literary analogues in the modern novelist's anatomical descriptions of matter and motion. The analogies become even more precise with Joyce, where his depth analysis of the visible world becomes the external counterpart of his depth analysis of the human mind, the famous interior monologue: both monologue and anatomy consciously dissect "unconsciously penetrated space." One can only conjecture, for example, about the number of readers who have ever really

---

[1] Arnheim, *Film as Art,* pp. 13-14.
[2] "The Work of Art in the Age of Mechanical Reproduction," *Illuminations,* ed. Hannah Arendt and trans. Harry Zohn (New York, 1968), pp. 238-39.

observed the movements of a running dog until they read Joyce's anatomization of them in *Ulysses:*

> The dog ambled about a bank of dwindling sand, trotting, sniffing on all sides. Looking for something lost in a past life. Suddenly he made off like a bounding hare, ears flung back, chasing the shadow of a lowskimming gull. The man's shrieked whistle struck his limp ears. He turned, bounded back, came nearer, trotted on twinkling shanks. On a field tenney a buck, trippant, proper, unattired. At the lacefringe of the tide he halted with stiff forehoofs, seawardpointed ears. His snout lifted barked at the wavenoise, herds of seamorse. . . .The dog yelped running to them, reared up and pawed them, dropping on all fours, again reared up at them with mute bearish fawning. Unheeded he kept by them as they came towards the drier sand, a rag of wolf's tongue redpanting from his jaws. His speckled body ambled ahead of them and then loped off at a calf's gallop. [P. 46]

Joyce's friend and early critic Frank Budgen thought that a better word picture of a dog did not exist, and even this extract from the long description is sufficient to confirm Budgen's high estimation of Joyce's achievement. The dog's movements are marvelously observed, and yet at each phase of its many activities we have the sensation of seeing double, of seeing movements proper to a dog and proper to other animals as well. We experience this sensation because we watch the dog through the eyes of Stephen Dedalus, who in a series of metaphoric superimpositions transforms the dog into other animals at each phase of its progress across the beach. Since each transformation depends on a motion common to both the dog and another animal, we are simultaneously aware of two animals within each phase: dog and rabbit ("like a bounding hare, ears flung back"); dog and buck ("with stiff forehoofs, seawardpointed ears"); dog and bear ("dropping on all fours, again reared up at them with mute bearish fawning").

In this procedure we note Stephen's characteristic manner of confronting objects in time. This manner entails a recognition of the temporal continuum, the flux, the surface chaos, and at the same time an attempt to deny, halt, and transcend this flux through the associational and metaphoric powers of the mind and imagination. Each change that the dog undergoes suggests the object's endless permutation in time; yet each change is focused and fixed with such vivid and concentrated intensity that it almost becomes a compartmentalized end in itself. A slight change in position equals a slight modulation in the animal's indentity, which is quickly replaced by another position and another identity; each moment held and relinquished, recreated in the imagination and replaced. Stephen's eye tracks its object in a series of discrete yet continuous snapshots which in its consecutive ordering is not unlike the series composed by Eadweard Muybridge's famous battery of cameras when he photographed the movements of a running horse in 1877.

The contrast between Muybridge's literalism and Stephen's imaginative re-creation highlights the important difference between a scientific rendering and an artistic one. Through Stephen's description, Joyce shows us his way of solving the problem inherent in all anatomical descriptions, the problem of giving the individual units of a continuous motion their just due without reducing the entire animated complex to an arid and mechanical time-motion study. This problem is for the modern practitioner of concretized form actually part of a much larger problem. It is, in fact, part of the very crisis which lies at the center of a neutral and analytic way of seeing and which each novelist who embodies this way of seeing must deal with in his own special manner. For the tendency in the most extreme forms of anatomization, as in the most extreme forms of all the aspects of the cinematographic manner, is not only to separate the phenomenal world from the mind of man but also, in so doing, to reduce this world to an inhospitable machine, a dehumanized exteriority.[3]

And we see Joyce moving in the direction of a purely phenomenal rendering in the motion depictions from *Dubliners* (quoted above), and in the time-motion parodies from the "Ithaca" section of *Ulysses*, in which the ambulations of Stephen and Bloom in and out and about the Eccles Street kitchen are dissected into a succession of distant and monumental stases. But here, with the

---

[3]Magny arrives at a similar notion, but with different terminology. What I have described as "cinematographic" she describes as "impersonal." She uses this term to refer to the American novels (by Steinbeck, Dos Passos, Hemingway, and Faulkner) that appeared after World War I and reveal the influence of film. She supports my position here, however, when she says of John Steinbeck that "his art is perpetually threatened by the gravest danger facing the impersonal novel—dehumanization" (*Age of the American Novel*, p. 171).

running dog of the "Proteus" episode, the effect of the description is anything but mechanized. Joyce allows Stephen both to describe and to impose himself upon the object of his description; the dog and its transformations are embodied and thus contained within the verve and ripe concision of Stephen's protean language. In this way the artist's imagination controls and ultimately conciliates matter, motion, and the entire galloping menagerie.

Now to a certain extent the technical structure of motion is an element in virtually every description of physical action, but when we examine the work of the pre-Flaubertian novelists, we are still hard pressed to find anything comparable to the anatomies of motion that we find in Joyce. Unlike the cinematographic novels, the novels of Stendhal, Fielding, and Austen, for example, tend to subordinate the process of the motion (how it happened) in any given action to the function and purpose of the motion (what happened and why it happened). Here, for instance, in *The Red and the Black* (1831), we observe a scene of swift physical violence in which old Sorel catches his son Julien reading a book instead of minding the sawmill:

Nothing could have been more disagreeable to old Sorel; he might perhaps have pardoned Julien his slender figure, unsuited to hard labor and unlike his elder brothers'; but this passion for reading was hateful to him, as he didn't know how to read himself.

He called Julien, vainly, two or three times. The young man's absorption in his book, much more than the roar of the saw, prevented him from hearing his father's terrible voice. Finally, despite his age, the old man jumped lightly onto the tree trunk which was being sawed and from there to the crossbeam which helped support the roof. A violent blow sent Julien's book flying into the stream; a second cuff, just as heavy, fell on his head and caused him to lose his balance. He was about to fall a distance of ten or fifteen feet into the middle of the machinery, which would have ground him up, but his father caught him, with his left hand, just as he was falling:

—All right, loafer! still reading your damn books while you're supposed to be watching the saw? Read them after work, when you're wasting your time with the priest, why don't you?[4]

We are told how old Sorel jumps from the tree trunk to the crossbeam and, briefly, the way in which he moves his body (he

---

[4]Stendhal, *The Red and the Black*, Norton Critical Edition, ed. and trans. Robert M. Adams (New York, 1969), p. 13.

"jumped lightly"). But Stendhal does not describe the series of motions between the crossbeam and the blow that sends "Julien's book flying into the stream"; nor do we see the series of postures and gestures that would constitute the entire concretization of the struggle between the father and the son. What does Julien look like when he loses his balance? How does old Sorel appear as he maintains his own balance and saves Julien from falling? While these questions seem finicky and technical when applied to Stendhal, they are just the sort of questions that a modernist treatment of the scene would answer. Stendhal simply does not want to place the narrative emphasis upon *how* the action occurred at each moment of its progress; rather, he concentrates on the origins of the action (old Sorel's jealous hatred of his son's reading) and the end and purpose of the action (the blow that knocks the hated book from his son's hands and the expression of the disgust that old Sorel feels for Julien). Everything between the intention and the final phase of the act itself is, according to a modern and cinematized practice, severely abridged.

The difference between pre- and post-Flaubertian fiction become dramatically apparent not only in the work of Joyce but even more so in that William Faulkner, a literature of melodrama and extravagance where the laws of matter and motion are both grand and furious. Here (*The Hamlet*, 1940), for example, we find a Texas horse dealer in the middle of a sale, trying hard to hang on to his "merchandise":

The pony recovered almost at once and pawed itself to its knees and heaved at its prisoned head and fought itself up, dragging the man with it; for an instant in the dust the watchers saw the man free of the earth and in violent lateral motion like a rag attached to the horse's head. Then the Texan's feet came back to earth and the dust blew aside and revealed them, motionless, the Texan's sharp heels braced into the ground, one hand gripping the pony's forelock and the other its nostrils, the long evil muzzle wrung backward over its scarred shoulder while it breathed in labored and hollow groans. Mrs. Littlejohn was in the yard again. No one had seen her emerge this time. She carried an armful of clothing and a metal-ridged washboard and she was standing motionless at the kitchen steps, looking into the lot. Then she moved across the yard, still looking into the lot, and dumped the garments into the tub, still looking into the lot. "Look him over, boys," the Texan panted, turning his own suffused face and the protuberant glare of his eyes toward the fence. "Look him over quick. Them shoulders and—" He had relaxed for an instant apparently. The animal exploded again; again for an instant the

The Anatomy of Motion 117

Texan was free of the earth, though he was still talking: "—and legs you whoa I'll tear your face right look him over quick boys worth fifteen dollars of let me get a holt of who'll make me a bid whoa you blare-eyed jack rabbit, whoa!" They were moving now—a kaleidoscope of inextricable and incredible violence on the periphery of which the metal clasps of the Texan's supenders sun-glinted in ceaseless orbit, with terrific slowness across the lot. Then the broad clay-colored hat soared deliberately outward; an instant later the Texan followed it, though still on his feet, and the pony shot free in mad, staglike bounds. The Texan picked up the hat and returned to the fence and mounted the post again.[5]

Of all the serious novelists that emerged in the thirties and forties of this century, Faulkner is perhaps the most elaborate and prodigious exponent of the cinematized narrative. Since he spent a good part of his middle and late years in and out of writing assignments for the Hollywood studios (1932-1945),[6] it is only fitting that retinal imagery, camera angles, and montage sequences are to be found everywhere in his novels and stories (though here we should remind ourselves, as in the case of Joyce and many other cinematographic novelists, that a direct causal relationship is hard to demonstrate convincingly).

Faulkner, like all the modern anatomists, seizes a complex and intricate physical operation and proceeds to render it through a kind of temporal dismemberment. As in Joyce the process of apprehension is slowed down to an unnatural degree so that gestures and motions that would ordinarily take place within seconds seem to take much longer to complete themselves. The first two sentences, for instance, virtually a third of the passage, describe a single jump of the horse, which is divided into three separate phases, each with its own special stop-action tableau; the first sentence up to the semicolon shows us the Texan hanging on; after the semicolon we see him in the air; in the second sentence he is on the ground once more, still hanging on.

In Joyce, however, each phase of the action usually represents a discrete and compartmentalized focal point of temporal and spatial energies, each point sustaining only an abrupt and discontinuous relationship with preceding and succeeding phases. In Faulkner, on the other hand, each phase of the action seems to

---

[5]*The Hamlet* (New York, 1940), pp. 292-93.
[6]Joseph L. Blotner, "Faulkner in Hollywood," in *Man and the Movies*, ed. W. R. Robinson (Baltimore, 1967), pp. 261-303.

cling obsessively to what has already happened. One may say, I think, that in Faulkner's world no moment is so trivial or inconspicuous that it can ever be forgotten; that each present moment not only seems continuous with a history of past moments but is, indeed, almost retroactive, stretching its confines, as it were, to contain within it bits and pieces of what the narrator insistently refuses to forget.[7] That is why Faulkner's sentences are so characteristically long and why, too, each sentence seems so richly clogged, overstuffed with parenthetical detail. Each represents an expanded instant, a time-space summary equilibrating both "is" and "was" in a kind of verbal juggle.

We see, for example, in just the first two sentences alone how the reiteration of certain key words and actions has the effect of binding and merging the different units of motion; repeated words like "man," "horse," "earth," "Texan"; or the way "pawed itself to" is echoed by "fought itself up"; or the way "feet came back to earth" carries over into "sharp heels braced into the ground." And further into the passage we find a similar repetitive principle employed with obvious and comic insistence when we watch Mrs. Littlejohn through each phase of her morning wash, from the kitchen steps to the tub, as the narrator reminds us within each phase—three times in all—that she was "still looking into the lot."

These examples tell us that Faulkner is perhaps the most time-haunted of all the great modern American writers, that the active ghost of each past moment lives on into the present; and that motion is perceived here not only in time but, even more important, in the light of memory, the linking, gathering, and integrating faculty that provides a common denominator for almost all of Faulkner's different narrative voices. It is memory that not only unifies the different phases of a physical action but, as we have seen in the case of Mrs. Littlejohn, seizes and binds the different

[7]Faulkner said: "To me, no man is himself, he is the sum of his past. There is no such thing really as was because the past is. It is a part of every man, every woman, and every moment. All of his and her ancestry, background, is all a part of himself and herself at any moment. And so a man, a character in a story at any moment of action is not just himself as he is then, he is all that made him, and the long sentence is an attempt to get his past and possibly his future into the instant in which he does something" (*Faulkner in the University,* ed. Fredrick L. Gwynn and Joseph L. Blotner [New York, 1959], p. 84).

The Anatomy of Motion

manifestations of personality into a coherent whole, that singles out and fastens itself to the ruling passion of a character throughout all the different phases of his conduct in past, present, and future.

It is memory's affinity for whatever is constant in time that confers upon Faulkner's men and women their characteristically obsessive natures, as if each character walked in a kind of mesmerized self-absorbtion, carrying his values and purposes like a sacrament through every adversity of chance, matter, force, and temporal chaos. Surely we cannot conceive of any freak of circumstance in which the single-minded Texan will *not* be delivering his sales pitch and hustling his ferocious animals. He will carry his obsession even into the realm of the tall tale, as the narrator finds him "still talking"—though airborne!

The furious determination of the character to be nothing but himself whatever the situation often tilts Faulkner's descriptive techniques in the direction of comical, agonized, and sometimes apocalyptic extremes. While it is Joyce who renders action in the abrupt, staggered manner of the stop-motion camera, it is Faulkner who in his depictions of motion usually approximates the continuous, gliding, almost hallucinatory effect of true slow-motion photography. Slow motion is one of the most fascinating and, until recently, least explored aspects of film technique. Apart from some brilliant experimentation in the twenties and early thirties (notably in France, as in René Clair's *Entr'acte*, 1924; Jean Cocteau's *The Blood of a Poet*, 1930; Jean Vigo's *Zero for Conduct*, 1933), this device now seems relegated in the popular cinema to an exploration—and sometimes an exploitation—of the poetics of violent death (as in the films of Arthur Penn, Sam Peckinpah, and the more recent work of Nicholas Roeg). This current usage seems to have thoroughly displaced its overworked predecessor—slow motion for lyrical release or "bucolic abandon," which nowadays appears most frequently in those soft-focused hard-sell television commercials (those men, women, and albino children who run—slowly—and jump—slowly—through blurry flowers authorizing soap or sedatives).

But slow motion actually presents us with a good deal more than the simple retardation of natural or rapid movements. Rather it opens up an entirely new dimension of reality, an entirely other mode of existence. Through the expansion of movement, slow motion can reveal new and unknown qualities that, in Arnheim's words, "give the effect of singularly gliding, floating, supernatural motions."[8] And it is Faulkner who fully creates the literary equivalent of slow motion's oneiric character, particularly in the brief and outrageous aerial ballet of the Texan and the horse. This passage effects a fantasy of physics and mechanics as human and animal seem to defy matter and gravitational force to hurtle and whirl "in ceaseless orbit, with terrific slowness across the lot."

Here Faulkner's prose rises to a characteristically dense, opulent, free-for-all of grandiloquence which signifies to the reader that a character is attempting the impossible, a moment of comic yet gallant transcendence where the momentum of the character's personal determination thrusts him against an even greater and thoroughly uncontainable momentum—the life force itself (here represented by the horse). Like most of Faulkner's characters the Texan fails in his struggle but maintains his honor and integrity by refusing to relinquish his obsession, by continuing to be nothing but himself. He loses the horse, but lands on his feet, picks up his hat, returns to his post, and continues the sale without missing a beat.

The effects of cinematic slow motion in Faulkner and photographic stop motion in Joyce are probably inadvertent: these are essentially the results of novelists who are simply following through the assumptions of concretized form in an attempt to render, as it were, the interstices of the existentialized moment. As the century wears on, however, and the pervasiveness of cinema becomes an unavoidable fact of modern life, we are not very surprised to discover in the work of certain exponents of the cinematographic form an obvious intermingling between film consciousness and literary consciousness. Here (*Lolita*, 1955) Vladimir Nabokov provides the anatomized description with the name it has probably deserved all along:

> Oh, what a dreamy pet! She walked up to the open suitcase as if stalking it from afar, at a kind of slow-motion walk, peering at that distant treasure box on the luggage support. (Was there something wrong, I wondered, with those great gray eyes of hers, or were we both plunged in the same enchanted mist?) She stepped up to it, lifting her

[8]Arnheim, *Film as Art*, pp. 116-17.

The Anatomy of Motion

rather high-heeled feet rather high, and bending her beautiful boy-knees while she walked through dilating space with the lentor of one walking under water or in a flight dream. Then she raised by the armlets a copper-colored, charming and quite expensive vest, very slowly stretching it between her silent hands as if she were a bemused bird-hunter holding his breath over the incredible bird he spreads out by the tips of its flaming wings. Then (while I stood waiting for her) she pulled out the slow snake of a brilliant belt and tried it on.[9]

Anatomization appears in all of Nabokov's work; sometimes it is accompanied by film terminology, sometimes not. Here, however, this novelist asks us pointedly to see something in a cinematographic manner, as he often does in his other film-oriented novels, *Laughter in the Dark* and *King, Queen, Knave*. But whether his effects are cinematic (effects of oblique perspective, retinal imagery, fragmented visual fields) or painterly (effects of extravagant color and tone, scenographic layouts), this passage, like so many others in his work, presents to the reader's eye what is virtually a formal exercise in vision. Nabokov gives us an *aesthetic* of motion where each gesture, each minute detail of human phenomenology is savored for its texture and line: the slow-motion walk, the "peering" at a distance, the "high-heeled" lift of the feet, the bend of the "beautiful boy-knees," the silent and bemused raising of the vest, the slow pull of the "brilliant belt."

Faulkner's technique for rendering moments of transcendence becomes the dominant note of Nabokov's visualization. Like Faulkner, Nabokov employs anatomization, with its strange physics and startling mechanics, to transport reality into a different dimension. Obviously, for the narrator each moment of the event cannot last long enough, space cannot dilate far enough. Notice how he protracts time by modulating the raising and spreading of the vest through three separate, but only slightly differentiated, phases; first "raised by the armlets"; then "stretching it between her silent hands"; finally, in a simile, we see it again as it "spreads out by the tips of its flaming wings." Notice, too, how the narrator achieves a similar temporal expansion by bringing Lolita up to the suitcase, and then extends the moment by slightly backtracking to tell us how she got there; how she moved her legs "while she walked through dilating space

[9] *Lolita* (New York, 1955), p. 122.

with the lentor of one walking under water or in a flight dream." These are the literary analogues of those temporal conflations in Eisenstein (the raising of the bridge in *October*, 1928), Godard (the lovers' farewell kiss in *Vivre sa vie*, 1962), and Penn (the death of Bonnie Parker and Clyde Barrow in *Bonnie and Clyde,* 1967), where a single climactic action is repeated many times, each time with a slight shift in camera angle and at a fractionally different tempo, in an attempt to imbue the single moment with qualities of myth, revelation, and transcendence.

As is often the case in Nabokov's visual renderings, it is impossible to separate reality-as-experienced from reality-as-recalled. Was the event slow and dreamy for the narrator, Humbert Humbert, when it happened? Or does it only seem slow and dreamy now, as he writes his memoirs? It is difficult to say. (If the dreaminess applies to both the past and the present, then we are experiencing the reality of the event twice removed.)

Still, the special qualities of recollection make themselves felt: for what but the leisures of nostalgia enable the narrator to slow the event down according to his pleasure, to thicken the sensuous texture of each phase, and to cast that peculiarly Nabokovian luminosity over the whole of it? Recollection also enables the narrator to transform the event into the simplicities and primary colors of something that resembles a Slavic fairy tale—the stalking hunter, the incredible bird of flaming wing, the slow and brilliant snake, the enchanted mist. (Is Nabokov thinking of the Russian legend of the magic firebird that haunted the imagination of that other great White Russian expatriate, Igor Stravinsky?) This imagery enriches the visualization with the aura of legend and lifts up and all but recasts the quotidian banality of the middle-class bric-a-brac: "the open suitcase," "the luggage support," and that "expensive vest."

Almost, but not quite. The vest, the support, and the suitcase mar and ultimately mock the perfection of Humbert's memory. And even the images of bird-hunter and bird-victim strike an ominous note that both reader and author are quick to pick up, even if Humbert himself is too bemused by his dreamy memory to notice them. The images of hunter and prey, victim and victimizer, modulate in various forms throughout the narrative. While it is Humbert, for instance, who stalks Lolita, it is ultimately Lolita who seduces, ensnares, and destroys him; she may be caught by him, for a time, but he too is caught by her—and forever. Above all, there is the grandiloquence of Humbert himself, both fine and absurd, enshrining jewellike memories and then undercutting them with phrases like "what a dreamy pet!" or "a copper-colored, charming and quite expensive vest."

Readers of Nabokov's work are familiar with the author's habitual ambiguity toward his heroes and his rhetorical gambit of identifying himself with the raptures of the central character and simultaneously disengaging himself from these raptures through a variety of parodic devices. It would, I think, falsify Nabokov's conception of the transforming powers of memory to reduce Humbert's recalled visualization here to an aspect of his foolish and obsessive solipsism, which refuses to accept Lolita as she is and makes her, instead, an adjunct to his fantasy. After all, similar visualizations appear throughout much of Nabokov's work, and much of Humbert's solipsism clearly belongs to the author. The quoted passage, for example, is one of his favorite moments in the novel.[10] Nabokov usually engages the transformations and distortions of memory quite seriously as a valid means of preserving perishable moments in art. In this sense, then, the element of parody is actually the author's way of distancing himself and the reader from the memory: distance does not diminish the memory but simply frames it and, as it were, hangs it on the wall. Nabokov does not want the reader to participate in Humbert's vision, but to *see* it, and parody helps to create the necessary atmosphere of sequestration. "I think that what I would welcome at the close of a book of mine," the novelist has told us, "is a sensation of its world receding in the distance and stopping somewhere there suspended afar like a picture in a picture."[11]

The anatomization of Nabokov conflates and thus clarifies a tendency that was already implicit in the similar anatomizations of Joyce and Faulkner. Nabokov shows us that the final aim of the anatomist is not only to slow down, dissect, and control a process of motion but that it is ultimately to bring that process to a halt, to transform each phase of that process into an infinite present. And

---

[10]Vladimir Nabokov, "On a Book Entitled *Lolita*," in *Lolita*, p. 318.

[11]Interview with Alfred Appel, Jr., *Wisconsin Studies in Contemporary Literature*, 8 (Spring 1967), 136.

this endeavor is really just one crucial skirmish in the much larger struggle that all three of these literary modernists have waged against the devastations of time. What joins these novelists, then, in spite of their great differences, is the attempt to find a literary procedure that will confront the temporal continuum in the full havoc of its mutability and yet transcend that continuum and that havoc. Anatomical renderings are one manifestation of the struggle to bring the temporality of the living moment into the controlled dominions of art. In Joyce and Faulkner the strain and anguish of the artist's struggle with the moment's transience are very apparent; in Nabokov, less so. In *Lolita* the temporal distance from the original moment only seems to increase the power of the narrator's memory to shape and spatialize this moment according to his own aesthetic design. Here time waits upon the injunctions of memory, and the struggle with the living moment seems to have receded into the background.

In the fiction of Alain Robbe-Grillet the retardation of the moment is more pronounced than it has ever been before; the signs of the seen objects' mutability seem to have all but vanished. The process of apprehension is no longer simply slow, it has become glacial:

The brush descends the length of the loose hair with a faint noise something between the sound of a breath and a crackle. No sooner has it reached the bottom than it quickly rises again toward the head, where the whole surface of its bristles sinks in before gliding down over the black mass again. The brush is a bone-colored oval whose short handle disappears almost entirely in the hand firmly gripping it.

Half of the hair hangs down the back, the other hand pulls the other half over one shoulder. The head leans to the right, offering the hair more readily to the brush. Each time the latter lands at the top of its cycle behind the nape of the neck, the head leans farther to the right and then rises again with an effort, while the right hand, holding the brush, moves away in the opposite direction. The left hand, which loosely confines the hair between the wrist, the palm and the fingers, releases it for a second and then closes on it again, gathering the strands together with a firm, mechanical gesture, while the brush continues its course to the extreme tips of the hair. The sound, which gradually varies from one end to the other, is at this point nothing more than a dry, faint crackling, whose last sputters occur once the brush, leaving the longest hair, is already moving up the ascending part of the cycle, describing a swift curve in the air

The Anatomy of Motion 125

which brings it above the neck, where the hair lies flat on the back of the head and reveals the white streak of a part.[12]

Examining this passage (*Jealousy*, 1957) in the light of its predecessors, we see at once that Robbe-Grillet, novelist, filmmaker, and literary polemicist, does not represent the beginnings of something "new" in the history of the novel—whether it be New Novel or new man—as much as he actually represents the intensification and ultimately, I suppose, the culmination of literary tendencies that are, at the very least, half a century "old." These are tendencies that cultivate the microscopic inspection of existential moments, and such tendencies were characterized with a good deal of disparaging wit by D. H. Lawrence as far back as 1923:

And there's the serious novel: senile-precocious. Absorbedly, childishly concerned with *what I am*. "I am this, I am that, I am the other. My reactions are such, and such, and such. And, oh, Lord, if I liked to watch myself closely enough, if I liked to analyse my feelings minutely, as I unbutton my gloves, instead of saying crudely I unbuttoned them, then I could go on to a million pages instead of a thousand. In fact, the more I come to think of it, it is gross, it is uncivilised bluntly to say: I unbuttoned my gloves. After all, the absorbing adventure of it! Which button did I begin with?" etc.[13]

Here Lawrence was describing the modern novelist's microscopic inspection of feeling, the interiorized counterpart of the modern novelist's microscopic inspection of the visible world that we have been describing; and what has been true of this novelist's treatment of the mind has been equally true of his treatment of the eye. By the "serious novel," Lawrence was specifically referring to the novels of Proust and Joyce, and since then other serious novelists have not only continued to find the unbuttoning of a glove a process of considerable fascination but have pursued the inspection of this process with increasing analytic intensity. If Lawrence's criticism of Joyce and Proust seems to us now somewhat premature, it may also seem to us both apt and prophetic when applied to the fiction of Robbe-Grillet. Here the threatening

---

[12]*Jealousy*, in *Two Novels by Robbe-Grillet*, trans. Richard Howard (New York, 1965), p. 66.

[13]"Surgery for the Novel—or a Bomb," in *D. H. Lawrence: Selected Literary Criticism*, ed. Anthony Beal (New York, 1966), p. 115.

tendencies always inherent in the anatomization of motion achieve their fullest realization. The physical world reduces to a state of visualized petrifaction—and then disappears altogether.

One must not, then, minimize the changing nature of the anatomical depiction from Joyce, through Faulkner and Nabokov, to Robbe-Grillet: each writer brings to his study of time and motion a small quantitative change that actually effects a considerable qualitative change. In Robbe-Grillet we note that the inspection of the individual phase is closer than before; the intervals between the phases longer than before; and the relationship between the phases less discernible than before. Moreover, the scale of action itself is significantly smaller than before. After Joyce's running dog, Faulkner's bucking bronco, and Nabokov's walking girl, we now confront a hand brushing its hair. Robbe-Grillet has finally dissected the process of motion into units so fine that any sense of continuous motion is now all but abandoned. His treatment demonstrates that what we have all along perceived as motion has actually been an optical illusion composed of an infinite number of minute and separable units. Robbe-Grillet now detemporalizes each unit and examines each one like a fragment of statuary.

Through at least the first half of the description we confront the visualization of an artist who has been called by many, and rightly so, cinematographic. We seem to be in the presence of a tightly framed and very sharply focused close-up: something is being looked at by someone; an eye is watching, and very closely. But in the second half of the description, beginning with the words "the left hand" and continuing for the rest of the paragraph, we confront an effect that is equally characteristic of this artist and one that is extremely problematic. The reader can read these sentences once, then again, and then again, and while he knows that the eye is still looking—it never stops—and that this eye is describing what is being looked at with uncanny precision, the action itself is extremely difficult to visualize. What exactly are we looking at?

In order to evoke a mental visual image of this action of brush and hair, we must continue to understand that it is, indeed, an action of brush and hair that we are looking at. But at this point in the passage the unit of action is so small, so thoroughly segregated from its context, from a "before" and an "after," that it

The Anatomy of Motion

becomes extremely difficult to recognize what it is that we are being asked to see. And this phenomenon occurs many times throughout the fiction of Robbe-Grillet. We often find ourselves viewing the size, shape, position and mechanical operation of something that cannot quite be given a name.

I do not think that these effects are simply the results of the general inadequacy of language to describe the material world with the clarity and intelligibility of the photograph. This inadequacy pertains more or less to all literary descriptions and is to a certain degree unavoidable. Robbe-Grillet, however, is quite consciously trying to create effects that could easily be avoided if his intentions were otherwise, and these are effects that continue to find their correspondences in the photographic arts. Every photographer is familiar with the effect that is created when the camera moves so close to its subject that the portion within the frame loses all meaningful relationship with the surrounding area from which it has been separated. The extreme close-up reveals a hypertrophied space and, like extreme slow motion, gives us a glimpse of unforeseen structures, textures, and graphics (see the camera studies of Edward Weston or Teshigahara's *Woman of the Dunes*, 1963). This new space rarely retains its representational value and often discloses, instead, a rectangle of abstract form. The second half of Robbe-Grillet's anatomization has an effect analogous to the hypertrophied space of the extreme close up: visualized motion is raised to the level of an abstraction and rendered virtually impervious to any system of specific signification. Here Robbe-Grillet approximates that extreme form of the cinematographic manner that we observed earlier as he attempts to do for action what we have already seen Sartre attempt to do for inanimate objects. Both artists attempt to extricate the constituents of the phenomenal world from the human context that customarily embodies them. But unlike Sartre, Robbe-Grillet also proceeds to diminish the ability of the seer to recognize anything in the seen object that corresponds to anything in himself; to demote this seer to the deactivated status of undefined watcher and describer.

Is such a diminishment of the seer's powers really possible? Every arrangement of words is also an arrangement of signs. Can any arrangement of signs ever be finally separated from what it signifies? Moreover, if a seer is present, as he is here, why does he choose to see one object rather than another? On what basis are these choices made? Robbe-Grillet may have greatly diminished the possibility of finding significance in his fiction, but that possibility cannot be entirely discarded. Far from creating the "total objectivity" that his earliest critics attributed to him, Robbe-Grillet himself has described his novels as attempts to create a *"total subjectivity"* and his describers as *"always* engaged in an emotional adventure of the most obsessive kind."[14] So ultimately we learn from the more recent Robbe-Grillet critics that the describer of the above passage is a jealous husband who only selects views that correspond to, and thus reveal, his obsessive jealousy.[15]

The first half of the passage is indeed suggestive enough to lend itself to such a reading. But what of the second half? What do these time-motion minutiae tell us about the husband's jealousy? What do they tell us about *any* aspect of his personality? Is he delirious? Mesmerized? Is he avoiding and repressing his jealousy by focusing on trivia? Above all, what sort of *human* can the seer possibly be if such a description can possibly be attributed to him?

Any number of readings are possible at many different points in the narrative—so *many* different readings, in fact, that each not only seems to cancel the other out but, in so doing, ultimately serves to create Robbe-Grillet's characteristic fictive texture of enigma, elusiveness, and portent. One thing, however, *is* reasonably certain: the first half of the quoted passage sets forth an image that can be seen clearly; the second half of the passage does not. The first half sets up possibilities of meaning that the second fractures and ultimately denies. This continual oscillation between clarity and distortion is perhaps the single constant in the descriptions of Robbe-Grillet. Passage upon passage simply refuses to do what it ostensibly sets out to do, evokes expectations in the mind of the reader only to frustrate them a moment later—and then evoke them once again.

[14] For an analysis of the "objective" Robbe-Grillet see Roland Barthes's "Objective Literature: Alain Robbe-Grillet," in *Jealousy,* pp. 11-25. Robbe-Grillet has changed his opinions about his own work over the years. The most recent view seems to be *"total subjectivity"*—see "New Novel, New Man," For a New Novel, p. 138.

[15] Leo Bersani entertains this notion and then (wisely, I think) qualifies it in *Balzac to Beckett: Center and Circumference in French Fiction* (New York, 1970), pp. 290-94.

The Anatomy of Motion

Robbe-Grillet's ultimate goal, then, becomes not only to disabuse the reader of his customary response to the world around him but to disabuse him of his customary response to literature itself. This becomes apparent, I think, as soon as we understand that the issue is not really whether the descriptions in his fiction represent the observations of a human eye with a specific psychology or the observations of a mechanical eye that simply records objectively; sometimes the description will seem to represent the exercise of one kind of eye, and sometimes that of another. The point, rather, is that *whatever* is described does not mean to refer to any existence anterior to the description itself. In the passage above, then, terms like *total objectivity* and *total subjectivity* only confuse matters. Instead, here and throughout his work Robbe-Grillet is inventing descriptive situations with their own internal logic that do not depend for confirmation on similar situations in any world beyond the world of the novel so much as they depend on the adventure of their own structural movements which usually go, as I have said, from clarity to distortion, from creation to decreation.[16] The author invents a series of self-destructive descriptions, or, in his own words, a literature of "disappointment":

> Description once served to situate the chief contours of a setting, then to cast light on some of its particularly revealing elements; it no longer mentions anything except insignificant objects, or objects which it is concerned to make so. It once claimed to reproduce a pre-existing reality; it now asserts its creative function. Finally, it once made us see things, now it seems to destroy them, as if its intention to discuss them aimed only at blurring their contours, at making them incomprehensible, at causing them to disappear altogether.[17]

So in the fiction of Robbe-Grillet we can observe the way in which one facet of cinematographic form can virtually use itself up. Starting with Joyce, each artist we have examined has manipulated the anatomized depiction with increasing self-consciousness: Faulkner romantically intensifies it, Nabokov plays with it as a form of parody, and Robbe-Grillet embalms it and finally lays it to rest. Joyce, Faulkner, and Nabokov, however, all use this technique to render some variety of human

[16]My view coincides with Bersani's, p. 294.
[17]Robbe-Grillet, "Time and Description in Fiction Today," *For a New Novel*, p. 147.

experience. In Robbe-Grillet, the ostensible subject is only the point of departure for the real subject—which is, as we have seen, the operation of the anatomized depiction itself. A technique of vision here becomes the object of vision—to the point where it dissolves in the intensity of its own self-regard. Of all the artists in this post-Joycean line, Robbe-Grillet is perhaps the most abstract and the most dogmatic. He is, in effect, a nihilist of form, and in *Jealousy* we watch him put his form to death—again and again and again.

Chapter VI
Depthlessness

FEW OF US actually see the world as we have come to know it; few of us have come to know the world as we actually see it. We develop and finally create the world we see by means of virtually everything that we are, everything that we have come to be out of a lifetime of growth, learning, and endless transaction with our surroundings and ourselves. In perceiving this world, brain and eye work together to construct the prototypical visual landscape that most of us take for granted, and have always taken for granted beyond all doubt and hesitation: a landscape of fixed position, stable appearance, and permanent identity.

Yet we are told by psychologists of perception that the eye alone does not see such a landscape, that the apprehension of an object's continuous identity and permanence in space is something that arises in the brain, not in the eye, something learned in the early stages of infancy through a complex process of trial and error, and from then on automatically assimilated, as it were, to the images on the retina that in themselves present very different visual patterns and textures. We are informed that the slack and unfocused eye of the infant sees a shimmering, amorphous, continually shifting field of light and shade in which effects of depth and distance are virtually unknown; a visual field very much like those "innocent" visual fields sought after by the impressionist painters.[1]

Of course, when we begin to speak of "innocent" vision and the very earliest stages of infancy, we are fast approaching areas of thought where the facts are few, the hypotheses tentative, and where speculation itself often leans towards mythology. In his famous study *Art and Illusion*, E. H. Gombrich, reminds us that even the impressionist painters could never entirely separate

[1] M. D. Vernon, *The Psychology of Perception* (Baltimore, 1963), pp. 13-14.

light and color from their sources in solid objects, and also that no sane man has ever reported having seen a visual sensation.[2]

Still, there are countless daily optical occurrences that when scrutinized with sufficient detachment, testify to the instability and impermanence of the same visual field that we otherwise continue to perceive as fixed and unchanging. These occurrences appear everywhere in the fiction of the novelists we have been discussing, and when they do, they tend to work upon us as little moments of ocular wit, spoofing and unsettling our customary acceptance of a solid landscape. In *Ulysses*, for instance, we are told that Bloom "held out his right hand at arm's length toward the sun. . . .The tip of his little finger blotted out the sun's disk" (p. 166). This effect works best, of course, only if you close one eye, but Joyce withholds this information and presents this little eclipse almost as if it were an effect of normal vision. In *King, Queen, Knave* Nabokov's protagonist, Franz, enters a railway car and finds it amusing when he spies a man "leafing through the magazine, and the combination of his face with its enticing cover was intolerably grotesque."[3] The man's face is ugly and the magazine cover displays the picture of a bathing beauty, and Franz understandably finds the juxtaposition of the two humorous. But the full effect of the joke is still inconceivable unless we ignore, as Franz obviously does, the leeway of space between the magazine and the face and align both on a single continuous plane. In *Nausea*, to cite a final instance, Roquentin watches the landscape through the window of a moving train: "The yellow house starts up again, it leaps against the windows, it is so close that you can only see part of it, it is obscured. The windows rattle. It rises, crushing, higher than you can see . . ." (p. 168), and so on, the entire ride made wild and strange as Roquentin ignores reason and ordinary experience which would tell him, of course, that the yellow house is actually motionless and that only the train is moving.

The occasions for optical effects such as these present themselves to us all the time. Sometimes we ignore them, but more often we are hardly aware of them. We usually do not view our

[2]*Art and Illusion: A Study in the Psychology of Pictorial Representation* (New York, 1960), pp. 298, 296-301, and *passim*.
[3]Vladimir Nabokov, *King, Queen, Knave* (New York, 1969), p. 11.

Depthlessness

visual field with the high degree of self-conscious detachment exercised by the literary characters above; we do not often make the characteristic refusal of the cinematographic novelist to recognize what he sees in terms of what he knows. And if we do not often make this refusal, the ocular effects experienced by these characters will more than likely prove disorienting to us, will work upon us like minute seismic shocks: we pull back from the visual field as, simultaneously, it pulls back from us. Quite suddenly we have broken our habitual and unconscious rapport with our landscape. Suddenly this landscape has become unfamiliar territory, and as we move farther away from this territory, we also move that much closer to the estranged vision of these characters.

When this happens we realize how little we know about whatever we see; how whatever we see remains impervious to whatever we are, everything we have become. It is at this point that we also realize what it means to be alone. And this realization lives at the center of the literary form we have been discussing, the form that thus provides the novelist with the technique for presenting the conditions of solitude.

The optical effects cited above are all examples of retinal imagery used specifically to obtain effects of depthlessness. In each selection—most obviously in Joyce and Nabokov, and partly, too, in Sartre—the strange and unsettling visualization depends almost entirely on the fact that the character perceives the seen objects in a condition of superposition precisely where normal vision would probably recognize no such condition. It is widely known that no single aspect of the retinal image directly reproduces the third dimension of space, depth, and distance. Our perception of the third dimension, like our perception of spatial permanence and continuity, is also a creation of the brain, which somehow manages to coordinate, in a manner not entirely understood by psychologists of vision, the two flattish and slightly disjunctive retinal images within the eyes and, in so doing, produces the various effects of spatial depth that constitute the stereoptics of the world we normally perceive.[4] This is not to say, of course, that the third dimension does not exist, but that we probably could not perceive it as such with the eye alone. (As

[4]Vernon, *Psychology of Perception*, pp. 125-30.

Stephen Dedalus puts the matter, "Flat I see, then think distance" [*Ulysses*, p. 48]). And just as the modern cinematized narrative cultivates the raw immediacy of the retinal image, so too does it cultivate this image's flattened-out, two-dimensional structural quality.

Needless to say, the depthlessness of the retinal image is equaled by the depthlessness of the photographic image. This quality probably represents the most obvious and emphatic way in which camera vision differs from normal vision: the photograph draws the background, as it were, toward the foreground and tends to equalize both on a single continuous plane, often creating those effects of overlapping objects, which in turn produce the blockage and truncation—or at least one form of these effects—so characteristic of film space. From our previous discussion, we now have little difficulty in recognizing in the literary examples above the fragmented visual structures of a literary space that has been organized in a cinematographic manner: a thumb blocking off part of the sun; a face bisected by the edge of a magazine; the window of a moving train framing a single section of a house as it obscures the rest.

The subtle but crucial effect of the flat image upon the nature and quality of the narrative form in film can hardly be overemphasized. According to Béla Balázs:

> On the stage the living, speaking human being has a far greater significance than dumb objects. They are not on the same plane and their intensity is different. In the silent film both man and object were equally pictures, photographs, their homogeneous material was projected on to the same screen, in the same way as in a painting, where they are equally patches of colour and equally parts in the same composition. In significance, intensity and value men and things were thus brought on to the same plane.[5]

In the film image, then, regardless of the object's position in relation to the character, both object and character as formal entities on the same plane will tend to impress themselves with an equality of insistence on the consciousness of the viewer. In this respect one obvious reason for the invention and regular employment of the close-up was, and still is, to direct the view-

---

[5]Balázs, *Theory of the Film*, p. 58.

er's eye to the most important element in a large flat visual field where phenomena of equal "significance, intensity, and value" compete with one another for the viewer's attention. In both the film form and the modern novel of concretized form, however, this new "democratized" structural situation produces essentially the same results: a new kind of equality between the seen character and the seen object and, in certain instances, a merging or crossbreeding between the two.

This means specifically, for both film and novel, that *things* become increasingly important and attain conspicuous and compelling presence in the narrative action. No longer mere props, things are activated into the drama, indeed, virtually become actors as they embody in themselves aspects of the character's psychology and life-style and enact the drama, as it were, in place of the character. In this new role things diminish in utility as they are neither subordinate to man nor serve him in his attempts to realize the significant social and moral acts of his life. At the same time things also increase in symbolic value as they stand equal to man, representing him in the world of the narrative, made resonant and animate by his living presence in them. Furthermore, as we have seen, the increasing tendency in much post-Joycean fiction has been for things to surpass humanity, for things to go off, as it were, on their own.[6]

But as things become more compelling, the depthless view also tends to diminish and circumscribe the full range and complexity of the interior life of the seen character. Here I am referring specifically to a certain effect that often appears in the cinematized novel. But in both novel and film the formal and material qualities of the seen character's physical appearance emerge in vigorous relief, and the character is now compelled to

[6]My discussion of "things" throughout this paragraph is based on Lukács' masterly overview of the use of "objects" in pre- and post-Flaubertian narrative tradition. Naturally Lukács uses a terminology very different from mine, but my basic themes are mirrored in "Narrate or Describe?" pp. 135–40: "Objects come to life poetically only to the extent they are related to men's life, that is why the real epic poet does not describe objects but exposes their function in the mesh of human destinies, introducing things only as they play a part in the destinies, actions and passions of men. Lessing understood this principle of poetic composition. 'I find that Homer depicts nothing but action,' he wrote, 'that he depicts all individual objects and people only through their participation in action'" (p. 137).

announce his psychic dimension, the vital "third" dimension of thought, feeling, and spirit, through the lines, colors, textures, and masses of his body (a situation somewhat alleviated in the sound film, but nevertheless inherent in all the photographic arts). In the fiction of the early modernists (Joyce and Hemingway, for example), these tendencies appear in qualified forms, but in the concretized art of the later novelists (such as West and Kesey), as we shall see, they tend to proliferate and intensify to the point where the seen character's physical appearance indicates hardly more than an internal void, a debased humanity: the character fuses with the brutal material components of his environment and becomes virtually indistinguishable from the objects associated with him.

Animation and Dehumanization

Early in *Ulysses* Bloom discovers the integrity and individuality of things as he watches the men setting type in the offices of the Freeman's Journal: "Sllt. The nethermost deck of the first machine jogged forwards its flyboard with sllt the first batch of quirefolded papers. Sllt. Almost human the way it sllt to call attention. Doing its level best to speak. That door too sllt creaking, asking to be shut. Everything speaks in its own way. Sllt." (p. 121). I take this as perhaps the most succinct and definitive statement of Joyce's attitude toward the inanimate object; each "doing its level best to speak," each speaking "in its own way," each "almost human" in the way that it calls attention to itself. The "speaking" of the object is its epiphany, its showing forth, the outward sign of its struggle to realize itself as that thing which it is and no other. As we have already seen, every component of Joyce's heterogeneous cosmos, each phase of human and animal existence, strives to distinguish itself in this manner, and so it is with the purely material order of being. Mysterious, cunning, enigmatic, comical, aloof—indeed, it would seem as if each dumb thing had been energized and animated from within with the very qualities of character we are likely to associate with Joyce himself. But the autobiographical element here is not the only reason for the way in which the object appears. Most objects in concretized fiction—in Joyce's and in others'—characteristically appear mysterious and aloof because the seer himself does not know what to make of them, because they are presented as part of the visual field from which he has severed emotional connections.

This is particularly the case when the object remains unattached to a particular character, as in the passage just quoted, but such a relatively free object is an uncommon occurrence in Joyce's world. Most often a thing is employed to express an aspect of the human being who engages it, and here the expressiveness of the thing becomes the link that binds the human to it, the link that equalizes the one with the other. In this relationship, however, we can still perceive the separatist strivings of the object, for as the character associates himself with a thing, he relinquishes that much of his power to act, gives it over to the thing, which proceeds to funtion, as it were, on his behalf—as it does in this sequence from *Ulysses* where Blazes Boylan flirts with the salesgirl from Thornton's:

> The blond girl in Thornton's bedded the wicker basket with rustling fibre. Blazes Boylan handed her the bottle swathed in pink tissue paper and a small jar.
> —Put these in first, will you? he said.
> —Yes, sir, the blond girl said, and the fruit on top.
> —That'll do, game ball, Blazes Boylan said.
> She bestowed fat pears neatly, head by tail, and among them ripe shamefaced peaches.
> Blazes Boylan walked here and there in new tan shoes about the fruitsmelling shop, lifting fruits, young juicy crinkled and plump red tomatoes, sniffing smells. . . .
> Blazes Boylan at the counter wrote and pushed the docket to her.
> —Send it at once, will you? he said. It's for an invalid.
> —Yes, sir. I will, sir.
> Blazes Boylan rattled merry money in his trousers' pocket.
> —What's the damage? he asked.
> The blond girl's slim fingers reckoned the fruits.
> Blazes Boylan looked into the cut of her blouse. A young pullet. He took a red carnation from the tall stemglass.
> —This for me? he asked gallantly.
> The blond girl glanced sideways at him, got up regardless, with his tie a bit crooked, blushing.
> —Yes, sir, she said.
> Bending archly she reckoned again fat pears and blushing peaches.

Blazes Boylan looked in her blouse with more favour, the stalk of the red flower between his smiling teeth.
—May I say a word to your telephone, missy? he asked roguishly. [Pp. 227-28]

The characters exchange words and entertain a thought or two ("a young pullet," thinks Boylan), but their words and thoughts do not tell us nearly as much as either their glances and gestures or, even more important, the objects connected with these glances and gestures. The rich areas of intonation and implication hidden behind the words of the characters, what they feel and want but do not say, are all mediated through gestures and things that here act as inanimate solicitors and promoters in establishing their relationship and infusing the entire atmosphere with a lush, grandly comic, and exaggerated eroticism.

The shop itself begins to acquire the atmosphere of the boudoir as the wicker basket is "bedded" with "rustling" fiber. The girl, though never described directly, is given both bodily form and maidenly attitude by the "fat pears" and "ripe shamefaced peaches." Boylan is confident and conquering in his "new tan shoes" and risqúe in handling the feminized and fleshy fruits, "young juicy crinkled." In this context even seemingly innocent expressions such as "head by tail" become unavoidably lubricious as they pick up a kind of erotic electricity by association with such obviously charged phrases. Finally, both object and gesture consort with a language of banal romance and antiquated courtliness ("gallantly," "roguishly," "blushing," "shamefaced") to show us not so much who these characters are as what they take themselves to be; that is, the author's notion of how these characters conceive of themselves in this specific situation: Boylan the "gallant" Lothario, the salesgirl the "blushing" maid. They are acting out a series of faded, and therefore comic, postures—and Boylan never more so than in his amusing but thoroughly stereotyped final gesture as he snares the "stalk of the red flower," her flower, "between his smiling teeth."

Anyone with even a passing familiarity with film practice is no doubt well aware of the way inanimate objects can be, and indeed have been, actively employed by directors as a form of dramatic economy not only to obviate a lengthy passage of dialogue but also, on occasion, to displace the actor himself. In this respect the close-up can do for the object what it can also do for the face: increase the sensory and emotional impact of the object's features by increasing its size; the close-up, that is, can "star" the object just as it can "star" the actor.

Sergei Eisenstein was particularly adroit in using the close-up to activate the object into the drama, to make the drama express itself through the object. He theorized at great length, for example, about the moment in *Potemkin* when the ship's surgeon, an employee of the czar's navy, was called upon to examine the maggot-ridden meat the sailors had refused.[7] According to Eisenstein very few viewers ever remember the face or manner of the surgeon, though his full figure appears in numerous shots, but very few ever forget his glasses, the pince-nez with which he examines the meat. This is the only action the surgeon is called upon to perform, and it is undertaken specifically by the pince-nez itself as, in close-up, we examine the wriggling vermin going in and out of focus through its glass lens. The shot ends with the lens out of focus so that the vermin cannot be seen (thus representing the surgeon's distortion of reality), and the surgeon declares the meat fit to eat. This decision eventually leads to the sailors' revolt during which the surgeon is thrown overboard. Rather than show him struggling in the water, Eisenstein again cuts to the pince-nez, tangled amidst the ship's ropes and dangling above the water, thus dramatizing the struggle of its owner below as well as the certainty of his death (hanging from the ropes as from a gallows).

Eisenstein referred to this replacement of the actor by the object as a *"pars pro toto"* effect where the part is at one and the same time also the whole.[8] This sort of visual shorthand, the cinematic equivalent of the literary synecdoche, not only reappears with striking consistency throughout all of Eisenstein's films but by now has become virtually a commonplace in the expressive vocabulary of filmmakers everywhere.

The device is also something of a commonplace in *Ulysses*. We not only think of Joyce's anatomy of Dublin in terms of its human population but also in terms of its equivalent object population, dependent on its human counterpart in a tremulous and shifting

[7] Eisenstein, *Film Form*, pp. 132-34.
[8] Ibid., p. 132.

relationship, yet assuming a vigorous prominence in its own right. Like the human citizenry, this object population can also be divided into two sexes: male things (topcoats, canes, crutches, keys, pens, umbrellas, shoes, and a rather staggering variety of hats) and female things (handbags, notions, fruits, petticoats, corsets, stockings, bloomers, boas, frills, and laces). Sometimes a single object will become the source of dramatic tension between characters, as the key to the Martello Tower causes tension between Stephen and Mulligan. Sometimes two objects will lock horns with each other, as they do when "the stickumbrelladustcoat dangling" of the eccentric Farrell rudely brushes from its angle "the slender tapping cane" of the blind stripling (p. 132). Sometimes an entire catalog of objects will be employed in an epical fashion as if to overwhelm the consciousness of the reader with the sheer profusion and variety of the phenomenal world (such as the famous inventories of the "Cyclops" and "Ithaca" episodes).

The object becomes most memorable, however, when it is permanently associated with a specific human being, when it is employed in the Eisensteinian manner, *pars pro toto,* as a kind of emblem, the material signature of the character himself: Mulligan's mirror and razor in the mock-up of a cross; Haines's "soft grey hat," bland and malleable; Boylan's rose and straw boater tilted at "a rakish angle"; Mollie's underwear, soiled yet provocative; and, of course, Bloom's famous soap, like its owner, sweet, mild, and thoroughly prosaic. The soap enters the narrative as a *pars pro toto* effect, but as Bloom's day wears on, the soap increases in significance—as Bloom thinks about it, pats it reassuringly, shifts it from pocket to pocket in a series of uncomfortable situations—until the inevitable finally happens: the soap, now more powerful than its owner, detaches itself from Bloom and assumes a life of its own:

(*He points to the south, then to the east. A cake of new clean lemon soap arises, diffusing light and perfume.*)

THE SOAP

We're a capital couple are Bloom and I:
He brightens the earth, I polish the sky. [*Ulysses,* p. 440]

Now none of the objects mentioned above ever achieve a realization comparable to the epiphany of the soap here in Nighttown. Yet the actual speaking of the soap represents the logical extension and conclusion of the object's animation, that autotelic condition toward which all the other objects seem to strive, but rarely attain. With the soap, however, we enter the world of dreams, demonology, and surrealist fantasy modes (cinematically represented in the early work of Buñuel, Clair, Epstein and Cocteau); those worlds where inanimate things do indeed seem to represent the locks and keys of deeper, darker forces just beneath their surfaces.

But just as important as the animated object is the externalized character. The latter is the counterpart of the former, and the cinematized fiction that includes one will invariably include the other. Like the animated object, the externalized character also appears to be mysterious and aloof because he is only seen, and, because only seen, this character will also emphasize the immense separation between himself and the seer. The seer in his isolation will often attempt to reconstruct (sometimes inaccurately) the internal life of the seen character. On certain significant occasions, however, no reconstruction will be possible, for in these instances the seer will often confront a dehumanized "flat," a thing in the shape of a man, and when this happens, everything that the seer sees will be synonymous with everything that the seer needs to know. The dehumanized character represents another extreme instance of the cinematographic manner in which we note a drastic reduction of the kind of ordinary novelistic information that would enrich and enliven the visual detail from within, deepen the lines and masses of the surface with notations—for example, of the character's social, familial, and psychic backgrounds, or his interconnections with his neighbors and local institutions, or his personal ideology (what Lukács called the character's "intellectual physiognomy");[9] everything, in brief, that we associate with the living history and internality of the seen character. This sort of information, while never dispensed with, is often minimized and simplified, as we shall see,

[9]Lukács, "The Intellectual Physiognomy in Characterization," *Writer and Critic,* pp. 148-88, and *passim.*

especially in the fiction of the post-Joycean novelists who employ these dehumanized effects in their most radical form.

While it is true that many of Joyce's character portraits are presented in the conventional, fully rounded manner (that is, with visual and expositional detail together), particularly in *Dubliners*, it is no less true that he employs depthless treatments throughout most of his work. Even the early stories provide extensive illustration of the externalized approach and of what was to become perhaps his most characteristic method of rendering one character as seen by another:

> While she spoke she turned a silver bracelet round and round her wrist. She could not go, she said, because there would be a retreat that week in her convent. Her brother and two other boys were fighting for their caps and I was alone at the railings. She held one of the spikes, bowing her head towards me. The light from the lamp opposite our door caught the white curve of her neck, lit up her hair that rested there and, falling, lit up the hand upon the railing. It fell over one side of her dress and caught the white border of a petticoat, just visible as she stood at ease. [*Dubliners*, p. 32]

In the later work (*Portrait*, two-thirds of *Ulysses*) the visual detail may take on a richer symbolic implication, but even there the interior life of the seen character is essentially no more apparent than it is here ("Araby," 1905), nor will the relationship between the seer and the seen character be so very different; that is to say, it will usually be the relationship between a virtually bottomless mind and a relatively flattish physical surface linked essentially by an eye beam of mental consciousness (in certain ways, a structural situation analogous to a motion picture projector and its screen). In most of Joyce's work, early or late, most of what we learn about the seen character we will learn as we learn it here in "Araby" vis-à-vis the thoughts and feelings of the seer.

I think it is generally true of Joyce's fiction that the more sharply visualized the character, the less we tend to know about him or her. The visualized characters are generally minor characters (as is the girl in "Araby"). The least visualized characters, however, are usually the seers and they are the ones we come to know best. All the centers of consciousness in the stories, as well as Stephen, Bloom, and Molly, of course, are not nearly as pictorialized and

Depthlessness 143

opaque as the characters that they themselves perceive. The most obvious example is Stephen in *Portrait*, whose perspective is so unyielding that while we never manage to know what he looks like, he becomes the most fully, and perhaps only, developed character in the novel. We do not see these observers, we see with them. They are not characters in a film so much as they seem to be characters *at* a film; or to put it another way, each is like the camera through which we perceive a series of depthless images.

The extent of the separation between the seer and the seen is partly redeemed by the seer's active eye beam of mental consciousness, groping, testing, reflecting, and interpreting the received visual information, balancing off moments of illusion with moments of insight. As is so often the case in Joyce, the "Araby" passage provides us with both an object and a consciousness, one tentatively fastened to the other. Here the way that the seen character appears at the moment of apprehension is, in a sense, indistinguishable from the way that the seer would like her to appear, from the way that he thinks and feels about her. The seer describes her as part of a formal visual composition of curves, masses, lights, and shadows, for that is the way she actually appears at that moment, but he also elects to single out this particular visual disposition, so graceful and poetic, for he is in love with her to the point of adoration.

Still, the treatment is too studied and painterly to be fully representative of Joyce; it is perhaps more Flaubertian than Joycean as the eye moves from head to petticoat and takes in the whole figure of the girl. The fragmented figure is more typical of Joyce's ocular habits than is the treatment in "Araby":

Old Jack raked the cinders together with a piece of cardboard and spread them judiciously over the whitening dome of coals. When the dome was thinly covered his face lapsed into darkness but, as he set himself to fan the fire again, his crouching shadow ascended the opposite wall and his face slowly re-emerged into light. It was an old man's face, very bony and hairy. The moist blue eyes blinked at the fire and the moist mouth fell open at times, munching once or twice mechanically when it closed. [*Dubliners*, p. 118]

Here ("Ivy Day in the Committee Room," 1905) one character is not seen by another but rather is viewed directly by the author himself. The texture, perspective, and lighting are harsher, more oblique, more deformed than in the previous visualization. The treatment here is also more overtly cinematographic than in "Araby" since Joyce visualizes most of the movement by focusing on old Jack's disembodied face as it lapses in and out of the shadows. Both treatments, however, are done largely in black and white—as are many of the visualizations in Joyce's stories—which both emphasizes their lack of warmth and adds to their flatness by casting a homogenous tonality over the whole of the visualization. (In films, too, the black and white image tends to appear colder, flatter, and more abstract than the color image.)

The two visualizations are also alike in one other way: just as the girl turns the silver bracelet on her wrist "round and round," so too does Jack move his mouth "mechanically" once or twice when closed. Like so many of Joyce's Dubliners—and not only here in the early stories, but throughout the later work as well—these two characters have an obsessional tic, some personal mannerism that they exercise automatically over and over again in the way that a machine performs one function over and over again. Something has happened to these people, some inner resiliency has been lost, some vital and very human flexibility, some variousness, has gone out of them. What they have lost, at least in part, is their capacity to change, and this has been taken from them by the city itself. The automatic tic is the outward sign of an inward "paralysis," that "paralysis" of the human spirit which, as Joyce himself indicates, was the unifying theme of his first collection of stories.[10] This mechanization, or dehumanization, of the seen character points towards an extremity of depthless portraiture and results in one of Joyce's most striking visualizations:

Corley was the son of an inspector of police and he had inherited his father's frame and gait. He walked with his hands by his sides, holding himself erect and swaying his head from side to side. His head was large, globular and oily; it sweated in all weathers; and his large round hat, set upon it sideways, looked like a bulb which had grown out of another. He always stared straight before him as if he were on parade and, when he

---

[10] "My intention was to write a chapter of the moral history of my country and I chose Dublin for the scene because that city seemed to me the centre of paralysis" (Joyce to Grant Richards [1906], *Letters*, ed. Ellman, II, 134).

Depthlessness

wished to gaze after someone in the street, it was necessary for him to move his body from the hips. At present he was about town. Whenever any job was vacant a friend was always ready to give him the hard word. He was often to be seen walking with policemen in plainclothes, talking earnestly. He knew the inner side of all affairs and was fond of delivering final judgments. He spoke without listening to the speech of his companions. [*Dubliners*, p. 51]

Joyce's treatment of Corley ("Two Gallants," 1906) represents a special instance. Most of the other Dubliners do not appear in such a dehumanized form, for most of them have not yet devolved to such an extreme condition of brutality and spiritual impoverishment. Corley is a Dublin street loafer, small-time gigolo, parasite, and pimp (or so it is implied). Even though his description incorporates the traditional expositional information that would take us beyond his external appearance, this information does very little to mitigate the severity and distortion of his delineation. Nothing we learn about Corley either here or at any other point in the story tells us very much more about him—his psychology, temperament, emotional style—than what is already implicit in the two-dimensional graphics and ugly mechanics of his body. Exposition, conversation, and behavior simply corroborate the initial testimony of the visualization itself: the automatonlike rigidity of the torso equals a rigidity of the spirit; the geometric abstraction of head and hat ("like a bulb which had grown out of another") reduces and streamlines the natural irregularities of the human form to connote a displaced and debased humanity. This latter detail in particular quite *literally* flattens out Corley's figure (or at least it is as close as the printed page can come to such an effect) as the geometry of head and hat place a firm outline about these shapes and bring them into the two-dimensional space of the photographic arts.

In general, all depthless treatments tend to distance and ultimately alienate the seer (if one is present) and the reader from the full comprehension of the seen character. But the externalized treatments of minor characters like old Jack and the girl from "Araby" do not rob these characters of an interior life so much as they indicate the extent of the difficulties of the seer and the reader to acquire access to such a life. The highly pictorialized renderings in concretized fiction often connote problems in personal communication and rapport, but not necessarily a total absence of humanity. The dehumanized variety of the depthless treatment, however, not only distances seer and reader from the character, but usually makes this character impervious to further inspection, makes the flat surface the terminal point of virtually all there is to know about the character. I think that Joyce's treatment of Corley tells us that he would no more wish to enter Corley's mind than he would wish to enter that of a stone, a chair, or a steamroller. In this respect the dehumanized visualization is often the sign of the author's moral antipathy toward his character.

Corley is one of Joyce's urban grotesques; Alleyne ("Counterparts," 1905), who shakes his fist "like the knob of some electric machine," is another; so too are those ubiquitous sign carriers (from *Ulysses*) whose heads seem to have been displaced by the letters on their placards, "H.E.L.Y.S." In these treatments the passive vision that lies at the center of the depthless perspective conjoins naturally with a still older literary tradition of character distortion that reaches back to the naturalism of Zola, Norris, and London, and still further back to the Gothic modes of Dickens and Gogol, in which the bizarre transformations of man and the environment brought about by the emerging big cities of the nineteenth century enter works of narrative fiction with impressive impact. The fiction of these diverse writers converges in a specific response to the members of the new economic classes created by the new technology and abounds in portraiture of blue- and white-collar workers from the factories, the mines, the office cubicles of the law firms and civil service departments, who are described through comparisons with animal, vegetable, and mineral components, thus indicating at least a partial displacement of the human by the subhuman.[11]

Joyce and many other modern exponents of concretized form—Faulkner, West, Dos Passos—draw heavily upon this trad-

[11] For detailed discussion of these transformations, see Dorothy Van Ghent's remarks on Dickens in "The Dickens World: A View from Todger's"; Vladimir Nabokov's analysis of *Dead Souls* in *Nikolai Gogol* (New York, 1944), pp. 75-86; and Martin Turnell on Zola's *Germinal* in *Art of French Fiction*, pp. 164-73. Both Van Ghent and Nabokov introduce the concept of the demonic, which I use in my discussion of the contemporary American Gothic novel.

ition, not departing from tendencies already present in the earlier manner but rather intensifying and expanding them. In the modernist works, for instance, natural metaphors, like Zola's wild beast analogies or Gogol's man-into-garden-vegetable motifs, tend to diminish in frequency in favor of purely mechanistic and mathematical comparisons—human components replaced by components of wood, metal, or plastic, or the outlines of the human form abstracted into various geometric shapes. Moreover, the modern novelist will often extend the scope of the malformation and the malfunction, including distortions from the working class along with dehumanized types from all areas of modern urban existence. (Corley, after all, has no profession, nor can the slight tics of old Jack and the girl from "Araby" be directly related to their occupations.)

Indeed, the entire literary tradition of urban dehumanization in both its modern and premodern forms represents a moral and humanist response to the decay of human value in a mechanized environment. This tradition charts the varying stages in the corrosion of the human spirit through its fusions with a world of dead matter and views the rise of the modern city in inverse proportion to a decline in human dignity and, indeed, a sense of the sacramental itself.

In his brilliant discussion of the emergence of the modern city, Oswald Spengler suggestively describes the growth of the urban landscape as a millenium-long evolutionary movement away from the natural and organic shapes of the countryside and toward the abstract, geometric shapes and "soulless material" of the modern metropolis, the "daemonic stone-desert." And while there are many causes for the modern observer's disaffiliation from his visual field and for the passive vision that tends to accompany this recession, certainly not the least of these causes resides in the transformation of man's physical circumstances by industry and technology into Spengler's "stone-desert." The shape of Corley's body and the artistic imagination which envisages such a shape are both the products of, and the reactions to, a life that has been bred amid the shapes, sizes, and angles of vision provided by the architectonics of an urban landscape, "that artificial, mathematical, utterly land-alien product of a pure intellectual satisfaction . . . the city of the city-architect. In all civilizations alike, these cities aim at the chessboard form, which is the symbol of soullessness."[12]

Joyce was certainly a man of the cities who enjoyed many facets of city life, but this did not prevent him from portraying the adverse effects of such a life upon the quality of the citizenry. In a very precise sense a man like Corley fits perfectly into the formal decor of his city-home. He is in his element and like Joyce's other brutal and mechanized types—Alleyne, Mrs. Mooney ("The Boarding House," 1905), Boylan—Corley performs easily in his environment and, on occasion, even triumphantly, a small but well-oiled mechanical unit in the greater machine which is Dublin itself.

But what of Bloom, Stephen, and the very young protagonists of the early stories ("The Sisters," "Araby," "An Encounter")? These types, the seers, the watchers, are the polar antitheses of the grotesques. Sensitive, deep-feeling, the seers are characteristically outsiders, estranged from most of the other citizens and, by virtue of their loneliness, at least partially excluded from the deformations of the city. Or are they? When Joyce elects to visualize these characters—and for the most part they are significantly faceless—how do they appear?

On the farther side under the railway bridge Bloom appears flushed, panting, cramming bread and chocolate into a side pocket. From Gillen's hairdresser's window a composite portrait shows him gallant Nelson's image. A concave mirror at the side presents to him lovelorn longlost lugubru Booloohoom. Grave Gladstone sees him level, Bloom for Bloom. He passes, struck by the stare of truculent Wellington but in the convex mirror grin unstruck the bonham eyes and fatchuck cheekchops of Jollypoldy the rixdix doldy. [*Ulysses*, pp. 433-34]

Such a visualization helps to explain why in presenting an essentially positive character like Bloom, Joyce will not, and perhaps cannot, resort to the visual modality any more than is absolutely necessary; it also suggests why Joyce in the last phase of his career, when presenting a historical and cosmological vision of humanity in itself more positive than any he had yet conceived, minimizes the importance of this modality more conscientiously than ever before.

[12]All quotation in this paragraph is from Oswald Spengler, "Cities and Peoples," *The Decline of the West*, ed. Helmut Werner and Arthur Helps, trans. Charles Frances Atkinson (New York, 1932). p. 248.

Depthlessness

In the description above, the human form is treated with the elasticity of a rubber band as Bloom's image passes a shop window where it is reflected three times: first by a concave mirror at one side, which mournfully stretches him out ("Booloohoom"); next by the shop window itself which returns a neutral image ("Bloom for Bloom"); then by a convex mirror, which gaily compresses and widens the margins of his body ("Jollypoldy"). We see the various images of Bloom through an appropriate arrangement of vowels and consonants that alternately expand and contract, thus duplicating in language the shapes of the images in the mirror.

Bloom's deformation is even more exaggerated than Corley's, and certainly if we were asked to deduce everything that we know and could know about Bloom solely on the basis of his very brief external visualizations, here and throughout *Ulysses*, we could hardly arrive at a character portrait deeper, nobler, or more sympathetic than Corley's. In the interior monologue, however, the formal opposite of the depthless perspective, we get a very different portrait of Bloom, a partrait in depth. The few external views of Bloom, like the one above, tend to discredit his character, ridicule and humiliate him, sketch out the ignominious profiles of cuckold, buffoon, and petit bourgeois. On the other hand, in his rich, vigorous, and witty monologues a faceless and unvisualized Bloom expands and deepens in moral and emotional quality as his associations of thought and feeling carry us to those bottomless regions of the mind where we confront the motions of his soul, both individual and universal, that unite Bloom with his race and the history of his culture; those archetypes that translate Bloom beyond the transience of a phenomenal self and into the permanence of universal myth where he is one with heroes and gods (Odysseus, Jehovah, Christ, Vishnu, Shakespeare, Elijah). Viewed from without, Bloom is simply another object in Joyce's phenomenal landscape, limited, visible, immediate, fragmented, impermanent, a chaos of multiple appearances and minute deformations. (For example, three very different images appear in the shop window. Which one represents the authentic Bloom?) Viewed from within, the shades and changes of the many appearances are contained and resolved in the underlying unity of an archetypal identity, as Bloom is fixed in the timeless space of mythopoeic association.

Accordingly, from *Dubliners* to *Finnegans Wake* Joyce's literary and intellectual development reveals an inexorable interiorization of his materials as his focus of interest moves away from the visible, phenomenal world, away from visualization itself, and deeper into the recesses of the human mind and closer to the sources of myth, which he finally embodies by means of a self-reflexive, multiplex verbal music, word fusions from a polyglot vocabulary more evocative of multivalent concepts than of any specific visualized space. In *Finnegans Wake* we are located entirely in the nightworld, the dreamscape of the sleeping members of the Earwicker family, who are at once distinct individuals and archetypes of the Family of Man. Significantly, this last book, Joyce' most mythic, hopeful, and sacramental work, is also his least visualized.

Black Graphics

Interiorized procedures are most apparent in late Joyce (*Finnegans Wake*) and represent of course a movement away from concretized form and point out certain limitations in this form (as well as, perhaps, in the film form itself). In early Joyce (*Dubliners*) and middle Joyce (*A Portrait of the Artist as a Young Man*, most of *Ulysses*), we find for the most part the procedures of an exterior-interior artist achieving a shifting balance between depictions of the visible world and the internal life of the mind. The main line of development in concretized form—the line that runs from Flaubert to Joyce, Faulkner, Hemingway, Dos Passos, Camus, Sartre, Nabokov—has, in a variety of ways, always cultivated this shifting interaction between subject and object.

Film, too, has cultivated this interaction through the double-sided nature of the camera. One has only to attend films regularly, however, to realize that one often gets a more varied and immediate experience of the seen than of the seer. Many works of cinematographic fiction will often reverse these proportions, and here one may well feel that one is not getting so much of the object's subjectivity as he is of the subject's objectivity. But we must never forget that in both film and cinematographic fiction the emphasis is continually shifting between subject and object, and thus it is not always easy to generalize about where the primary emphasis will most often lie in any given film or novel. Does Zola's fiction tell us more about the mind of the seer than a film like 8 ½? Does Nabokov's? How much more does Joyce's tell us?

Two important literary movements, however, have significantly shifted the balance of emphasis in favor of the object, have pursued a line of literary procedure directly opposite to late Joyce, that is, away from the interior and toward the exterior. I refer specifically to certain practitioners of the New Novel in France—Robbe-Grillet, Simon, Le Clézio—and the group of American novelists known variously as black humorists, surreal fantasts, and perhaps more accurately, in point of history, as the practitioners of the contemporary American Gothic novel: West, Kesey, Hawkes, Heller, Ellison, James Purdy, and Flannery O'Connor. Both movements represent perhaps the most radical employment of the depthless perspective on the current literary scene; we find in both the centrality of things and an extreme flattening of the seen character. The fiction of both movements is also permeated with the full variety of cinematographic effects that result from the separation of the seer from his visual field.

Yet both movements are essentially different from each other and should be thought of separately. The New Novel emerges out of a very advanced reaction against the Flaubertian novel of psychological realism and adopts a philosophical position that argues against the mind's attempted assimilation of any element in its visual field as well as the mind's endeavor to find any element of itself reflected therein. It is not antirealistic (or so its proponents maintain), but antipsychological, and it attempts to obviate the traditional dialogue between the seer and his visual field, basic to psychological realism, by minimizing the role of the seer and thus neutralizing the visual field.

Instead, the American Gothic novel represents an extreme intensification of the tradition of urban distortion and displacement and adopts an ethical position that views and presents the visual field as a kind of social nightmare, not at all neutral, but vibrant with subrational and even satanic forces. It is not antipsychological, but antirealistic, and thus represents a radical abstraction of traditional psychological realism by projecting the unconscious forces of the mind outward, as it were, upon the surface of the visual field and reshapes the natural form of this surface in compliance with the nature of these forces—and thus results in an *exteriorized* and *visualized interior*. While the New Novel attacks the basic humanist contention which holds that man is central and significant, the American Gothic novel, itself an expression of an outraged humanism, attacks the naive humanist contention which holds that man is virtuous and rational.

The original progenitor of the contemporary American Gothic novel is, of course, the classic Gothic novel, which flourished in the latter half of the eighteenth and early nineteenth centuries. As practiced by Walpole, "Monk" Lewis, Ann Radcliffe, and Charles Maturin, this literary assemblage of weird castles, ghosts, dungeons, mysterious chases and disappearances, with its "horrific," vaguely medieval, and quasi-supernatural settings, had an incalculable influence on some of the best European and American literary minds—both poets (Byron, Shelley, and Coleridge) and fiction writers (Dickens, Gogol, Hawthorne, and Poe)—throughout the nineteenth century and into the twentieth. In all of its novelistic manifestations, both modern and premodern, the Gothic tradition has always cultivated modes of expression that veer toward the melodramatic and the typological, the projective and the hyperbolic, as opposed to the realistic traditions of the novel (Flaubert, James, Conrad, Joyce), which tend to cultivate modes that are historical and mimetic, analytic and normative.[13] Concretized narrative forms can appear and have appeared in both the hyperbolic and the normative traditions, in the former, intermittently, and in the latter almost to the exclusion of all other forms.

The classic Gothicists are pre-Flaubertian artists and their novels are not concretized. Gogol, Dickens, and Dostoevsky, however, are transitional figures. In all three novelists the manners of an omniscient novelist—pre-Flaubertian tendencies—still make themselves felt. These authors only intermittently hide behind the seeing eye of a character or the neutral eye of a presentational narrator who visualizes each existentialized mo-

---

[13]My remarks on the Gothic novel are based on Leslie A. Fiedler's study in *Love and Death in the American Novel* (New York, 1960), pp. 106-48.

Depthlessness 153

ment from a fixed, articulated, and therefore limited position and angle in space. These qualities of camera vision, however, do appear in the work of the contemporary American Gothic novelists. There is, then, a crucial overlap, between the two traditions, and I think that a concretized realism converges with a concretized Gothicism precisely at those points where the seer's recession from his field of vision is so complete that this field seems no longer merely strange and unfamiliar but now seems monstrous and threatening—entirely beyond his control—in proportions exactly equal to the terror and helplessness he feels within himself; in other words, where the seer finds in the world about him a projection of what he had always found in himself, but only in the wildest and most secretive moments of his darkest nightmares.

This convergence is most apparent in Joyce's treatment of characters like Corley and Alleyne, and I think it is equally apparent in Faulkner's treatment of the gangster Popeye in *Sanctuary* (1931):

> He saw, facing him across the spring, a man of under size, his hands in his coat pockets, a cigarette slanted from his chin. His suit was black, with a tight, high-waisted coat. His trousers were rolled once and caked with mud above mud-caked shoes. His face had a queer, bloodless color, as though seen by electric light; against the sunny silence, in his slanted straw hat and his slightly akimbo arms, he had that vicious depthless quality of stamped tin.... He squatted in his tight black suit, his right-hand coat pocket sagging compactly against his flank, twisting and pinching cigarettes in his little, doll-like hands, spitting into the spring. His skin had a dead, dark pallor. His nose was faintly acquiline, and he had no chin at all. His face just went away, like the face of a wax doll set too near a hot fire and forgotten.[14]

Although Faulkner worked equally well throughout his career in both the hyperbolic mode (*Absalom, Absalom!*) and the normative mode (*Intruder in the Dust*), he did not produce another novel as thoroughly sinister and exteriorized as *Sanctuary*; nor did he create many characters as thoroughly dehumanized as Popeye (certain members of the Snopes clan, however, while less menac-

---

[14]William Faulkner, *Sanctuary* (New York, 1932), pp. 5-6.

ing, appear to be cut out of the same flattened out and mechanized materials). I think that Irving Howe is correct when he contends that the manner and atmosphere of *Sanctuary* represent the consequences of "Faulkner's fastidious distance from his own materials...his hatred for the world of his own novel."[15] And Faulkner himself seems to have confirmed this view, as is well known, by dismissing his book as a potboiler.[16]

Yet in spite of, and indeed because of, the very maverick qualities that isolate *Sanctuary* from the rest of Faulkner's work, it remains one of his most gripping creations and, I think, his single most influential novel. I take this book as the first modern American literary instance of a social order consistently viewed as a nightmare fantasy, and thus the twentieth-century initiator of that line of novels I have designated as the contemporary American Gothic. For one moment in his career Faulkner's distaste for his own literary materials, and perhaps for the very reading public that would (and did) welcome such materials, had reached that pitch of intensity where he could render them with the mixture of outrage and bitter satire so characteristic of such novels as *Catch 22*, *Wise Blood*, *Invisible Man*, and *One Flew over the Cuckoo's Nest*. In all of these novels, the human cruelty and suffering either undergone or perpetrated by the characters have attained proportions so cosmic that only literary forms of extremity and distortion are capable of both representing and containing them, of making them felt and keeping them at a distance. The weird laughter that runs through *Sanctuary* (in the brothel scenes, at Red's funeral) and its latter-day counterparts is the last recourse of an astonished sanity before an inexplicable horror.

And the essential point about Popeye is that he *cannot* be explained. Faulkner watches him endlessly throughout the narrative, carefully describing his every move and gesture, but he does not examine his motives. Unlike the ordinary exteriorized characters in cinematized fiction, Popeye is not merely distanced from us, he is virtually immune to inquiry. Faulkner employs an extremity of depthless portraiture—and here the term is Faulkner's ("he had that vicious *depthless* quality of stamped tin")—to indicate that we are not simply watching a man but something

---

[15]*William Faulkner: A Critical Study* (New York, 1962), p. 194.
[16]See Faulkner's Introduction to *Sanctuary*, pp. 1-2.

Depthlessness 155

other than a purely human nature, and therefore a nature not entirely susceptible to the inspections of reason, analysis, or any law of human predictability. Popeye is not only alien to nature (he shrinks back in terror from bird whistles) but to any form of human contact. His relation to others is mediated through objects; the gun with which he kills, and the corncob with which he rapes Temple Drake: *pars pro toto*. His impotence is both literal and figurative. Just as Popeye's nature is embodied in objects, so objects are embodied in his nature. His body is a hybrid form, a man in the shape of a child's toy with "little doll-like hands" and "no chin at all." "His face just went away, like the face of a wax doll set too near a hot fire and forgotten." We could laugh at such a Bergsonian automaton (and in a certain sense, I think we are supposed to laugh) if it were not for the fact that this doll is also a killer. But this is only part of the point. What a comparison between a man and a thing really indicates—and not only in *Sanctuary*, but wherever it appears in the contemporary American Gothic—is that the nature of the man's evil is not simply human, not simply embodied in any specific individual, but that it extends throughout the entire material complex (for example, above, in "wax," "tin," "doll," "electric light"). Popeye cannot be fully explained, for he is not entirely responsible for who he is or what he does: rather, he is the embodiment of a demonic world order, the agent through which flow forces of cosmic violence, a violence that also flows through all the rapes, tortures, burnings, shootings, hangings, and miscarriages of justice that constitute the entire social world of *Sanctuary*.

Because his psychology is so monolithic and his actions so unmodulated in their viciousness, the character of Popeye, like many of the characters in this kind of fiction, yields itself easily to allegorical and schematic interpretations.[17] As many critics have pointed out, Popeye is Faulkner's embodiment of an amoral modernism, of material and technological encroachment, and certainly the signs of urban distortion are readily apparent not only in the comparisons between Popeye and things but also—as

---

[17]See, for example, George Marion O'Donnell's allegorical schema for *Sanctuary* in "Faulkner's Mythology," in *William Faulkner: Three Decades of Criticism*, ed. Frederick J. Hoffman and Olga W. Vickery (East Lansing, Mich., 1960), pp. 82-93.

in Joyce's distortion of Corley—in the outline that Faulkner draws about his body, in the rigidity and angularity of the "cigarette *slanted* from his chin," and "his *slanted* straw hat, and his slightly akimbo arms." The general effect is again to push the foreground figure against the background, *"against* the sunny silence," to flatten him out—like "stamped tin"—as one object amid other objects in a two-dimensional field. The space occupied by Popeye is always photographic space.

This photographic dimension is perfectly consonant with the fact that Popeye's slanted hat and slanted cigarette are, of course, part of the ritualized postures of the movie gangster. In this sense I think it is important to realize that *Sanctuary* is Faulkner's *Hollywood* novel, his first best-seller, the only one of his works to be filmed twice and the book that first brought him to the Hollywood studios where he worked on the screenplay that eventually became *The Story of Temple Drake* (1933, and remade in 1961 as *Sanctuary*). The entire narrative surface of this novel seems to have been composed not just with any camera eye but with a specifically American camera eye. *Sanctuary* is not only Hollywood material in its cinematographic technique and in its contents—that mixture of lurid sex and hopped-up physical violence that has always been the staple of the Hollywood film ever since the days of the nickelodeon—but in its very mode of expression: melodramatic, typological, hyperbolic, a bold and brilliant immediacy of physical surface readily yielding up to formula and abstraction. These elements, of course, not only constitute the mode of expression of the basic Hollywood genre film—the gangster, the western, the thriller—but they also appear in many forms of popular art and entertainment, all of which the contemporary American Gothic has adapted and transformed in developing its own special world view; for instance, the comic strip (*Miss Lonelyhearts, One Flew over the Cuckoo's Nest*), the vaudeville revue (*Malcolm, Catch 22*), the pulp novel (*A Cool Million*).

Nathanael West, who in terms of finished achievement and depth of talent may be considered the most important member of this post-Faulknerian group, incorporated all of these popular elements into his work. Moreover, West is also known to have acknowledged the influence of Faulkner on his writing, and certain critics have already pointed out the specific similarities between *Sanctuary,* Faulkner's Hollywood novel, and *The Day of the Locust* (1939), West's Hollywood novel, which significantly has Hollywood for its subject.[18]

Earle was a cowboy from a small town in Arizona. He worked occasionally in horse-operas and spent the rest of his time in front of a saddlery store on Sunset Boulevard. In the window of this store was an enormous Mexican saddle covered with carved silver, and around it was arranged a large collection of torture instruments. Among other things there were fancy, braided quirts, spurs with great spiked wheels, and double bits that looked as though they could break a horse's jaw without trouble. Across the back of the window ran a low shelf on which was a row of boots, some black, some red and some a pale yellow. All of the boots had scalloped tops and very high heels. . . .He had a two-dimensional face that a talented child might have drawn with a ruler and a compass. His chin was perfectly round and his eyes, which were wide apart, were also round. His thin mouth ran at right angles to his straight, perpendicular nose. His reddish tan complexion was the same color from hairline to throat, as though washed in by an expert, and it completed his resemblance to a mechanical drawing.[19]

In this description of the movie extra Earle Shoop, West exaggerates a point of comparison between depthless portraiture in fiction and the geometric face of the Hollywood star; that is, an image on a two-dimensional surface that helps to convey an essentially typological and formulary narrative to a mass audience whose mental capacity supposedly does not overreach that of an average twelve-year-old American child. The actual shape of such an image for such an audience has often been (and, in a certain sense, often must be) compelling and uncomplicated, immediate and simplistic, and the geometry of Earle's face is a comic abstraction of any number of American film types, such as, those long gaunt oblongs of the prototypical cowboy (from William S. Hart to Gary Cooper); or the ovoids upon circles of the plump male comic (Harry Langdon, Oliver Hardy, W. C. Fields); or the wide-browed, sharp-jawed, inverted triangles of the gangster and the urban hard types (Cagney, Kirk Douglas); or the

---

[18]See Carvel Collin's "Nathanael West's *The Day of the Locust* and *Sanctuary*," in *Nathanael West: A Collection of Critical Essays*, ed. Jay Martin (Englewood Cliffs, N.J., 1971), pp. 144-47.

[19]*The Day of the Locust, The Complete Works of Nathanael West* (New York, 1966), pp. 322-23.

arabesques and hourglass shapes of the dumb blonde and femme fatale (Harlow, Mae West).

Such comparisons, of course, can only extend so far: the American film actor, like film actors everywhere, communicates with far more than just the lines and masses of his face and conveys a greater depth of emotional life than any simple body geometry could possibly indicate. Not so with Earle, however: West arranges the lines of Earle's face to indicate a mathematical void, a shape equivalent to the Spenglerian "chessboard form ...the symbol of soullessness." What appears in isolated and qualified instances in Joyce, and in a solitary novel by Faulkner, appears in virtually all of West's fiction and in the fiction of others like him (Kesey, Heller, Purdy) as a cohesive and unified world view: a visual field consistently presented in the form of a demonology. Virtually all West's seen characters are described in terms of material, mechanistic, or mathematical comparisons, faces and figures possessed by a world of things.[20]

The things themselves always represent a form of social or personal biography, vibrant with the dark forces that the human surfaces often conceal. Earle's sadistic and quasi-homicidal nature, for example, is quite literally behind him in the window of the saddlery shop and is represented *pars pro toto* by the spurs, spikes, and high heels, the "torture instruments" and the boots. Earle, like so many of West's creations, is provided with a synthetic, strikingly manufactured physical appearance which becomes his product, the merchandise through which he markets himself in the society, the public mask through which he continues to define himself until what the mask conceals, but cannot always contain, finally breaks through: an inner world of subrational violence, hysteria, and self-destruction. Lunacy and murder are the common denominators behind the flat, brilliant, and varied surfaces of West's characters.

The description of the silly face and the vicious objects presents in a polarized form the aesthetic and generic centers of West's universe: comedy and terror, the innocuous cartoon face from the depths of which the monster emerges. Thus, the true cinematic

[20]"Man's collaboration with *things*, the paraphernalia of his suffering, is realized in the metaphor where West's vision takes effect" (Josephine Herbst, "Nathanael West", in *Nathanael West: A Collection of Critical Essays*, p. 15).

Depthlessness

counterparts of the American Gothic demonologies are the related fantasy modes of the horror film and the animated cartoon. West has often been called a comic writer and so have many of the recent practitioners of the demonic manner, but this description hardly begins to indicate the depth of the horror that lies at the heart of their cartooning:

She knows what they been saying, and I can see she's furious clean out of control. She's going to tear the black bastards limb from limb, she's so furious. She's swelling up, swells till her back's splitting out the white uniform and she's let her arms section out long enough to wrap around the three of them five, six times. She looks around her with a swivel of her huge head. Nobody up to see, just old Broom Bromden the halfbreed Indian back there hiding behind his mop and can't talk to call for help. So she really lets herself go and her painted smile twists, stretches to an open snarl, and she blows up bigger and bigger, big as a tractor, so big I can smell the machinery inside the way you smell a motor pulling too big a load....

But just as she starts crooking those sectioned arms around the black boys and they go to ripping at her underside with the mop handles, all the patients start coming out of the dorms to check on what's the hullabaloo, and she has to change back before she's caught in the shape of her hideous real self....

She stops and nods at some of the patients come to stand around and stare out of eyes all red and puffy with sleep. She nods once to each. Precise, automatic gesture. Her face is smooth, calculated, and precision-made, like an expensive baby doll, skin like flesh-colored enamel, blend of white and cream and baby-blue eyes, small nose, pink little nostrils—everything working together except the color on her lips and fingernails, and the size of her bosom.[21]

This is one of Ken Kesey's creations (in *One Flew over the Cuckoo's Nest*, 1962), Big Nurse, the tyrannical overlord of a mental hospital, and here we watch her swoop down on the attendants she has caught loafing on the job. In this description, character and thing are so thoroughly merged that, apart from the context, it is hard to tell whether we are looking at a woman transformed into a tractor or a painted doll that has suddenly begun to smile and snarl. The hospital is "like a cartoon world," says Kesey's narrator, "where the figures are flat and outlined in black, jerking

---

[21] Ken Kesey, *One Flew over the Cuckoo's Nest* (New York, 1962), pp. 4-5. Subsequent references to this novel appear in text.

through some kind of goofy story that might be real funny if it weren't for the cartoon figures being real guys" (p. 31). And we recognize the abstract and mechanized graphics of the cartoon form in the exaggerated "swelling up" of the Big Nurse, "those sectioned arms" like tentacles, and the "swivel" effect of her big, doll-like head. But the "painted smile" that "stretches to an open snarl" and the transformation into the "hideous real self" and then back again into the "expensive baby doll"—these are the elements of the classic movie fright tale, specifically the moments of metamorphosis, those moments of ultimate terror and demonism where either the underworld arises and dead matter animates itself (the mummy in the tomb flicks open a wrinkled eyelid, the monster composed of corpses rises from the operating table) or the human merges with the lower orders (man into wolf, Dr. Jekyll lap-dissolving into the bestial Hyde).

The world of the horror film joins the world of the cartoon precisely at that point where one order of being superimposes itself and merges with another (the dancing trees, talking ducks, and singing locomotives of any cartoon). After all, one has only to remember the Bergsonian formula for the comic effect (man into machine) to realize how finely drawn the lines between comedy and terror can sometimes be, and one only needs a detached eye to laugh at a horror film—which for some people has always been a form of low camp humor anyway—just as one only needs a naive eye to be disturbed by the cartoon (*Snow White* and *Pinocchio* are often thought to be "too frightening for children").[22]

The visual forms of the contemporary American Gothic novel find correspondences in both of these film forms. In cartoon, horror movie, and novel, it is the transfusion between the different orders of being that provides the cosmic and metaphysical center of each imagined universe. In the novel, however, this tranfusion is usually the sign of a total moral, social, and psychic collapse. It is the modern humanist's vision of hell before which

[22] The basic differences between these two forms, however, are obvious: the photographed horror film evolves from a context full of relatively naturalistic detail, while the world of the cartoon figure (who is first drawn, then photographed) is essentially a geometric abstraction. Mickey Mouse, like most cartoon creatures, can never really be frightening, for he represents neither a real mouse nor a real human being, but rather is sui generis. His ears, for example, are simply black circles; also, his hands have neither human fingers nor animal claws—just something resembling white gloves.

the seer or center of consciousness, characteristically presented as the one relatively normal figure wandering amid a lunatic world of urban grotesques, is essentially helpless and ineffectual (Miss Lonelyhearts, Malcolm, Todd Hackett in *The Day of the Locust*, and the nameless "I" of *Invisible Man*). In the end this single normal character is either destroyed by the berserk and evil forces that rule his universe (as are Malcolm and Miss Lonelyhearts); or he evades them in some way (as does Ellison's "I," Heller's Yossarian, and Kesey's Broom Bromden in *One Flew over the Cuckoo's Nest*); or he succumbs to them and becomes part of their evil (as does Fenton Riddleway in Purdy's *Dreamplace: 63*). But in no instance does he have the power either to manipulate or control these forces.

The relation of the seer to this anarchic and demonized visual field is perhaps best epitomized in the situation of West's most anguished hero, Miss Lonelyhearts. The madness and the hopelessness of the subject-object responses in the following description may be viewed as paradigmatic of the entire genre:

> Miss Lonelyhearts found himself developing an almost insane sensitiveness to order. Everything had to form a pattern: the shoes under the bed, the ties in the holder, the pencils on the table. When he looked out of a window, he composed the skyline by balancing one building against another. If a bird flew across this arrangement, he closed his eyes angrily until it was gone.
>
> For a little while, he seemed to hold his own but one day he found himself with his back to the wall. On that day all the inanimate things over which he had tried to obtain control took the field against him. When he touched something, it spilled or rolled to the floor. The collar buttons disappeared under the bed, the point of the pencil broke, the handle of the razor fell off, the window shade refused to stay down. He fought back, but with too much violence, and was decisively defeated by the spring of the alarm clock.
>
> He fled to the street, but there chaos was multiple. Broken groups of people hurried past, forming neither stars nor squares. The lamp-posts were badly spaced and the flagging was of different sizes. Nor could he do anything with the harsh clanging sound of street cars and the raw shouts of hucksters. No repeated group of words would fit their rhythm and no scale could give them meaning.
>
> He stood quietly against a wall, trying not to see or hear.[23]

---

[23]Nathanael West, *Miss Lonelyhearts, The Complete Works of Nathanael West*, pp. 78-79.

Chapter VII
Montage

LONG BEFORE MOVIES got to be everything they were going to be, many writers and critics were quick to perceive that the techniques of the new art form would ultimately help to transform the older art forms. As early as 1908 Leo Tolstoy insisted at great length upon the new areas of narrative technique opened up by the advent of film:

You will see that this little clicking contraption with the revolving handle will make a revolution in our life—in the life of writers. It is a direct attack on the old methods of literary art. We shall have to adapt ourselves to the shadowy screen and to the cold machine. A new form of writing will be necessary. I have thought of that and I can feel what is coming.

But I rather like it. This swift change of scene, this blending of emotion and experience—it is much better than the heavy, long-drawn-out kind of writing to which we are accustomed. It is closer to life. In life, too, changes and transitions flash by before our eyes, and emotions of the soul are like a hurricane. The cinema has divined the mystery of motion. And that is greatness.

When I was writing "The Living Corpse," I tore my hair and chewed my fingers because I could not give enough scenes, enough pictures, because I could not pass rapidly enough from one event to another. The accursed stage was like a halter choking the throat of the dramatist; and I had to cut the life and swing of the work according to the dimensions and requirements of the stage. I remember when I was told that some clever person had devised a scheme for a revolving stage, on which a number of scenes could be prepared in advance. I rejoiced like a child, and allowed myself to write ten scenes into my play. Even then I was afraid the play would be killed.

But the films! They are wonderful! Drr! and a scene is ready! Drr! and we have another! We have the sea, the coast, the city, the palace. . . .[1]

Here Tolstoy isolates the element of motion in the motion picture: "The cinema has divined the mystery of motion," he tells

[1] Quoted by Jay Leyda in "A Conversation with Leo Tolstoy," *Kino: A History of the Russian and Soviet Film* (London, 1960), pp. 410-11.

Montage 163

us, "and that is greatness." And not only its greatness, one wants to add, but part of its unique character as well, one of the special attributes of its idiom. Tolstoy understands what is not always understood when one refers to the unique treatment of motion in the cinema. What he is talking about clearly has very little to do with the physical actions of the photographed subject—speeding car, galloping horse, or whatever—but rather refers to the motion, or pulse, that is created by the relationship between the shots, by the change from one shot to another. He is referring, then, to the structural motion of the filmed narrative itself. In his own way Tolstoy is describing montage.

Montage is the syntactical ordering of the images in a film. Montage in this sense is vital to the narrative life of film. Without it there is only the strict reproduction of a single continuous time and space. With it there are different times and different spaces; there is one thing after another, sequence, narrative.[2] Practically speaking, montage is the editor's or director's arrangement (mounting) of the various photographed perspectives (shots, the images recorded by all the different camera setups) according to a predetermined concept; according, that is, to his plan, his vision of the order and length of time in which he wishes each perspective to be projected on the screen. The movement from one

[2]At no point do my remarks here and throughout this section mean to imply that montage is the "essence of cinema," or even to reduce the full range of cinematographic resourse to this single function. Least of all do I wish to enter that battle royal—dear to film theoreticians (but not to me)—that has been raging now for over a quarter of a century between those advocates of montage (or fragmentation), like Arnheim, Lindgren, and their followers, and those advocates of antimontage, like Bazin and *his* followers (i.e., those advocates of a continuous visual field sustained by either a single camera perspective or a moving camera). The truth is that most narrative films have found their formal existence at neither of these polar extremities, but rather at some point in the middle of the formal-aesthetic scale. Here an individual director—on the basis of a given dramatic context and his personal vision of such a context—may employ in infinitely varying degrees either fragmented or continuous visual fields wherever he finds one or the other to be needed. I do insist, however, that montage in its most elementary form (a simple change from one view to another) exists to some degree, greater or lesser, in almost every narrative film that has been made since 1908 and even in those very same great films—like Chaplin's, Renoir's, Von Stroheim's—famous for their low degree of fragmentation. It is this elementary usage that I have in mind when I say that montage "is vital to the narrative life of film." (For an overview of these matters that is admirable in its lucidity, sanity, and balance, see V. F. Perkins, *Film as Film* [Baltimore, 1972], pp. 9-58).

perspective to another, a cut, is the primary unit of narrative motion in film. Tolstoy actually refers to the cut with his expletive "Drr," the leap from one thing to another. The total number of cuts in any film creates what Tolstoy meant by the "life and swing of the work," the rhythm of its space, the shape of its temporality.

Montage, then, is finally the essential difference between the single photograph and the finished motion picture comprised of many photographs, between the solitary angle of vision and the composite perspective, between what can loosely be called photography and what can strictly be called cinema. The still camera and the resulting single picture is to the cinema and the resulting motion picture in the photographic arts what, by analogy, description is to narration in the literary arts. By description in fiction I mean the depiction of character, setting, or action, or any combination of these, as a separate and distinct picture, an isolated moment in the activity of the narrative. Description, then, is a component of the narrative, while narrative itself is a demonstration of character, setting, plot, or theme in the form of a sequential and integrated telling (pre-Flaubertian) or action (post-Flaubertian).

Thus far in our discussion, we have been mostly concerned with the descriptive procedures in concretized form, analyzing and illustrating the visualized results of what, and how, a center of consciousness or a relatively neutral authorial voice is able to see from a single circumscribed position in space and time. Adventitiousness, anatomization, and depthlessness represent essentially those aspects of cinematographic form that can legitimately be referred to as modes of description. In this final chapter however, I want to examine those methods of narration per se that are most characteristically associated with this form: the "life and swing" of the modern concretized narrative, the movement from one point in time and space to another, from one concretized perspective to another.

How do time and space go in such a narrative form? The following passage (from *Portrait*) is not only characteristic of narrative motion in Joyce but is also precisely analogous to narra-

He stood still in the middle of the roadway, his heart clamouring against his bosom in a tumult. A young woman dressed in a long pink gown laid her hand on his arm to detain him and gazed into his face. She said gaily:
—Good night, Willie dear!

tive motion in film:

> Her room was warm and lightsome. A huge doll sat with her legs apart in the copious easy chair beside the bed. He tried to bid his tongue speak that he might seem at ease, watching her as she undid her gown, noting the proud conscious movements of her perfumed head.[3]

Here, in the movement from one scene to the next, we perceive the characteristic Joycean tempo, the swing of his typical narrative manner. The passage begins as Stephen stands "in the middle of the roadway," proceeds immediately to the encounter with the prostitute, and then upon her first utterance switches—cuts, "Drr"—to her room, where the reader suddenly finds his visual attention pressed hard upon the huge doll "with her legs apart," which, *pars pro toto,* represents the character of the room and, of course, the prostitute herself. In the abrupt leap from the roadway to the room, we have an example of modern narrative movement. It is movement with a gap between its phases. For Joyce to fill in this gap would be to show us a literary space that was solid, continuous, and stable. But Joyce creates, instead a characteristically modern space, a dynamic, discontinuous space that seems quite literally to twitch and jump before our eyes. No longer stable and continuous, space is charged with the quality of motion and now seems to jerk and leap past us from one moment to the next in the manner of a syncopated clock. What Joyce is doing here is disposing his space in time, arranging it according to a temporal sequence. Film theorists refer to this effect as the temporalization of space, for while every separate shot in a film is nothing more or less than a picture of a part of space, each part of space is ordered and then perceived in time.[4] The cinematic novelist, like the filmmaker, often cuts up his space and splices the resulting spatial fragments together as part of a temporal continuum.

A temporalized space is space "alive," space as *process,* developing, changing, infinitely flexible, quick with advances and recessions, expansions and contractions, openings and closings, accumulations and dissolutions. In the passage above, as in a film, space seems first to expand in the middle of the roadway

---

[3]James Joyce, *A Portrait of the Artist as a Young Man* (New York: Viking Press, 1965), p. 100. Subsequent references to this edition will appear in text.

[4]See Ralph Stephenson and J. B. Debrix, *The Cinema as Art* (Baltimore, 1965), pp. 132-34.

and then abruptly to contract to the room and the close-up of the doll. We are not always aware of such spatial disjunctions as we move through the seemingly stable and continuous space of our daily activities, and we do not under ordinary conditions experience space in the cinematographic manner. But—and I think this is essential—that is always the way we can, and often do, *think* about it. The space-time montages in Joyce and in the film are readily reflected in the activities of a freely associating mind, and it is the mental motion of Stephen's mind, probably not film montage at all, that Joyce is attempting to reproduce in the passage above. We experience the roadway and the room and nothing in between, for this is all that matters to Stephen, all that constitutes the full moral and emotional import of what is happening to him.

It is the montage component in any given film—and particularly in those films where the cutting sequences are most fragmented—that always reminds us of the associational structures of a rapid mental process. For we must remember that each picture in a film shows us not only a physical reality but a mental reality as well, a point of view—either that of the character or of the director himself—and that the instantaneous movements from one point of view to the next and the spatial transformations which occur as a result of each movement find their affinities in the speed, flexibility, and transforming power of human thought and feeling. Tolstoy seems to understand this perfectly when he senses that films are "closer to life. In life, too, changes and transitions flash by before our eyes, and emotions of the soul are like a hurricane." In this manner the "mystery of motion" that Tolstoy refers to must be understood as a mental motion, a motion of the living mind in process.

What links the characteristic narrative procedures in *Portrait* and *Ulysses* with the characteristic narrative procedures in film is the highly subjective character of the procedures in both media. It is only in film and cinematographic fiction that we find such magical deformations and elisions of physical reality:

His own head was unbent for his thoughts wandered abroad and whether he looked around the little class of students or out of the window across the desolate gardens of the green an odour assailed him of cheerless cellardamp and decay. Another head than his, right before

Montage

him in the first benches, was poised squarely above its bending fellows like the head of a priest appealing without humility to the tabernacle for the humble worshippers about him. Why was it that when he thought of Cranly he could never raise before his mind the entire image of his body but only the image of the head and face? Even now against the grey cutrain of the morning he saw it before him like the phantom of a dream, the face of a severed head or deathmask, crowned on the brows by its stiff black upright hair as by an iron crown. It was a priestlike face, priestlike in its pallor, in the widewinged nose, in the shadowings below the eyes and along the jaws, priestlike in the lips that were long and bloodless and faintly smiling. [*Portrait*, p. 178]

The disembodied head of Cranly is, of course, only one of the many examples of a truncated spatial organization that helps to define the nature of space in a cinematographic narrative, and the positioning of this head "*against* the grey curtain of the morning" is in itself another of the depthless effect so characteristic of this form. It is, however, the imaginary linking, Stephen's surreal merger, of these two essentially disparate entities that exemplifies one aspect of Joyce's montage technique: the arrangement of space according to the character's structure of perception. In this case the arrangement results in that form of camera magic where one image is superimposed upon another. In this passage a fragment of internal or mental space (the head) is superimposed upon a fragment of external space (the sky). The following example reverses the procedure and cuts from a fragment of external space to a fragment of internal space:

How pale the light was at the window! But that was nice. The fire rose and fell on the wall. It was like waves. Someone had put coal on and he heard voices. They were talking. It was the noise of the waves. Or the waves were talking among themselves as they rose and fell.

He saw the sea of waves, long dark waves rising and falling, dark under the moonless night. A tiny light twinkled at the pierhead where the ship was entering: and he saw a multitude of people gathered by the waters' edge to see the ship that was entering their harbour. [*Portrait*, p. 26]

Here the motions of the fire cast wavelike shadows on the wall, which are in turn replaced by the purely imaginary waves in Stephen's dream. Joyce executes the transition from one space to the other without explanation, but also with a minimum of discontinuity because the cut is unified by the formal similarity of the two kinds of waves. In the following example from *Ulysses*, however, Joyce does not make any cut at all but, still in a cinematic manner, dissolves one image over the other. A dissolve is that form of film linkage in which one image is gradually superimposed upon another, and as the first grows dimmer and finally fades away the second grows clearer and replaces it entirely:

He passed Saint Joseph's, National school. Brats clamour. Windows open. Fresh air helps memory. Or a lilt. Ahbeesee defeegee kelomen opeecue rustyouvee double you. Boys are they? Yes. Inishturk. Inishark. Inishboffin. At their joggerfry. Mine. Slieve Bloom.

He halted before Dlugacz's window, staring at the hanks of sausages, polonies, black and white. Fifty multiplied by. The figures whitened in his mind unsolved: displeased, he let them fade. [Pp. 58-59]

In Bloom's mind the white chalk figures on the blackboard of the school are linked with black and white hanks of meat hanging in the window of the butcher's shop. The former fade away in Bloom's mind as the latter slowly grow more vivid and finally replace them. Where the cut in the previous passage was based on the similarity between the shape of the linked objects, the transition here, which is almost as smooth, seems to be based not only on shape but also on the similar color combinations of the linked objects. In all of these renderings space becomes almost hallucinatory (in the second, quite literally) as the mind becomes sovereign architect over its own physical reality, possessing and reshaping this reality according to the mind's moment-to-moment fears and desires.

Just as Joyce's spatial arrangements tend to be mental arrangements, so too his temporal arrangements tend to present themselves through the special tempo and dispositions of an individual mind. Time is no longer rendered as the human body seems to experience it in everyday life, chronologically, as a forward-moving, continuous flow; but rather time is dramatized as the mind experiences it, flashing from one temporal perspective to another in a series of swift transitionless jumps.

By far the longest section in *Ulysses*, virtually one quarter of the novel, is the "Circe" episode, in which Joyce projects the unconscious life of his protagonists outward, and all memory and desire seem to shift and glide before the eye of the reader in a dramatic and fully externalized form. At the beginning of one montage, for instance, Bloom imagines himself in conversation with his father, who promptly castigates him for wasting his money and drinking with gentiles. ("One night they bring you home drunk as dog after spend your good money" [p. 438]). Bloom, filled with guilt, remembers one such drinking bout from his youth. Upon the instant, the memory exteriorizes itself and Bloom suddenly appears

(In youth's smart blue Oxford suit with white vestslips, narrowshouldered, in brown Alpine hat, wearing gent's sterling silver waterbury keyless watch and double curb Albert with seal attached, one side of him coated with stiffening mud.) [P. 438]

Later in the same fantasy, upon remembering the night he flirted with Josie Breen at Georgina Simpson's housewarming, Bloom now enters as a

(Squire of dames, in dinner jacket, with watered-silk facings, blue masonic badge in his buttonhole, black bow and mother-of-pearl studs, a prismatic champagne glass tilted in his hand.) [P. 445]

Still later he recalls how, after his marriage, he and Molly accompanied the Breens to the Leopardstown races, and again a change in costume immediately embodies his thought and the new moment in time:

(In an oatmeal sporting suit, a sprig of woodbine in the lapel, tony buff shirt, shepherd's plaid Saint Andrew's cross scarftie, white spats, fawn dustcoat on his arm, tawny red brogues, fieldglasses in bandolier and a grey billycock hat.) [P. 448]

Throughout the fantasy, as his mind wanders up and down the years, Bloom undergoes other sartorial transformations to correspond to other points in time, and when his fantasy finally comes to an end, it does so in the manner of a film as the image of Mrs. Breen "fades from his side" (p. 449)

In film we measure time as a dimension of space. We learn to know different parts of time by looking at different parts of space, for in film we can finally see nothing but space. We see a young man sitting in a room, and then we see a dissolve to the same man sitting in the same room, but now his hair is gray and wrinkles line his face. Nothing has been said and we have not looked at the clock, and yet we know the years have passed, for our eyes have observed them as a temporal imprint upon a physical surface.

When Joyce visualizes and exteriorizes time, our eyes can literally wander about in time, as if it were, part of a solid and seemingly permanent landscape. In film, time is a quality that solidifies, just as space is a quantity that flows. Thus, in both film and the cinematographic novel, we can speak of either *space temporalized* (as in the passages from *Portrait*) or *time spatialized* (as in the "Circe" episode). Now, when properly speaking of narrative montage in film and novel, we do not speak of space *and* time, but rather we speak in the modern Einsteinian manner of space-time.[5]

Yet none of the quoted passages represents Joyce's most radical form of narrative montage. In these passages the discontinuity between one point in time and space and another is unified and sanctioned, as it were, by the consciousness of a specific character: we always know approximately where we are to the degree that we have come to know the habitual cast of the character's mind and the general nature of the dramatic situation in which he finds himself. But who sanctions and unifies the abrupt change of perspective in the following dialogue between Mulligan and Haines in the "Wandering Rocks" episode?

—We call it D.B.C. because they have damn bad cakes. O, but you missed Dedalus on *Hamlet*.
Haines opened his newbought book.
—I'm sorry, he said. Shakespeare is the happy hunting-ground of all minds that have lost their balance.
The onelegged sailor growled at the area of 14 Nelson street:
—*England expects* . . .
Buck Mulligan's primrose waistcoat shook gaily to his laughter.
—You should see him, he said, when his body loses its balance. Wandering Ængus I call him. [*Ulysses*, pp. 248-49]

[5]My remarks in this paragraph are based on the discussion by Stephenson and Debrix, *Cinema as Art*, pp. 132-36: "The two fundamental aspects of film, space and time, thus intermingle, interchange, interact. On the one hand the spatialization of time, on the other the temporalization of space. What a film shows us is space and nothing but space, so that this space has perforce to be used to express time. And yet on the other hand this space has to be *disposed* in time, has to be fitted into a temporal pattern. Again this temporal pattern is a continuously flexible one and enables us to move about in time as though it were space. These characteristics, at any rate, occurring so continuously and so flexibly, are peculiar to the cinema and make it something new and different both from reality and from any other art" (p. 136).

Does the cut to the "onelegged sailor" represent a thought in the mind of Haines? Mulligan? Both? Or does the entire conversation in the restaurant represent a thought in the mind of the sailor in Nelson Street? Obviously, the events described here do not take place in the mind of any one of the characters; and it is clear that the two separate actions have ostensibly nothing to do with each other. It is the mind of the author himself that sanctions and unifies the passage. Joyce has juxtaposed two distinct and quite disparate actions in order that we may perceive them simultaneously and thus understand that they are happening at the same time, but in different places. This is perhaps the most difficult and provocative of all of Joyce's montage procedures, for the effect is always, as it is here, that of dissonance, dislocation, and, on occasion, adventitiousness. It is also perhaps the richest of these procedures, for from within the dissonance emerge new and unexpected harmonies and unities.

This is exactly the kind of montage effect advocated in the writings, and often executed in the films, of Sergei Eisenstein, the most extreme and intensive of all the montage theorists and practitioners. Orienting his aesthetics in Marxist and Hegelian dialectics, Eisenstein tersely asserts that "montage is conflict,"[6] the collision of one image or perspective (thesis) against a totally disparate and unrelated image or perspective (antithesis) to form a new concept (synthesis) in the interaction of their union. Conventional montage practice—as it might appear, for example, in a Hollywood film—arranges the different perspectives so that the movement from one to the next will be seamless or, as it were, invisible, and the narrative flow unimpeded: that is, *without* conflict. Eisenstein, however, wishes to create a sense of dissonance between the images, not to advance the narrative, but in order to stimulate a richer, more thoughtful and complicated response in the mind of the viewer, to encourage him to think about the relationship between the shots, to perceive, in fact, the complex of thought and feeling that was in Eisenstein's mind when he decided upon the order of their relationship. In *October* (1928), for example, Eisenstein represents Kerenski's soldiers, the ancien régime, by shots of their medals and uniforms, which

---

[6]Reiterated throughout all of his writings—for instance, in "The Cinematographic Principle and the Ideogram," *Film Form*, p. 38.

he then juxtaposed against shots of wine glasses and tin soldiers. Separately, the two sets of shots bear almost no relation to each other; together, they bring Kerenski's soldiers into association with notions of decadence, shallowness, and puppetry. Eisenstein's methods were essentially a means of conveying an argument graphically, of transforming physical surfaces into a dimension of abstract discourse.[7] At their worst, the results of this abstract, or dialectical, montage effect (Eisenstein gave it many names) were often incoherent. At their simplest and most accessible they represented an immediate and effective form of agitprop; at their best they initiated a new film form, the cinematic analogue of the essay. (Variants of this approach to montage continue to appear, to a greater or lesser degree, in the work of many contemporary film artists, most notably Jean-Luc Godard.)

When Joyce interposes the conversation between Haines and Mulligan with the cry of the "onelegged sailor," he also, in the manner of Eisenstein, wishes to create a dissonance, a disturbing and startling effect, to show us that what we see and feel cannot sustain any prolonged order or linear sequence in time. Unlike Joyce's other techniques (such as the interior monologue), this is not an effect that will bear "getting used to." Like much of the great modernist art in the first quarter of the century—that is, like Schoenberg collocating the "wrong" notes, or like Picasso superimposing the front of a woman's face over her ear—Joyce's effect here is meant to give us a shock, a jolt of displacement, a sense of things not meshing: first we should feel uncomfortable—and only then begin to understand. We should begin to sense the underlying harmonies within the dissonance, the hints of continuity emerging from within the contraries, the possible reasons why Joyce brings these perspectives together in the first place.

We should sense that Joyce only cuts to the "onelegged sailor" immediately after Haines utters the word "balance," and then jumps back to the conversation when Mulligan remarks on Stephen's drinking habits and his body losing its balance. Obviously, through a punning juncture of verbal and visual effects ("balance" and balancing sailor), the disparate actions are united

---

[7]See Karel Reisz and Gavin Millar, *The Technique of Film Editing* (New York, 1968), pp. 33-40.

Montage 173

in an amusing and witty concept of mental and physical equilibrium. Moreover, Haines, an Englishman, expects to hear Mulligan's version of Stephen's Shakespeare theory, and his anticipation is reflected in the sailor's cry "England expects." On the other hand, the crosscut juxtaposes two very different kinds of Englishmen—a well-to-do snob and a bitter, begging sailor—and when Mulligan laughs, after both Haines and the sailor speak, the sequential ordering of the lines leads us to believe (though Mulligan himself is unaware of it) that Mulligan is laughing *at* Haines, not with him, as he sees the disparity between the two Englishmen. He then seems to have an extra reason for laughing, one that Haines is unaware of, and this in turn reminds us that Mulligan often amuses himself at the expense of the unsuspecting Haines.

But does Joyce have any, or all, of this in mind when he crosscuts the different perspectives? The point, I think, resides not so much in exactly what Joyce intended when he brought the perspectives together but that in bringing them together he knew that the combination itself would unlock any number of different meanings in different minds, meanings perhaps similar to those just discussed and certainly many others as well. Joyce might not have been aware of all of these meanings, but he must have known when he made such a dissonant combination—and it represents the quintessence of his way of working throughout and beyond *Ulysses*—that the combination itself was ripe with a multiplicity of associative possibilities. Dialectical montage, then, provides Joyce with a way of *abstracting* from his concretized form without ever really departing from it, of creating an atmosphere of intellection and symbolic resonance while working in and through a series of concretized actions. Now Joyce can inject his thought without interjecting his voice.

Dialectical montage, the conjunction of opposing perspectives, represents Joyce's widest application of the montage concept, an application on the largest scale which no longer results in specific visualized effects but which still may be considered a generalized principle of the cinematographic manner.[8] We see the montage

---

[8]While visualization appears, of course, to some degree in all eighteen episodes of *Ulysses*, certain episodes contain precious little of it, tend to make their main effects upon the ear rather than upon the eye and to manipulate the language in a centripetal manner, not as a reflector of the phenomenal world but rather as a

concept operative, for instance, in the nature of the portmanteau word as a conflict of linguistic perspectives, thus providing *Finnegans Wake* with its structural premise. This concept also represents the essential organizing principle behind the larger units of narrative action that comprise *Ulysses;* most notably, of course, it is the concept which juxtaposes the ancient story that Homer wrote against the modern one that Joyce wrote, which juxtaposes the spatiality of myth against the temporality of history, the past against the present.

For Joyce and many other novelists in the first quarter of this century, the montage principle represents a way of presenting truncations and limitations within the field of vision at the same time that it provides a way of going beyond them; it dramatizes partialized fields without a sacrifice of authorial neutrality. Montage allows the author something very like the luxuries of omniscience, the unique status of the epic artist, yet without the need for the bias that usually accompanied this position in the past. It allows him to open up the single perspective by juxtaposing it with other perspectives; it provides for scope and depth, crosscurrents of dialectical tensions, balances and contrasts, new conflicts and new continuities. In this sense montage is for the novelist of concretized form an act of liberation and transcendence, offering him the one viable literary means in the twentieth century for releasing epic and panoramic energies while also allowing for a modern, or relativistic, epistemology.

The montage artist encompasses for himself, and restores to the reader, a totality of life experience, a whole truth—yet a totality and a truth comprised of fragments and limited perspectives. William Faulkner's statement about the nature of reality in his own work could apply equally well not only to *Ulysses* but to those other novels that also embody the montage principle:

I think that no one individual can look at truth. It blinds you. You look at

---

self-reflector, a revealer of new and unexplored sonic and rhythmic possibilities (e.g., "The Sirens," "Oxen of the Sun"). Obviously in trying to grapple with a book like *Ulysses,* one has to make distinctions between those procedures and forms that are (*a*) not cinematographic at all, (*b*) those that are cinematographic in both principle and effect (like the truncated visual fields, the adventitious and peripheral details, the effects of anatomization and depthlessness, and space-time montage), and (*c*) those that are cinematographic in principle only but not in effect (like the portmanteau word).

Montage

it and you see one phase of it. Someone else looks at it and sees a slightly awry phase of it. But taken all together, the truth is in what they saw though nobody saw truth intact. . . . It is . . . thirteen ways of looking at a blackbird. But the truth, I would like to think, comes out, that when the reader has all these thirteen different ways of looking at the blackbird, the reader has his own fourteenth image of that blackbird which I would like to think is the truth.[9]

When we speak of montage on a scale this large and in such a generalized way, we are actually speaking of a modern structural tendency that has been widely commented on and is perhaps best known to us under other names: "composite" or "multiple perspective," "cubist perspective," "spatial form," "simultaneity."[10] But whatever critical rubric we may prefer, the student of modernism knows by now that the widest application of this principle represents a way, perhaps the major way, of unifying that diversity of revolutionary and unprecedented cultural achievement and experimentation that occurs from roughly 1914 through the early thirties. It gives us a way of gathering together a poem by Pound or Eliot, a film by Eisenstein or Pudovkin, a painting by Picasso or Braque, the physics of Einstein, the perspectivist philosophy of Ortega, and a book by Joyce written "from eighteen different points of view and in as many styles."[11]

In the history of the novel critics have marked the original appearance of the montage principle with the crosscutting in the famous Agricultural Fair scene in *Madame Bovary*, and Eisenstein himself was only too pleased to point out montage precedents in the work of such practitioners of concretized form as Zola and de Maupassant, and most notably in all the novels of that great transitional figure between the pre- and post-Flaubertian modes Charles Dickens.[12] It is, however, only in the first quarter of this

[9]Gwynn and Blotner, *Faulkner in the University*, pp. 273-74.

[10]For a discussion of multiple perspective, see Charles I. Glicksberg's *Modern Literary Perspectivism* (Dallas, 1970), pp. 17-28; for cubist perspective see Sypher's *Rococo to Cubism*, pp. 257-311; for spatial form see Joseph Frank's "Spatial Form in Modern Literature," in *A Grammar of Literary Criticism: Essays in Definition of Vocabulary, Concepts, and Aims*, ed. Lawrence Sargent Hall (New York, 1965), pp. 417-25.

[11]Joyce to Harriet Shaw Weaver (1921), quoted by Ellmann in *James Joyce*, p. 526.

[12]For a discussion of the scene in Flaubert, see Joseph Frank's "Spatial Form in Modern Literature," pp. 420-21; Eisenstein's famous essay "Dickens, Griffith, and the Film Today" is in *Film Form*, pp. 195-255.

century that the montage principle comes into its own, fully emerges as the preeminent period style for the modernist fiction of the twenties and early thirties. In this era the widest variety of montage effects—in both their generalized and specific forms, temporalized space and spatialized time as well as multiple narrative views—appears in the art of Andrey Biely (*St. Petersburg*), Faulkner (*The Sound and the Fury, As I Dying*), Huxley (*Point Counter Point*) and David Jones (*In Parenthesis*); and then as a generalized cinematic principle, but not as a visualized effect, in the fiction of Gide (*The Counterfeiters*) and in certain novels of interior form, such as those of Virginia Woolf (*Mrs. Dalloway, To the Lighthouse*).

Beyond the first great period of the modernist endeavor, however, there is a noticeable reluctance by the novelist to pursue the kind of large and multifaceted truth that marked the era of Faulkner and Joyce. At the same time there is also a significant decline in the serious employment of the montage technique. Even some of the concretized artists that we associate with early modernism could not be legitimately described as montage artists; Hemingway, for instance, could not, nor could Fitzgerald. Nor can most of the important artists since the original modernist movement be considered montage-oriented: these artists include such major post-Joycean practitioners of concretized form as Camus, West, and Nabokov; as well as major interior artists such as Beckett or Borges. Of all the cinematographic effects that we have discussed, montage, generally speaking, has probably fared the least well on the contemporary scene as the serious artist has preferred to work less boldly but perhaps more confidently within the novel of limited perspective, the sustained drama of a single center of consciousness. The obvious and important exceptions to this general observation would be the attempts at multiplane effects by Sartre in his tetralogy, *The Roads to Freedom*, and most recently in certain novels by Michel Butor, notably *Degrees*. Montage also appears, perhaps most famously, in the work of John Dos Passos (as in the following passage from *Nineteen Nineteen*, 1932):

> The blood ran into the ground, the brains oozed out of the cracked skull and were licked up by the trenchrats, the belly swelled and raised a generation of bluebottle flies,

Montage

and the incorruptible skeleton,
and the scraps of dried viscera and skin bundled in khaki

they took to Châlons-sur-Marne
and laid it out neat in a pine coffin
and took it home to God's Country on a battleship
and buried it in a sarcophagus in the Memorial Amphitheatre in the Arlington National Cemetery

and draped the Old Glory over it
and the bugler played taps
and Mr. Harding prayed to God and the diplomats and the generals and the admirals and the brasshats and the politicians and the handsomely dressed ladies out of the society column of the *Washington Post* stood up solemn

and thought how beautiful sad Old Glory God's Country it was to have the bugler play taps and the three volleys made their ears ring.[13]

Dos Passos by his own admission came under the influence of both Joyce and Eisenstein.[14] The crosscutting of four different levels of American experience in the *U.S.A.* trilogy (completed 1937)—in sections of straight narrative (the individual view), "Newsreel" (the topical view), biography (the public view), and "Camera Eye" (the private view)—indicates the scope of the book's technical achievement and provides one of the few serious examples of sustained multiple perspective in the post-Joycean era. *U.S.A.* is a fine accomplishment, and yet we would no doubt think it even finer if we could push from memory the more radical and complex montage achievements of *Ulysses, As I lay Dying,* and *St. Petersburg.* In certain ways Dos Passos embodies the last resurgence of the bold technical experimentation that marked the modernism of the twenties, but in comparison with its predecessors, his famous technique also reveals an intellectual softening, a dilution and simplification of the very montage procedures that once appeared in forms of concentration and difficulty.

Joyce employs his disparate perspectives in a dialectical manner to create a sense of dissonance. Dos Passos creates a simpler

[13]*Nineteen Nineteen,* in *U.S.A.* (New York, 1937), p. 472-73.
[14]Harry T. Moore reported Dos Passos's remarks in a discussion with students: "Dos Passos further said that his work had been influenced by Defoe, Fielding, Smollett, and Joyce, as well as the film director Eisenstein" (Preface, *Dos Passos, the Critics, and the Writer's Intention,* ed. Allen Belkind [Carbondale and Edwardsville, Ill., 1971], pp. xi-xii).

and more obvious effect by arranging his disparate perspectives in an additive manner to create—or at least to move toward—a sense of assonance, to make them accumulate steadily and, as it were, flesh out his general attitude. And in most instances this attitude is the characteristic Dos Passos blend of irony, cynicism, and anger. The prose is intentionally cast into a hard-drilled mechanical rhythm that seems to transform all nuance of gesture and feeling into a form of process data, a hard fact that becomes virtually immune to value or sentiment. In the passage above, the body of a man (the warm materiality of "blood," "belly," and "the incorruptible skeleton") is transformed into an "it," into the function of a shallow public ritual, a cliché ("God's Country," "Old Glory"); and by the time the body comes to Arlington Cemetery, it has already been sucked into the stream of "and . . . and . . . and," and virtually reduced to a kind of blather, a drivel of coordination.

Because Joyce's perspectives, even within their union, strive to maintain their integral distance from one another, their combined effects are always multileveled and always manage to evoke a variety of resonances and analogies. The Dos Passos montage operates essentially on a single level, and no matter how disparate the juxtaposed perspectives seem to be, they always manage to come together and merge in one strong, clear gesture of social protest. Where Joyce seems to arrive at dialectical montage by way of Flaubert and Dickens, Dos Passos seems to arrive at additive montage by way of an essentially American tradition, the tradition of Melville and Whitman, the epic catalogers and list-makers of American space.

From *Leaves of Grass* to *Of Time and the River,* and even beyond, a long line of serious American novelists and poets has tried to cultivate large and amorphous literary forms in an effort to embody their sense of the diversity and plenitude of American space, the vastness in which they live, and, even more, the vastness that lives in their minds and imaginations: a dream of a great American space that has neither beginning nor end; for Cooper it was a forest; for Melville, an ocean; for Whitman, an open road that wanders beyond all boundaries and finally ends where it began, in the poet's song. "I take SPACE," said another American poet, Charles Olson, "to be the central fact to man born in America. . . . I spell it large because it comes large here. Large, and without mercy."[15]

Thus, montage effects seem to come naturally, as it were, to American artists, and these effects are almost always additive, for the American's sense of his space has been invariably quantitative; its boundlessness has run along a giant horizontal: *Moby-Dick, Leaves of Grass, U.S.A.; The Birth of a Nation* and the westerns of John Ford; the Sears Roebuck Catalog; a canvas by Jackson Pollock; the *Holidays Symphony* of Charles Ives (originally conceived for four different orchestras, each playing from a different point in the Grand Canyon!).

In the thirties the American artist's drive to encompass the infinitude of the American space joins with a sense of social outrage, of a dream betrayed, of a greatness pillaged by a minority of the rich and the powerful. Now the large-scale literary forms and the additive montage effects serve the various forms of anguish, bitterness, and lament and thus shape the characteristic profile of the protest literature of the thirties: the novels of Dos Passos; Steinbeck's *The Grapes of Wrath*; Agee's *Let Us Now Praise Famous Men*; Farrell's *Studs Lonigan* trilogy. Traces of additive montage remain in the long prose-poem novels of Thomas Wolfe and still appear even as late as the "time-machine" interludes in Mailer's *The Naked and the Dead*.

In the fiction of William Burroughs the additive montage tendencies that appear throughout American fiction are brought to something very like their final ends. There is always the risk in any montage effect that the perspectives will be so thoroughly segregated from any specific spatial and temporal context that they will not make any sense when placed in sequence. Burroughs uses montage in its most radically additive manner to create effects of all-but-controlled accident and confusion, concrete fragments almost devoid of any knowable context, accumulating in a kaleidoscopic jumble (as in *Naked Lunch*, 1959):

a thousand boys come at one in outhouses, bleak public school toilets, attics, basements, treehouses, Ferris wheels, deserted houses, limestone caves, rowboats, garages, barns, rubbly windy city outskirts behind mud walls (smell of dried excrement). . . .

[15]*Call Me Ishmael* (San Francisco, 1947), p. 11.

Time jump like a broken typewriter, the boys are old men, young hips quivering and twitching in boy-spasms go slack and flabby, draped over an outhouse seat, a park bench, a stone wall in Spanish sunlight, a sagging furnished room bed (outside red brick slum in clear winter sunlight)....

The Old Man scream curses after him . . . his teeth fly from his mouth and whistle over the boy's head, he strain forward, his neck-cords tight as steel hoops, black blood spurt in one solid piece over the fence and he fall a fleshless mummy by the fever grass. Thorns grow through his ribs, the windows break in his hut, dusty glass-slivers in black putty—rats run over the floor and boys jack off in the dark musty bedroom on summer afternoons and eat the berries that grow from his body and bones, mouths smeared with purple-red juices.... [16]

I have chosen these extracts virtually at random, for Burroughs is the creator of single unrelenting effect, and everywhere in his books that effect is essentially the same. The classic American large-scale gestures are all present—the catalogs, the names, the places, the hard prose that lapses from time to time into a kind of lyric crooning, the language used as a kind of universal enveloper of all time and all space—and yet all of this serves a satanic vision of death, disgust, and universal decomposition, of a landscape in the midst of coming apart.

Burroughs employs montage to show us people and objects, times and spaces, in the process of crossing the thresholds and boundary lines of their physical identities, of flesh literally dissolving to its molecular parts, and then remerging into new hybrid forms. If the Joycean montage was a verbal analogue of a cubist approach to perspective (different perspectives sustained within a dialectical tension), then Burrough's montage is the verbal analogue of an action painting in which a myriad of tiny perspectives are merged and all but obliterated to serve the feeling of the artist.

Burrough's montage perhaps best illustrates the present tendency in our culture which seeks to dissolve oppositions, distinctions, boundary lines—between form and content, artist and audience, literature and junk, art and antiart. Burroughs transposes this tendency to the cosmic scale and gives us a vision of

[16]*Naked Lunch* (New York, 1959), pp. 94-95.

universal breakdown, of total superimposition where everything seems to be everywhere at the same time. It is the vision of a chaos that succeeds a decreation.

I think it is clear from the foregoing that while concretized form has endured, montage in its richest, most intensive (and perhaps truest) form has not. Dialectical montage—montage as conflict—remains essentially the period style of early modernism, one of the few ways that we have of representing and ultimately defining that period as a cultural entity. Stephen Spender has argued that one of the central achievements of this period was the artist's attempt to present a "vision of the whole" and that the following period represents a reaction against this vision—and in effect, I would add, against montage itself:

> It is also the characteristic of the reaction against modernism, which accepts the idea that there can only be "minor" fragmented art. Thus today when poets and critics say that they aim at elegance and correctness of form, they reveal that they have accepted the idea of writing within a fragmentary part of the fragmented situation, instead of trying to comprehend the situation itself in a single vision that restores wholeness to the fragmentation, even by realizing it as disaster, as the waste land, or night-town. . . . *Ulysses* and *Finnegans Wake* may not be complete successes. It is difficult to imagine how they could be, considering that the aim of Joyce in *Ulysses* was to invent an imaginative form which would express the whole experience of modern life, and in *Finnegans Wake*, the whole of history. They were gigantic achievements which include elements of gigantic failure. But to dismiss them as mere "experiments" . . . is to overlook what remains truly important and challenging about them: that they attempt to envisage the past as a whole complexity enclosed within a consciousness conditioned by circumstances that are entirely of today. They state a challenge which perhaps they did not meet and which perhaps cannot be met, although they indicate the scale of the challenge. And what has come after [these] works . . . is fragments of a fragmented view of civilization, and is on an altogether lesser scale.[17]

I think that the montage concept, though Spender makes no mention of it, can be seen as the principal technique for the embodiment of the modernist's vision of wholeness. And if we think that the quality of the literature that comes after this vision

---

[17]Stephen Spender, "The Modern as a Vision of the Whole," *The Struggle of the Modern* (Berkeley and Los Angeles, 1965), pp. 81-83.

represents a falling off from what went before it, one of the ways in which we might measure the extent of this decline would be to measure the extent of the artist's unwillingness to employ the montage principle—which is to say, his unwillingness to take risks, to restore "wholeness to the fragmentation."

Epilogue

He did not think much or trouble much. So long as he kept this sheer immediacy of blood-contact with the substantial world he was happy, he wanted no intervention of visual consciousness. In this state there was a certain rich positivity, bordering sometimes on rapture. Life seemed to move in him like a tide lapping, lapping, and advancing, enveloping all things darkly. It was a pleasure to stretch forth the hand and meet the unseen object, clasp it, and possess it in pure contact. He did not try to remember, to visualise.

—D. H. Lawrence, "The Blind Man"

And yet I am happy. Yes, happy. I swear, I swear I am happy. I have realized that the only happiness in this world is to observe, to spy, to watch, to scrutinize oneself and others, to be nothing but a big, slightly vitreous, somewhat bloodshot, unblinking eye. I swear that this is happiness.

—Vladimir Nabokov, *The Eye*

Comment C'est

THE CUSTOMARY FORM of a book teases us with the false notion that its subject concludes with its final page. Let us not be so easily misled: cinematographic literary forms are as much with us today as they were over a century ago, and there is no good reason to believe that they will not continue to be with us for at least some time to come.

Perhaps we have even gotten more than we bargained for. Film was a new fact for a modern like Faulkner, but for a contemporary like Nabokov it is already a given fact, one of the preeminent facts of the present cultural scene. If the cinema has not yet become the richest art of our time—has not yet given us everything we had hoped for—it has undoubtedly become the most popular art and possibly the most influential. Nowadays it becomes increasingly more attractive for the other arts to play follow-the-leader with the movies and often to do so with hybrid results that can seem embarrassingly self-conscious and, on occasion, labored to grotesquerie. The form of a great novel may indeed be like the form of a movie, as we have seen, but to write a novel in conscious imitation of a movie often only results in a kind of literary second fiddling, an attempt to do in one medium what can obviously be done better in another.

As movie equipment becomes less expensive, it becomes easier for certain contemporary writers to do what their eccentric writing methods told us they should have been doing all along: telling stories with a camera. Joyce's use of cinematic form virtually precedes his belated and ambiguous awareness of film, while Robbe-Grillet, as if in conscious recognition of the contemporary writer's quandary, leaves off writing his meticulous imitations of camera setups in order to set up a real camera and make movies (*L'Immortelle, L'Eden et après*). After all, if you want to describe physical surfaces with clarity and exactitude, the photographic image will not only do the job more effectively than words, but, as the ads say, will save you time and energy as well. Nowadays, when nobody is anything if not a technocrat, it is obvious that some writers want to enjoy not only the aesthetic economies of film mechanics but the wonders of it as well: arcane movie equipment like "dimmer banks" and "integral bipacks" doubtless has a hermetic and technological chic that the pen or typewriter cannot hope to rival. Beyond this, it is almost too obvious to speak of the enormous sums of money associated with the movie business, or, just as obvious, the size of the movie-going public itself, which is, or certainly can be, commensurate with any writer's most extravagant fantasies of power and exhibition. I suppose there is really no other way to explain why one of our most gifted writers, Norman Mailer, periodically abandons his good writing to make bad movies.

However, most contemporary writers who practice cinematographic forms have no intention of making films. They practice these forms because it suits their expressive purposes to do so and because the literature they have read and admired, the cinematic literature of the recent past, acts as both a formative context and stimulus for their own activities. The reason why this literature has come to be the way it is, as I have argued, has probably had more to do with changes in philosophic attitude and cognition than with the advent of the motion picture. One may even suggest, in fact, that both concretized literary forms and the modern passion for the film represent advanced expressions of the epistemology that we have been subtilizing and refining now for well over a century. We do not necessarily approve of our idea of reality, but can we live by any other? We now take it for granted that we cannot come to know or do a thing without first looking at it; that the meaning of what we see will be inseparable from the way in which we see it; and that no one acts in the world any more without awareness and forethought. Engagement without reflection, doing without knowing, has become in our time an unspeakably unnatural practice.

Yet who of us would want to admit that this, and only this, is what we have come to? Many of us are still hopeful and buoyant enough to conceive of a culture of spontaneity, involvement, and rapport as something very like a lost paradise of the human spirit. We want to believe in an earlier, better, more "primitive" life as something more than an anthropologist's dream, something

Epilogue: Comment C'est

more than some old wives' tale that has survived the past to haunt the present—because we know that we may disbelieve in this life only at the risk of total despair. The great tales and fables of Western culture have given us so many instances of cautionary advice about the perils of curiosity, self-consciousness, even ocular vision itself, that we cannot help but retain some notion of their opposites as equally viable attitudes.

When Psyche was visited every night under the cover of darkness by Eros, she took pleasure in her love as long as she could not see her lover. When she held a glowing lamp, the light of her sad enlightenment, above the sleeping body of Eros, she *saw* and knew the nature and object of her love and in that very instant lost it: the sleeping god awoke and vanished. The moment Psyche understood her experience, the experience itself became impossible, took a different and less satisfactory form never to be the same again. When the hunter Actaeon looked upon the body of the goddess Diana bathing in a stream, the horns of his voyeur's passion sprouted through the top of his head. Ravished by a rude eye, the goddess transformed the hunter into a stag to be devoured by his own hounds, analogues of his greedy, self-consuming lust. Gods do not like to be looked at any more than they like to give their names (even Moses got mystification from the Burning Bush), and the sacred will not tolerate too much human understanding of its forms and operations. When a mystery is seen and thus understood, it is no mystery; and the understanding of the sacred is its profanation. This is what Theseus knew when with reverential eyes he looked away from the transfiguration of Oedipus in the sacred groves at Colonus.

The most evocative myth of our Judeo-Christian culture—perhaps it is the central myth—also dramatizes the difference between blind devotion and corrupt sight. Genesis tells us that before the Fall, Adam and Eve "were both naked" and "were not ashamed"; that is, they were naked but did not know it, did not see each other *as* naked, just as anything that we love and trust by instinct cannot ever, in any objective sense, be empirically seen or rationally known. When the Serpent, the most knowing ("subtile") of all wild creatures, entices Eve to eat of the forbidden tree, he explains that her "eyes shall be opened" and that the tree itself is "pleasant to the eyes." And when she and Adam eat of the fruit, we are indeed told that "the eyes of them both were opened, and they *knew* that they were naked (italics in original)." Immediately Adam and Eve perform the first act of human separation from the world: "they sewed fig leaves together, and made themselves aprons." Each hides a part of himself from the other, and when the Lord comes looking for them, they hide from him too.

The Fall of Adam and Eve is a fall from unknowing rapport and blind union—with each other and their Maker—and a fall into sad wisdom and open-eyed estrangement. Their story is a parable of human emergence into self-consciousness and a demonstration of two different kinds of knowledge. Before the Fall there is only the subrational wisdom of affection, where the exercise of the eye is diminished in the passion of one's rapport with an object (spouse, garden, God). After the Fall there are only stratagems, tact, and forethought, where the exercise of the eye becomes a function of empirical wisdom and daily life a form of constant scrutiny.

In all the old stories, both pagan and Christian, assertion of the conscious eye is both gain and loss. Each effort of mind and eye to comprehend the world results in the subject's increased knowledge of, and independence from, its object; yet each effort also results in a corresponding decrease in wonder, harmony, and union. There is, of course, more in these myths than I have indicated, but I think the point is already clear: the way we live now represents the very forms and variants of the mental conduct for which the gods punished Actaeon, Psyche, Adam and Eve. Our characteristic cultural activities and forms of entertainment—films, television, a theater of images, a concretized fiction—emphasize the visual modality above all others because for well over a century now we have cultivated and enriched a spectator's idea of the world, a psychology of the voyeur, a philosophy and a feeling tone of the tourist and the *isolato*. We have held Psyche's lamp high above the body of reality for so long a time now that it is hard to conceive of our daily lives in terms other than those of a kind of desperate, ongoing scopophilia.[1]

---

[1] In this paragraph, I am intentionally ignoring the experiments in participatory art forms that emerged during the sixties—the Living Theater, street theater,

Epilogue: Comment C'est

The loss of rapport with one's world, the separation of the seer from the seen, has been one of the central assumptions of the fiction we have called modern for as long as any of us can probably remember. As we have already noted, this assumption most often appears in the novel in either one of two forms: an interior form or a cinematographic form. This latter form has, of course, been the main subject of this discussion, but in either of these forms we can discover the full panoply of characteristically modern themes and attitudes that result from a position of self-conscious estrangement from the world: passivity, isolation, solipsism, memory obsession, relativism, disorder, terror, and nihilism.

Not a pretty picture, but then no modern reader comes to this literature, *his* literature, expecting pretty pictures. I once knew a woman who did not want to read modern literature, not because she found it difficult, but because she found it hopeless. She could understand it well enough, but it did not make her want to live. I suppose we could say that this woman was reading fiction for all the wrong reasons, that one should not go to a book for "uplift" anyway and that perhaps this woman wanted to find in modern fiction exactly what she could not find in modern life. But, on the other hand, we know exactly what she was talking about—and that she was right: much of our best literature has been without hope.

Still, many of us would no doubt find this woman's complaint old fashioned, not in her analysis of modern literature, but in the

---

Happenings, wrap-around movie screens, do-it-yourself novel kits, etc.— because these movements no longer seem to apply to the present cultural situation, which is fundamentally a continuation of the situation as it existed *before* the sixties (When was the last time any of us attended a Happening or even read about one?). I think these new art movements failed to root themselves in the culture not only because their respective presentations often lacked craft and imagination, or because the political crisis that helped to bring them into being is no longer with us in the same exacerbated form, but precisely because our ingrained cultural style of ocular distance and passivity would not allow us to take pleasure in them. I think these forms often embarrassed most of us because they made us aware that we did not know how to make ourselves respond to them.

The real cultural legacy of the sixties has been a preference for mixed-media forms of presentation, in other words, a resurgence of one of the characteristic artistic endeavors of the twenties.

fact that she could still care enough to make a fuss about it. When we can tick off the themes and attitudes of our fiction as I have above, like so many items on a shopping list, then perhaps the time has come for us to admit that these words no longer move us to vigorous response and that now we would like to know what else is new in the world. We have heard these words (or words like them) reiterated so often for so long—perhaps all our lives—that now the very sound of them only provokes a familiar numbness: who wants to hear this schoolboy's codification of contemporary anguish all over again? Who even wants to hear again our recognition of the acknowledged origins of this anguish? Industrialization, urbanization, a debilitating nuclear technology, the loss of a unifying structure of value and belief, and so on, and so on. Is this litany any help at all? Where we are now seems so far from where we have been that I am not at all certain that it helps us any longer to know how we got there. How does one go back? What does one go back to? We have lived so long with a literature of estrangement—indeed, within the conditions of an estranged life—that it is virtually impossible for many of us to know what it must have been like to live with some other kind of literature, some other kind of life. What is new, then, about our present situation is that we no longer worry about the fact that we used to think it was awful. If we thought our condition to be worse than it is, it would no doubt begin to get better. The fact that it does not begin to get better tells us that things could get a lot worse and that the way we live now has become easy to endure. If we have any new problem at all, it is that we have learned to accept our old problem: our suffering has become a bore even to ourselves.

Too cynical? Perhaps. After all, one should realize that any body of thought that has been absorbed as thoroughly as the content of modernism is bound to lose some of its force. Besides, that lamenting woman was responding to modernism as such, and in this, too, she has again proved herself to be old fashioned. In the past thirty years or so we have seen the rise of a new body of literature with a new theme and a new attitude. We call this new literature "postmodern," and its new theme seems to provoke not hopelessness but apathy, not despair but tedium; in other words, its emotional spring has been calibrated to gauge our present mood.

Epilogue: Comment C'est

The new theme of the new literature has been precisely the formal nature of literature itself. The structures and techniques of fiction have become the new subjects of fiction. Our cultural style of self-conscious estrangement and ocular distance has finally separated us from the literary form that for two centuries was the one we liked best, the one that was so necessary a part of our cultural well-being—so much a source of pleasure and rapport—that we thought we could take its presence for granted. For two centuries the novel was a necessary part of our lives, for it was the one literary form that assured us that we were a necessary part of it, that we could always count on it to show us what we were, the way we lived, how we got on in the world, how the world we lived in really worked. We read a novel and found that it read us, put a mirror to our gazing faces.

At least that is what we thought. How could we have been so gullible, so vain, so blind? The new fiction asks us to open our eyes and *see* the novel for what it is, to remove it from the orbit of our rapport, to disengage it from the ardor of our passionate absorption in it. We see now that the novel was no mirror but that all along it had been only a fiction, a structure of words transparent enough to make us forget that they were only words. No mirror here, just language, style, technique—a magician's act. The new fiction shows us how the tricks were done and how we were all taken in.

By "new fiction," I am referring, of course, to the fiction that made its most auspicious debut in France after the Second World War, most notably in the work of Queneau, Sarraute, Butor, and Robbe-Grillet, and rapidly found critical and philosophical support in the French academy (perhaps no other avant-garde in history has gained so dubious a distinction so quickly). It now finds adherents in both North and South America: in the work of Barth, Barthelme, Gass, and Pynchon; and in the work of Borges, Cortázar, Donoso, and Márquez. The Irish-Gallic writer Samuel Beckett seems to be the lone cosmopolite in the group. Combining all of these greatly varied talents into a single school, or movement, is of course, only a way of facilitating critical discourse, and a way too of adding a small measure of artificial order to a literary scene that is still too much with us to be fully understood. (The differences, for instance, between Beckett and

Robbe-Grillet are, I think, more important than their similarities). Where many of these artists—but not all[2]—bridge geographical and metaphysical gaps is in their common awareness that their mode of conveyance, the novel form itself, has now become synonymous with the object to be conveyed, the story that is told.

To be sure, the new modernism has its sources in the old modernism, in the formal experimentation of Proust, Joyce, and Faulkner, in the stylistic innovations of Gertrude Stein and the young Hemingway. No one, however, who has ever read the fiction of these artists (save perhaps for the fiction of Stein) could ever believe for even a moment that he was reading *only* an exercise in language and form. One was always aware of the words themselves, but one was also aware of what the words

---

[2]While all of these artists come together in their experimental and nonmimetic approaches to the problems of fiction, they also separate into two distinct groups around the issue of literary belief. The first group—the more traditional of the two—attempts to promote the credibility of its narrative content (the characters and the action), however fantastic and unprecedented, and usually asks of its readers the customary "willing suspension of disbelief." The second group—far more tendentious than the first—seeks to destroy narrative credibility (in character and action) and compels its readers, willing or not, to an exercise of disbelief. The first group includes the Latin American writers, who are to my mind now writing the most original and viable new fiction in the West and provides us with highly personal and imaginative recreations of many of the older forms of fantasy, Gothicism, and romance (e.g., science fiction and adventure thrillers in Borges, modes of surealist juxtaposition in Cortázar). The theme of literary-form-as-literary-subject appears in this group only intermittently (and perhaps even less than that in Borges), but when it does appear (as in Cortázar's admirable *Hopscotch*), it does so as a dramatic component within the narrative context, a component that enriches rather than diminishes the meaning of the narrative. The burden of my remarks throughout this epilogue does not really apply to this group at all, but rather to the second group, which includes most of the French contingent and represents an extension of what I have already called, following Robbe-Grillet, a "literature of disappointment" (see pp. 129–30). I would place the American writers in either one group or the other and sometimes in both: the "scientific fiction" of Pynchon in the first group, the later work of Barth (*Lost in the Funhouse*, *Chimera*) and Gass (*Willie Master's Lonesome Wife*) in the second. The peripatetic Barthelme seems to hustle tentatively from one group to the other with each new literary invention (into group one with brilliant pieces like "Report" and "The Indian Uprising" and into group two with doodles of language and syntax like "Sentence" and "Bone Bubbles"). In a similar manner Beckett's *Trilogy* probably belongs in the first (though I'm less sure here; *The Unnamable* seems ripe for a conversion), while *Comment C'est* and *Texts for Nothing* fit easily into the second.

Epilogue: Comment C'est

were saying, and one found in this fiction what one had always found in the fiction of previous eras: character and narrative action. If the modern heroes—Swann, Bloom, Quentin Compson, Nick Adams—did not provide us with "uplift" or opiates, one had no trouble in identifying with them and participating in the life of their feelings. There was also in the despair of much of this fiction, as in all true despair, a kind of dark vitality and even a grandeur. If this fiction did not make us want to live, it reminded us of what it was to live, exposed us to the full dark power of despair and shook us into deep feeling. In this there was a kind of pleasure

The new fiction does not move us to this kind of deep feeling (or perhaps to any kind) because it does not allow us to participate in the life of a character and a narrative action. It negates character and action by systematically compelling us to scrutinize the means that produced them. It asks us to forego the experience of the novel by compelling us to examine the processes of the novel, that is to say, it asks us to forego the game by making us read the rules.

In this sense the intentions, if not always the effects, of fiction like *Jealousy, Lost in the Funhouse,* and *Comment C'est* may be understood, in part, as polemical, adversative, antidotal, and purgative. The most recent examples of cinematographic form, for instance, function as virtual emetics for the reader's experience of an older kind of concretized narrative. Those practitioners of the new fiction who can legitimately be called cinematographic—Simon, Le Clézio, Butor, and of course, Robbe-Grillet—seem to perform a rite of exorcism on the methodologies of Joyce, Faulkner, and Hemingway. Where the earlier fiction asked us to see, the new fiction seems to ask us *only* to see—to see, as it were, with a vengeance. It reiterates much of the earlier technique but now in hypertrophied and grotesque form. It tries, however unconsciously, to rid us of our old visual enthusiasms by allowing us to have them—and nothing else. The effect of this literary purge is a kind of death by satiation.

It is not easy to take pleasure in the visualized narrative of, say, *Sanctuary* after one confronts the hypertrophy of such a manner in the descriptive surfeit of, say, *Jealousy*. Certainly not after one has read the numberless accounts of bric-a-brac and bibelots, rooms and furniture; the frozen displays of material surface and human gesture; the curious blurrings and ellipses of landscape and behavior. Such a work reads as if the customary content of a novel—character, plot, narrative, drama—had been dismantled into its component parts, scrambled up, and then left to lie about the pages of a book like what is left on a battlefield after the contesting armies have pulled out.

I know that this description exaggerates, but there are times when giving complete literary justice to a work demands a larger effort than most of us are going to want to make, and especially when we know that the work itself is not going to reward us for making it. In this respect some of the new novelists might remind us more than a little of Ovid's Medea, a wild witch who was allowed to dismember old King Pelias because she promised his daughters that she would later reassemble him into a younger, stronger king. But Medea flew off with her job only half done, leaving the remains of Pelias still hot and twitching in his daughters' hands. Like Medea, the new fictionalists often perform death without regeneration, and some of us, like those stunned and angry daughters, might want to know whether it was worthwhile hacking up the old king if the executioner will not provide us with a new one.

It is hard to believe that many readers will find solace in all the "pure form" arguments that we hear nowadays; or that it will help much to learn how the new fiction, by finally ridding itself of character, plot, and drama has at last "caught up" with nonprogrammatic music and abstract painting; or how we are not supposed to ask any longer what a novel means but are simply to "enjoy it for its own sake" as a self-referring "project" in language and syntax. Unfortunately, it is a little hard to rejoice when all this "purity" finally overtakes the one literary experience that we valued for its impurity, whose unique value and definition depended on its formalized expression of our world, not of its own technical devices. Don't intelligent critics like Susan Sontag and Richard Gilman ever stop to wonder about such embarrassing fundamentals as whether language really lends itself to the same kind of stripping and draining that we agreeably associate with the nonrepresentational deployment of colors and musical sounds? After all, it is virtually impossible to separate a word from its meaning without violating its essential nature—its *true* purity, if you will—which consists precisely in its paradoxical and

Epilogue: Comment C'est

double-sided identity as both a reflection of something in the world and a distinctive aural presence. Nowadays, the new novelists (and some new critics too) are all for repressing the "worldly" side of the word, but you do not have to be even nearly as intelligent as Susan Sontag to know that such a repression results not in a new word but in a sound. Does a novel full of such sounds constitute anyone's idea of pleasure? Isn't *Finnegans Wake* still the greatest example of the postmodern manner in fiction, not because its narrative continually dissolves and evaporates into music, but precisely because its music continually toughens and clarifies into narrative, because all that chiming, ringing, and soaring sound, at its best, strives toward the revelation of some story, some character, some thing?

Because words are tied to their implications and associations, there is only so much one can do with the form of the novel before one works it down into gibberish and vacuity. If current practice is any standard, the form of the novel does not seem to be infinitely malleable. You can neologize the words, scramble the chronology, spatialize the syntax, transfer the story to tape or toilet paper, but as long as your medium is language, it is hard to see how you can prevent the reader from trying to get what the words themselves, no matter what you do to them, will be trying to give him: and that is the whole history of their meaning in past usage. Moreover, how can you ask your reader to view the novel as a construct of words that do not refer to anything outside themselves if the reader himself has not spent his life among the deaf and the dumb? Why is it that every time we open a serious new novel nowadays, we must pretend that we have never been born?

How *are* we to read these new books? One critic and practitioner of the new fiction, Ronald Sukenick, exemplifies the confusion at the heart of the "pure form" arguments when he insists that "we have to learn to think about the novel as . . . existing in the realm of experience rather than of discursive meaning and available to multiple interpretations, or none, depending on how you feel about it—like the way that girl pressed against you in the subway."[3] Perhaps this is what is really meant by "pure form," perhaps it all comes down to "the way that girl

---

[3]"The New Tradition," *Partisan Review,* 39 (Fall 1972), 583.

pressed against you in the subway." When literature approaches the final phase of its being, the truest perfection of its form—a "pure form" stripped of all "discursive meaning"—it becomes miraculously synonymous with life itself, the rawest of raw materials, a verbal Rorschach, and you can take it or leave it, "depending on how you feel about it." But perhaps when all of this begins to happen, when literature approaches such a condition, you may very well begin to wonder (doubtless as you stand in the subway) whatever happened to the novel as a work of art?

I think Sukenick reveals, perhaps unwittingly, what really does happen to it, that this version of "pure form" is really not much different from the mess we are living in every minute of the day; that "pure form" is really a way of disposing altogether of the novel as a work of art. Rather than talk about "pure form" at all, then, perhaps we need to say something much less exalted: perhaps we need to say that recent fiction is a way of getting us from a fiction that already exists to one that has not yet been written; at the very least it is certainly a way of bringing past fiction to the end of its tether.

I suppose that the sooner we admit at least this much to ourselves, the sooner we can stop asking of recent fiction what it obviously has no intention of giving us: a restoration of earlier kinds of novelistic satisfactions. What I want to know, then, is where will we take our pleasures in narrative fiction now that the novel itself no longer seems interested in giving them to us? I do not think that it will surprise anyone to learn, nor am I the first to point it out, that for some time now people who care about the novel have been going to the movies. Almost since its inception, and with incredible ease and rapidity, the film has been assimilating all the old narrative forms and dramatic materials that were once thought to lie within the special province of the novel.[4] Epic, saga, romance, chronicle, social history, biography, confession, the old tales of crime, passion, adventure, sentiment, and terror—all of this has now become part of the stock material and continuing repertory of the film. There is probably more rich and

---

[4] "But the main impetus of narrative art may well pass from the book to the cinema, even as it passed from the oral poet to the book-writer long ago" (Robert Scholes and Robert Kellogg, *The Nature of Narrative* [New York, 1966], p. 281).

Epilogue: Comment C'est

leisurely appreciation of character and environment, more development and sweep, more analytic depth and spatial panorama—more, that is, of all the old novelistic experiences and delights in great films like *Intolerance, Greed, Grand Illusion, Citizen Kane, Children of Paradise, The Seven Samurai, The Apu Trilogy, Jules and Jim, 8½, Dr. Strangelove,* and *The Emigrants* than in any of the recent fiction by Robbe-Grillet, Michel Butor, and J. M. G. Le Clézio.

A curious state of affairs, to say the least. The film at its best now recreates the experience of the traditional novel, while the contemporary novel at its most advanced now consorts with the coldness and passivity of the photographic plate.[5] Just as photography seemed to release painting from its representational functions, so perhaps the film was always meant to appropriate the mimetic tradition in literature and thus leave literature itself free to—well, to do what? Self-destruct?

If we believe that the New Novel means the end of the old novel, must we also take part in the current critical melodrama that casts any novel at all in the role of the Dying Swan? I don't know. Do the great forms really die? Did grand opera and the symphony, as it is so often argued, really exhaust their cultural tenure with the end of the nineteenth century? Some of the most innovative composers of our century—Stravinsky, Berg, Schoenberg—have continued to use these discredited forms in new ways. Did photography really kill off the representational modes of portraiture and narration in painting? For a while it certainly seemed so, but recent trends in art, pop art in particular, seem to indicate other wise. Many important novelists—Bellow, Ellison, Mailer, Roth, Malamud, Doris Lessing, Jean Rhys—in

---

[5]This is not to say, however, that the cinema is without its exemplary analogues of the self-reflexive mode in literature. Those works that explicitly focus on the camera and its usages as film subject have not been many, but each has contained memorable qualities. I would single out in particular the surreal wit of Keaton's *Sherlock Jr.* (1924), the technical vigor of Vertov's *Man with a Movie Camera* (1929), and the dramatic intensity of Bergman's *Persona* (1967). None of these films, however, has abandoned either character or narrative action (not even Vertov where the central character is the camera), and like the finest examples of literary postmodernism, each employs its self-reflexive moments to add to, not to detract from and thus "show up" the significance of the dramatic context (see my description of group one in note 2, this chapter).

spite of the most recent tendencies in fiction, still provide us with characters and a relatively traditional narrative line. On the other hand, the symphonies of Stravinsky are clearly of less interest to the musical public than are his mixed-media offerings (like *L'Histoire du Soldat* and *Oedipus Rex*), and Schoenberg's lone opera, *Moses und Aron*, gets far less critical attention (and fewer performances) than his hybrid compositions for voice and chamber groups. A Warhol or a Lichtenstein is often described as "camp" or "in a minor mode," while abstract expressionists are still "serious" and "very much in the mainstream." Bellow gets labeled "old guard," while the latest work of Thomas Pynchon, according to the current press, advances the novel "beyond *Ulysses*."

Perhaps any artistic form once established is always there for the artist who cares to use it—who can believe deeply enough in the ideas embodied in its form—but perhaps this form is not always there for the collective consciousness of a developing, changing culture. Forms do not die. "Death" is just our way of speaking, the metaphor we use when a form shifts position from the center of the cultural consciousness—from the center of critical concern, of media attentiveness—to some less eminent position tangential to the center. At this moment the novel seems to be in the process of changing its position in the cultural regard. The New Novel is both one cause and symptom of this process; in this sense, it is a novel of transition. It is also probably one indication that from now on all new novels, except perhaps for the very greatest, will matter a great deal less to us than they did in the past.

Index

Index

Adams, Robert Martin, 93–94n
Agee, James, 98
Antonioni, Michelangelo, 106–7
Arnheim, Rudolf, 61n, 111–13, 120

Balázs, Béla: on perception and the cinema, 31–33, 134
Balzac, Honoré de: on description in nineteenth-century fiction, 5; description in *Père Goriot*, 33–35
Barthes, Roland: on Robbe-Grillet, 128
Bazin, André, 86n, 107
Benjamin, Walter, 112
Bergson, Henri: and Joyce, 97–98
Bersani, Leo, 128–29n
Booth, Wayne C., 5n
Burroughs, William: narrative in *Naked Lunch*, 179–81

Camera. *See* Cinema
Camus, Albert, 82–83
Cervantes, Miguel de: characterization in *Don Quixote*, 9–16; *Don Quixote* and society, 11–16; narrative in *Don Quixote*, 8–16
Characterization: in Cervantes, 9–16; in Faulkner, 153–56; in Flaubert, 19–22, 25–27; in Joyce, 141–50; in Kesey, 159–61; in Lawrence, 46; literary and cinematic, 160–61; in West, 156–59; in Woolf, 51–52
Cinema: description in, 31–34, 37–39; and literary description, 53–68; as narrative form, 80–89; and perception, 31–32, 54, 61, 65–68, 106–08, 111–12, 119–20, 127, 129, 131–36, 150–51, 162–64, 165–66, 169–70; and photography, 72, 165–66; and society, 82–83, 185–198; special techniques defined, 87–89. *See also* Characterization; Description; Narrative
Collingwood, R. G., 15n

Conrad, Joseph: description in *Heart of Darkness*, 54–63; on description in own work, 4

Darwin, Charles, 17
Debrix, J. B., 165n, 170n
De Man, Paul, 31n
Depthlessness. *See* Description; Characterization; Perception
Description: in Balzac, 33–35; cinematic, 141–42; in Conrad, 59–63; in Dickens, 35–38; in Faulkner, 116–20; in Flaubert, 28–33, 90–91; in Hemingway, 99–101; in James, 54–59; in Joyce, 63–68, 90–97, 109–15, 136–41; in Lawrence, 43–47; literary and cinematic, 31–34, 37–39, 53–68, 80–89, 101–2, 106–8, 141–42; literary and scientific, 114; literary history of, 52–53; in Nabokov, 120–24; noncinematic, 39–53; and perception theory, 131–36; in Robbe-Grillet, 124–30; in Sartre, 102–6; statements by novelists about, 3–6; in Stendhal, 115–16; in Woolf, 47–53. *See also* Narrative; Perception
De Sica, Vittorio, 101
Dickens, Charles: description in *Oliver Twist*, 35–38
Dos Passos, John: and Eisenstein, 178; narrative in *U.S.A.*, 176–78

Eisenstein, Sergei, 33, 35, 175; and Dos Passos, 178; and Joyce, 75, 141; on narrative in cinema, 171–72; *Potemkin*, 139
Ellmann, Richard, 4n

Faulkner, William: characterization in *Sanctuary*, 153–56; description in *The Hamlet*, 153–56; and Hollywood, 156; on own work, 118, 174–75

Index

Fiedler, Leslie A., 152n
Film. *See* Cinema
Flaubert, Gustave: and audience, 22–27; and Cervantes, 8–9; characterization in *Madame Bovary*, 19–22, 25–27; description, 90–92; on description in own work, 4–5, 7, 18n; influence, 5–8; *Madame Bovary* and society, 16–19; narrative in *Madame Bovary*, 6, 16–27, 28–31
Form: cinematic and social, 82–83, 185–98; literary and scientific, 17–18; literary and social, 11–27, 144, 146, 147–50, 151–52, 154, 158, 175, 177–82, 185–88; literary forms as literary subject, 191–98. *See also* Cinema; Characterization; Description; Narrative
Francastel, Pierre, 39
Frye, Northrop, 17n

Godard, Jean-Luc, 108
Gombrich, E. H.: on art and perception, 131–32
Griffith, D. W., 38
Gross, John, 93–94n

Hebbel, Friedrich, 98
Heller, Erich, 18–19n
Hemingway, Ernest: description in *In Our Time*, 99–101; on own work, 99
Howe, Irving, 154

Images. *See* Description

James, Henry: on de Maupassant, 4; description in *What Maisie Knew*, 54–59; on own work, 4
Joyce, James: and Bergson, 97–99; characterization, 141–50; and the cinema, 71–82; description, 63–68, 90–97, 109–15, 136–41; and Eisenstein, 75, 141; and Flaubert, 6; influence on Dos Passos, 177; narrative, 63–68, 164–74. Works: *Dubliners*, 76–77, 91, 109–11, 142–49; *Finnegans Wake*, 74; *A Portrait of the Artist as a Young Man*, 3, 77, 164–68; *Ulysses*, 3, 63–68, 74, 75, 77, 78, 93–97, 111, 113–15, 136–41, 148–50, 168–74; filming of *Ulysses*, 74–75, 78
Joyce, Stanislaus, 76

Kael, Pauline, 74n
Kesey, Ken: characterization in *One Flew over the Cuckoo's Nest*, 159–60
Kracauer, Siegfried, 87n

Lawrence, D. H.: characterization in *Women in Love*, 46; description in *Women in Love*, 43–47; on description in the modern novel, 125
Lodge, David, 32n
Lukács, Georg: on characterization, 141; on description, 135n; on Flaubert, 91n

Magny, Claude-Edmonde, 32n, 114n
Malraux, André, 37–38n
Miller, J. Hillis, 17n
Montage. *See* Narrative
Mudrick, Marvin, 62n
Muybridge, Eadweard, 114

Nabokov, Vladimir, 132, 146n; description in *Lolita*, 120–24; on own work, 123
Narrative: in Burroughs, 179–81; in Cervantes, 9–16; cinema as, 80–89; in Dos Passos, 176–78; in Flaubert, 16–27; in Joyce, 63–68, 164–74; literary and cinematic, 53–68, 80–82, 87–89, 162–82; and perception, 14–16; and social forms, 11–13, 82–83
Novel: American Gothic, 151–61; literary precedents for modern, 5–16, 40–53; need for visual images in, 23–26; New Novel, 151–52. *See also* Characterization; Description; Narrative

Index

Olson, Charles, 178
Ortega y Gasset, José, 20n, 42; on Cervantes and Flaubert, 8

Perception: and cinema, 31–33, 54–68, 82–89, 97–98, 101–2, 111–12, 119–20; cultural myths about, 186–88; and literary forms, 14–16, 16–19, 23–27, 43–53; psychology of, 131–36. *See also* Description
Photography: and cinema, 72, 165–66; and literary forms, 80–82, 87–89; and perception, 131–36. *See also* Cinema; Perception
Pound, Ezra, 6
Proust, Marcel: on cinematic narrative in *Guermantes Way*, 83–87

Renoir, Jean, 38n
Robbe-Grillet, Alain, 105, 192n; description in *Jealousy*, 124–30; on own work, 128–29; on Sartre, 105
Rossellini, Roberto, 101–2, 106

Sartre, Jean-Paul, 132; description in *Nausea*, 102–6
Science: and literary forms, 17–18. *See also* Perception
Sontag, Susan, 194–95
Spender, Stephen, 181–82

Spengler, Oswald, 148–49
Stendhal: description in *The Red and the Black*, 115–16
Stephenson, Ralph, 165n, 170n
Sukenick, Ronald, 195–96
Svevo, Italo, 3

Teshigahara, 127
Tolstoy, Leo, 98n; on narrative in the novel and cinema, 162–63
Truffaut, François: perception and description in *Stolen Kisses*, 107–8
Turnell, Martin, 18n

Van Ghent, Dorothy, 146n
Vernon, M. D., 131, 133
Vision. *See* Perception
Visualization. *See* Description; Narrative

Watt, Ian, 16n
West, Nathanael: characterization in *The Day of the Locust*, 156–59; *Miss Lonelyhearts*, 161
Weston, Edward, 127
Woolf, Virginia: characterization in *Mrs. Dalloway*, 51–52; description in *Mrs. Dalloway*, 47–51; on own work, 49–50

Zola, Emile: Description in *Nana*, 40–43